The Majority Finds Its Past

The Majority Finds Its Past

PLACING WOMEN IN HISTORY

GERDA LERNER

OXFORD UNIVERSITY PRESS
Oxford   New York   Toronto   Melbourne

Oxford University Press

Oxford   London   Glasgow

New York   Toronto   Melbourne   Wellington

Nairobi   Dar es Salaam   Cape Town

Kuala Lumpur   Singapore   Jakarta   Hong Kong   Tokyo

Delhi   Bombay   Calcutta   Madras   Karachi

First published by Oxford University Press, New York, 1979

First issued as an Oxford University Press paperback, 1981

Library of Congress Cataloging in Publication Data
Lerner, Gerda, 1920–
The majority finds its past.
Includes bibliographical references and index.
1. Women—United States—History.   2. Afro-American women—History.
3. Feminism—United States—History.
4. Women's rights—United States—History.   I. Title.
HQ1426.L47   301.41′2′0973   79-14048   ISBN 0-19-502597-0
ISBN 0-19-502899-6 pbk.

This book is dedicated
to my students —
a new generation of women,
who take for granted
the time and space for thought
we had to win —

in faith and trust
that they will carry on

Preface

Most of the essays in this volume originated as lectures or conference papers. They were transformed, often through several versions, in response to audience reaction, criticism, and challenge from colleagues. Most scholarly work is subject to such beneficial exchange among scholars, but the quality and nature of feminist scholarship, at least as I have experienced it in the field of Women's History, is something quite different. We, who create Women's History, as we seek to uncover the female past and interpret it, are often an embattled lot, struggling for the right to teach what we research and to win professional recognition not only for our work but for the field in which we work. Our professional contacts with other feminist scholars therefore take on a significance far greater than that of the traditional scholarly exchange. We have become a community of scholars, vitally interested and involved in each other's work, trying to combat within ourselves and one another the competitiveness which is structured into our institutional and professional life and to substitute for it a new and as yet untested model of supportive and engaged scholarship. Feminist scholarship seeks to respect individual work, while searching for collective solutions to intellectual as well as societal problems. It seeks to break down and combat the artificial hierarchies, the elitism and narrow specialization so characteristic of our profession; it seeks constantly to broaden and deepen the connectedness between thinking and committed social action. The history we study offers us models for the kind of people we are trying to become and so some of the deep splits in personhood, from which so many of us have suffered, are healing. Thus, in preparing this volume of my own past work I am above all aware of an indebtedness far greater than can be acknowledged to my students, my lecture audiences, my colleagues in and out of academe—in short, to my sisters in Women's History. This work, whatever else it may be, represents an ongoing, continuing dialogue among many of us, concerning issues and questions as vital to our future as to our present. As I have all my life in different fields, I have in this work at times stood in opposition to prevailing trends, seemingly alone, yet I have never felt myself disconnected from that rising stream of consciousness, will, and force which seeks to have women realize their full human potential. It would be impossible to list here and acknowledge my indebtedness to all the individuals whose thought, help and support has made this work possible. Let me simply say, that I feel myself embedded in the collective effort and that I hope my own, sometimes lonely explorations have added to its strength.

I am grateful to Sheldon Meyer for his understanding and skillful editing of this volume and to Leona Capeless for her perceptive copy editing.

A Brief Note on Method

The essays, which have previously been published, are here reprinted with some cuts made to avoid repetition. In a few places ideas and concepts have been sharpened in the light of recent scholarship. In other places I have, from my current vantage point, critically commented in the footnotes on my earlier work. All bibliographical footnotes have been updated to bring them in line with recent scholarship.

The terms of reference by which Blacks have referred to themselves have changed in the course of history. In recognition of the emotional and symbolic significance of the choice of a name, which is part of self-definition for individuals as well as for groups, I have used the terms generally accepted by the group at a given time. Thus the term "Negro" is used when referring to the Negro Women's Club movement, while in other places "Black" is the term of reference. When the word "Black" means "Negro" I have capitalized it when used as a noun, but not as an adjective. Should the use of the word "Black" for "Negro" persist, it will undoubtedly be capitalized in the adjectival form, but such usage is still rare.

A similar wide range of usage with sensitive connotations concerns the terms "ladies" and "women." Here I use "ladies" to designate members of the leisured or upper and middle classes, and "women" to refer to all others. In the spelling of "Woman suffrage" and "woman's rights" I retain the usage current at the time of origin in the 19th century, as I do in referring to the 20th-century "women's movement."

Tomkins Cove, N.Y.   G.L.
April 1979

Contents

Autobiographical Notes,
by way of an Introduction

The essays in this volume were written over a span of eleven years in an attempt to develop a theory of Women's History. The first of these essays appeared in 1969, shortly before the birth of the then new women's movement and before most activists of the new feminism had begun to raise the demand for the restoration of the female past. Thus, this volume represents not only the personal intellectual growth of an individual historian, but also stages in the growth of a new field. In some ways, these essays contributed to the common consciousness, challenging earlier-held beliefs and assumptions; in some ways they represent an individual's answers to questions posed simultaneously by many historians.

Clearly, the very terminology used challenges and poses problems. Is the past gender-determined? Can there be a separate history of men and of women? And what is the content and meaning of the term "Women's History?"

Even in its surface meaning, the term "Women's History" calls into question the claim to universality which "History" generally assumes as a given. If historial studies, as we traditionally know them, were actually focused on men and women alike, then there would be no need for a separate subject. Men and women built civilization and culture and one would assume that any historical account written about any given period would recognize that basic fact. But traditional history has been written and interpreted by men in an androcentric frame of reference; it might quite properly be described as the history of men. The very term "Women's History" calls attention to the fact that something is missing from historical scholarship and it aims to document and reinterpret that which is missing. Seen in that light, Women's History is simply "the history of women."

The individual concerned with the search for what is missing from traditional history usually conceptualizes the problem that way, as a first step: The story of women "missing" from history is discovered, resurrected, and newly interpreted. Women are made to fit into the empty spaces of traditional history. Once engaged in this enterprise and confronting the vast untapped riches of primary sources, the historian becomes aware of the inadequacy of the concepts with which she must deal, of the limitations or inapplicability of the traditional questions she is asking. The search for a better conceptual framework for the history of women begins at that stage. One is led, step by step, to new definitions, to the search for more appropriate concepts, to dissatisfaction with periodization in traditional history. One searches for appropriate comparisons of "women" with other groups in society. One tries to find new conceptual models, borrowing concepts and tools from other disciplines. Women's History, at this stage, is no longer only a "field," rather it is a methodology, a stance, an angle of vision.

Women's History is a stance which demands that women be included in whatever topic is under discussion. It is an angle of vision which permits us to see that women live and have lived in a world defined by men and most frequently dominated by men and yet have shaped and influenced that world and all human events. Women's History challenges the androcentric assumptions of traditional history and assumes that the role of women in historical events—or the absence of women from them—must properly be illuminated and discussed in each and every case. Such an examination can also provide the basis for answering the other questions asked earlier. Is the past gender-determined? Is there a different history of men and of women? Another way of posing these questions is to ask, does gender determine a person's experience, activities, and consciousness? Few would disagree with the statement that gender, like class, race, and ethnicity, is *one* determinant in shaping the individual's life. The difficulty lies in making generalizations based on our one-sided knowledge of the human past. The study of the history of women is a necessity, if only for purposes of comparison.

Women's History, finally, is both a world view and a compensatory strategy for offsetting the male bias of traditional history. It is an intellectual movement of seriousness and considerable range, which aims for a new synthesis which will eventually make its continuation unnecessary.

I came into the study of history through my work on a biography of Sarah and Angelina Grimké. As a writer of short stories, articles, screenplays, and two novels, I planned to write a fictionalized biography. I was fascinated with the lives and characters of these two women, who had not had a biography written about them since 1885. I wanted to make them come alive as persons, as they had come alive to me while reading their diaries and letters. I wanted to trace their development and growth: creatures of society emerging into selfhood; selfless advocates of reform becoming, out of their own needs, organizers of women and finally creators of feminist thought. They spoke to me in a very personal way and I wanted to transmit what I received from these women of another century to readers of my day. I had researched for about a year and I had written eight chapters, but I was dissatisfied with my lack of research skills.

My formal education had ended about twenty years earlier, when I took my "Matura," the final exam qualifying a student for admission to university training, just after the accession of the Nazis to power in Austria. I passed the exam with distinguished honor; but instead of entering the university, I became a refugee and later made my way to America. Here I married, raised two children, and earned my living at every variety of women's jobs. And I always was a writer. It was as good an education as any for becoming a specialist in the history of women.

I worked with women at the work place and in the community and helped to organize them; I shared the experience of most ordinary women as an unskilled and later semi-skilled worker, as a housewife, a mother, a child-bearer, community activist. In all these roles and occupations I met an active and dynamic group of women, who worked quietly and without public recognition, usually without pay and frequently without an awareness of the significance of the work they were doing. I saw community organizations flourish, because there were a handful of such women in the community. Political organizations were influenced by their work, yet no one would ever know of their existence through the writings of historians or through the work of fiction writers. At the time in which I began to think of writing the Grimké biography, the movies were showing us as happy housewives puttering around spotless suburban kitchens, while the evil marriage wreckers, who always happened to be career women, gave up their happiness for ambition. The mass magazines and novels were preaching a similar message, which bore little resemblance to the life I knew. I had seen women during World War II, when they were thrust into positions of responsibility in fields in which they had little experience, maintaining the home-front economy. I knew the competent work women, even "mere housewives," were doing and so I knew from my own experience that literature, the media, and history did not reflect the realities of women's lives.

Earlier, in 1955, I had written together with the poet and playwright Eve Merriam, a musical, *Singing of Women,* which was performed off-Broadway. It was our idea to revive some of the heroic figures among American women and to celebrate their existence, their actuality. At that time what we had to say was not exactly popular; the musical, although well received and reviewed, did not have a commercial future. Still, in preparation for it I had read the autobiographies and biographies of the major 19th-century feminists. It seemed to me appropriate and perhaps not quite accidental that I should undertake to bring to life the two forgotten women who had started the woman's rights movement.

Although I was intellectualy prepared for the task, I was seriously handicapped by my lack of academic training and my inadequate knowledge of American history. My European classicist training had been rigorous and compared favorably with the best American high school and junior college education available, but the existence of the Americas had been barely acknowledged in it. The United States and its history and culture were marginal to the ethnocentric definition of humanist knowledge of pre-World War II Austria. In the twenty years since I had left school I had been reading voraciously, with the disorganized fervor of the autodidact; by then I knew enough to know my ignorance. Yet the culture shift I had made into a foreign language, a foreign history, and a new and different system of values, was in a sense an excellent preparation for the kind of work I would be doing. It was possible, in my day, to be a European intellectual, excellently trained and credentialled, and yet to be ignorant of the history and culture of several continents. The definition of knowledge and its content was obviously subject to prejudice and bias. It took the best part of my education for me to learn that what I was learning was based on unacknowledged bias and was in need of skeptical scrutiny and revision. What I was learning in graduate school did not so much leave out continents and their people as it left out half the human race, women.

I have always stood in awe of scholarship, and never more so than when I decided to formalize what I had referred to as "taking courses" at the New School of Social Research by enrolling for credit toward a B.A. It took four years to earn by part-time study the sixty undergraduate credits I needed. Appropriately, I majored in history and literature, learning the rudiments of research technique and historical verification. Incidentially, and without any planning or conscious effort on my part, it turned out that every paper I did on any subject whatsoever related to women. Looking over these undergraduate papers in art history, philosophy, literature, poetry, anthropology, history, and classics I realize now that I ran my own little Women's Studies major, only there was no such thing in existence then and there was no name for what I was doing. As my knowledge of historical method increased, so did my dissatisfaction with my manuscript. The discrepancy between the complexity of the historical data and my ability to interpret and fictionalize them became increasingly obvious. Sometime in my senior year I discarded the eight chapters of the fictionalized biography, decided to get professional training as a historian, and started all over again to work on a historical biography of Sarah and Angelina Grimké.[1]

While still an undergraduate at the New School I offered my first course in Women's History, "Great Women in American History" in the fall of 1962. The minimum required registration for a class was ten students and since I could not find ten people to take the class, it was cancelled. I offered it again in the spring of '63, secured a small, but sufficient enrollment, which included two retired men, and taught it another time in the fall term '63-64. To my knowledge this was the first class on the subject since a short-lived attempt had been made to teach such a class at Radcliffe in the 1930s. That spring I also gave a series of radio lectures on WBAI, entitled "Forgotten Women in American History." These were widely rebroadcast across the country and are still heard occasionally today.

In the fall of '63 I entered Columbia University as a candidate for the M.A. and Ph.D. in history. I was forty-three years old; my daughter had just entered college and my son was a senior in high school. My husband was busy with a successful career as a filmmaker and teacher of film. In those days, women my age did not, generally, attend graduate school, and I was somewhat apprehensive and so, I think, were some of my professors. My mentors were my own age or somewhat younger; my classmates were, by and large, the age of my daughter. I had shopped around before selecting a graduate school in order to be allowed to do the Grimké biography as my dissertation. Columbia was the only place where the department chairman was willing to tailor the institutional regulations so as to meet the needs of this eager, somewhat superannuated, and certainly "different" student. The topic, on which I had already been working for four years, was quickly approved for my dissertation and I was permitted to continue working on it, even before fulfilling my orals requirements. Due to this flexibility, I was able to earn both graduate degrees in three years from the time I entered, completing my course work, all the required examinations, the dissertation, and teaching for a year at the New School and for the final year at Long Island University in Brooklyn.

In a way, my three years of graduate study were the happiest years of my life. It was hard, absorbing work, constant challenges, but, mostly, it was the first time in my life I had time and space for thinking and learning. I could not have done it so quickly, if I had not had a supportive husband and son, who relieved me of many domestic responsibilities. Greedy for knowledge the way only people who have long been denied an education can be, I gave up all recreation, social life, and other interests. I was constantly aware of the twenty years I had lost and determined to compensate for them by increased concentration and effort. More than anything else I was driven by an urgency to learn what I needed to know in order to carry out a passionate ambition, which by then had taken concrete shape in my mind.

During the interview at Columbia, prior to my admission to the Ph.D. program, I was asked a standard question: Why did I take up the study of history? Without hesitating I replied that I wanted to put women into history. No, I corrected myself, not put them into history, because they are already in it, what I want to do is to make the study of women's history legitimate. I want, I said plainly, to complete the work begun by Mary Beard. This announcement was, not surprisingly, greeted by astonished silence. Just what did I have in mind saying I wanted to make women's history legitimate? And anyway, what was women's history? The question set me off into a lengthy explanation, on which I have played variations for the past fifteen years. I ended in somewhat utopian fashion: "I want women's history to be part of every curriculum on every level, and I want people to be able to specialize and take Ph.D.s in the subject and not have to say they are doing something else. I want women's history respected and legitimized in the historical profession."

At the time this was a fairly preposterous statement to make, not only in view of my late start and insignificant status in the profession, but also in view of the novelty of the enterprise. I must have presented a rather odd picture to my professors, an excitable middle-aged woman, making grandiose statements more appropriate to an immature freshman, and yet, unmistakably possessed of some inner urgency. My mentors had the good sense not to oppose me; in fact they helped me in many ways, but they tried their best to curb my high-flown ambition and settle me down to doing solid scholarly work on my dissertation. I have always appreciated that; it was what I had come to graduate school to learn, and I saw it as good preparation for what I had set my mind on doing. Still, from the beginning, I held a unique position among my fellow students and in the department. Had I been a young woman just out of college, I probably could not have withstood the social pressure, subtle ridicule, constant discouragement, and, not infrequently, open disapproval. There were no other women there who shared my interest or supported me; in fact some of the women students were more hostile to my constantly "harping" on women than were the men. After a while, I made a place for myself and even won the respect of some of the faculty for my knowledge in what one of them referred to as my "exotic specialty." But what I learned during those years, over and above what my professors taught me, was a strategy for extracting knowledge about women from whatever sources were presented to me. I developed a set of questions, which would elicit information about women, no matter what the subject was and no matter what the bias of the lecturer. I learned sometimes *from* my professors, often *against* them, and much by trial and error, but always I tested what I was learning against what I already knew from living. I was lucky to have had forty-three years of living behind me before entering graduate school; it was what enabled me to withstand its blandishments and to extract the maximum amount of useful knowledge from my instructors. I had sense enough to distinguish methodology from opinion; to acquire the former and skeptically test the latter. What I brought as a person to history was inseparable from my intellectual approach to the subject; I never accepted the need for a separation of theory and practice.

The pressure of time and my utopian goal were always before me. Early in my undergraduate studies I had first read Mary Beard's *Woman as Force in History*.[2] Somehow, I was able to disregard her poor presentation, her fervent, and sometimes ill-tempered rhetoric and to connect with her central idea: that women have always been active and at the center of history. I was struck, as by a sudden illumination, by the simplicity and truth of her insight. Mary Beard had arrived at that conviction the same way I had, by herself having been an engaged participant in women's work in society. In her narrative I recognized a world I knew from experience, a world in which women were active participants in the building of community and of institutions. Mary Beard's quarrel with the feminist theoreticians of her day and especially with their approach to history was due to her rejection of the idea that women were primarily victims. She went too far in that, and it led her to disregard large aspects of women's history—the structural, cultural, and sexual subordination of women and their exploitation. Beard's thinking reflects her isolation from criticism by feminist thinkers, her attachment to traditional sexual values, and, indirectly, the state of feminism during her most productive years. But implicit in Beard's work, whether she fully understood it or not, was the recognition of the duality of women's position in society—women are subordinate, yet central; victimized, yet active. Despite the fact that her rhetorical quarrel with the feminists of her day occupies much space in her writing, it is not central to Beard's thesis. Her greatest contribution is the insight that focusing on the concept of women as victim obscures the true history of women. Beard also insisted that the history of women had to reflect the variations in the status of women at any given time according to class. She did not blink the fact that women have been oppressors as well as oppressed and that class and sex interests have often been in conflict. Her methodological suggestions, her practice of comparative history, and her drawing on sources from other disciplines, such as anthropology and sociology, were a revelation to me. Long before the new feminism surfaced, reading Mary Beard raised my feminist consciousness.

Essentially, Mary Beard invented the concept of Women's Studies and Women's History. It was Mary Beard, first and foremost, whose critique of an androcentric academic establishment led her to envision new models of education for women. "Equal education for which women have clamoured," she wrote, "has merely meant the extension to women of men's education in their own history and judgements of themselves."[3] But such "history consists of threads . . . selected from men's activities in war, business and politics, woven together according to a pattern of male prowess and power as conceived in the mind of man. If the woman's culture came into this pattern in any way, it is only as a blurring of a major concept."[4] Here was a statement which expressed what during my graduate education I had experienced only vaguely as dissatisfaction with and resistance to what I was being taught. Traditional history fixed women into marginality; I knew and now found confirmation in Mary Beard's writing that this was not the truth.

As I began my first library research, I found the Mary Beard papers at the Sophia Smith Collection. These papers hold evidence of Beard's efforts for starting a Women's Studies course at Radcliffe College and of her protracted work collecting sources for the history of women and establishing a Women's History archives. I found there a two-page listing of questions, yet to be answered about women in history, and I found a very few sentences which became my guidelines, as I tried to proceed in this endeavor. In a very real sense I consider Mary Beard, whom I never met, my principal mentor as a historian.

Most educated women, as they pass through graduate school, have suffered from the absence of female role models. They have been made to feel their marginality in their numbers, in the rules, regulations, and the hidden "old boy network" of academe, and most of all in the content of their studies. The few learned women who made their success in that man's world had to become what Mary Beard called "men's understudies." She, for what seemed to her good and sufficient reasons, chose to remain an outsider to academe, challenging it with her writing, and turning, when frustrated, to popular media and broadcasts. Her strategy for bringing Women's History into the mainstream was complex. In her own work she moved from social and labor history to a comparative study of women of different cultures; to a study of women's humor; to a popular compendium of source material on women; to her major monograph.[5] She organized the search for sources; critiqued respected establishment enterprises like the Encyclopaedia Britannica; and moved on to proposing, designing and organizing Women's Studies courses. She developed a new model for the woman intellectual, fusing theory and practice.

Encouraged by her example, I was adapting it to my uses, my own time. Unlike her, I was not willing to choose amateur and marginal status in my profession. In order to write and research the history of women, historians must have the best of traditional training and practice their craft with rigorous skill, and then they must go beyond it. Yet I, too, searched for a new definition of professionalism, different from the male academic model. As usual, it was easier to know what *not* to do than it was to know what to do.

After my dissertation defense one of my professors congratulated me and offered what was undoubtedly well-meant practical advice. If I wanted to make a career in the profession commensurate to my talents, I needed only to keep quiet about my "so-called" specialty and stress the fact that I was a social historian and a specialist in reform history. Once established, I could then do whatever I wanted about women. I never took that advice. It was too late in my life to play career games. I was never going to be department chairman, dean, or president of one of the historical societies. I was never going to be able to make up for the time lost due to my late start. At age forty-six, I figured I had twenty years in the profession ahead of me, with luck, and so I made a twenty-year research plan, which I have followed, with only slight detours to this day. I reasoned I would have to have impact on the academic world in a number of ways in order to make Women's History accepted: by actual research and writing; by proving the existence of sources; by upgrading the status of women in the profession; by proving that there existed student demand in this subject and moving from there to designing courses and graduate programs. I made these plans in 1966 without knowledge of the spectacular progress that would be made in a short time due to the energy, zeal, and creativity of the women's movement and of Women's Studies.† I just planned for myself and, fortified with my shiny credentials, I decided once and for all to stop defending what I was doing. I would just go ahead, do my work and let it speak for itself.

I had the great good fortune, all during my dissertation research, of working in the finest private collection of women's history books then in existence, the library of Miriam Y. Holden. Miriam Holden, a member of the National Women's Party since World War I and a close co-worker of Alice Paul and Margaret Sanger prior to 1920, had dedicated herself to collecting printed sources on women of all nations, which were housed in her New York East Side brownstone. She had also worked with Mary Beard, Eugenia Leonard, and Elizabeth Schlesinger toward establishing a

† This progress and the rapid advance of Women's History scholarship accounted, certainly in some measure, for disproving at least one of my pessimistic predictions: just prior to the publication of this book I was nominated for the 1981/82 presidency of the Organization of American Historians, an honor which had not been bestowed on a woman for over fifty years.

national Women's History archives. They had written proposals, curricula, bibliographies, and position papers; they had nagged college presidents and alumnae trustees and had, for the most part failed to make a dent. Miriam Holden opened her superb library to a few scholars working on Women's History topics. I spent many weeks and months there, able to browse freely in works about women and by women spanning 300 years. In this library the history of women was a reality; the possibilities of comparative and inter-disciplinary approaches were evident. Here I connected with the feminist past of thought and activity. Working with such sources I began to formulate some of the basic questions. In order to clarify my own thinking, I wrote a number of articles; this is the way most of the essays in this book were written: working tools, stepping stones.

Revisionist theories usually begin with an argument with one's predecessors. In my case, these predecessors were 19th- and 20th-century feminist writers, who saw women's history as a manifestation of women's oppression and focused excessively on the struggle for women's rights. The most recent, and certainly indispensable book was Eleanor Flexner's *Century of Struggle,*[6] which cut a wide swath, although it was essentially written in the woman's rights framework. Flexner's essay and footnotes were invaluable in pointing out research directions; I had already followed most of her sources and now began to formulate my own research priorities. The essay "New Approaches for the Study of Women in American History" (#1) discusses the historiography available in 1969 and poses new questions and challenges. Drawing on Mary Beard, I argued that the idea of the oppression of women, while certainly a historical fact, is of limited usefulness to historical inquiry. More important are questions like: What were women doing? How were they doing it? What was their own understanding of their place in the world? The essay calls attention to the crucially important factors of race and class and cautions against speaking of women as though they were a unified entity.

"The Lady and the Mill Girl" (#2) was actually written earlier than "New Approaches." It uses comparative history to show how women of different classes experienced the past differently and often antagonistically. It also shows how reality can turn into ideological myth. The essay was in part an outgrowth of my research in ante-bellum reform movements, in part a response to the a-historical analysis of women's place in society in a book like Betty Friedan's *The Feminine Mystique* and in some of the early pamphlet literature of the women's liberation movement.[7] It seemed to me essential to show the connection of current events with the past. The essay locates the creation of the "feminine mystique" in the Jacksonian era and shows how the ideology of "women's place is in the home" changed from being an accurate description of existing reality into a myth. The essay hints at, but does not solve, the problem of finding a periodization appropriate to Women's History. It shows how the Jacksonian age, a period of democratic progress and increasing egalitarianism for men, turns into one of regression and repression for women.

"The Feminists: A Second Look" (#3), written in 1970, when the new feminism was just a few years old, subjects the movement and its ideology to comparative analysis with 19th-century feminism. The essay is concerned with developing appropriate criteria and calls attention to the historic antecedents in 19th-century utopianism of many of the most revolutionary-sounding demands of the women's liberation movement. At the time I still made a sharp distinction between myself as a citizen and active feminist and myself as a scholar of the history of women. I made that distinction even as I helped to organize and served with Berenice Carroll as first Co-President of the caucus of women historians, CCWHP (Coordinating Committee of Women in the Historical Profession), in 1969, and as I organized and co-chaired with Patricia Graham the New York caucus, New York Women Historians. This proves that one can be deeply interested and involved in writing the history of women, be a citizen feminist, and yet *not* be a feminist historian.

My dissatisfaction with the analytic tools available to me continued. I had, in 1968, completed a one-volume textbook for high school and junior college use, *The Woman in American History*. [8] The need for making judgments of selection in a work of this kind, the questions raised by my various editors, and my difficulty in communicating my point of view to them, had forced me to define my concepts more precisely. In "Women's Rights and American Feminism" (#4), I tried to develop a more precise terminology. A distinction is made between "the woman's rights movement," a movement to bring women into all the structures and institutions of male-defined society on the basis of equality, and "feminism," a broad-spectrum struggle for female autonomy and self-determination. The essay challenges the appropriateness of traditional periodization for organizing the history of women and suggests alternatives. Here the influence of Juliet Mitchell's pathbreaking essay, "Women: The Longest Revolution" is clearly in evidence. [9] Women's role as breeder and child-bearer emerged as a factor essential in an ordering of the history of women. The essay also develops more fully the need for separate consideration of class, race, and ethnicity in analyzing women's past.

Ever since my dissertation research, which had revealed to me virtually unknown sources of women's history, the idea of doing a source book of primary documents had interested me. I had such a book under contract with Bobbs-Merrill Co., as part of their American Heritage Series. It was to be entitled, "Woman in the Making of the Nation." I had begun to organize the research into chapters, arranged quite traditionally according to the major periods of American political history, when I undertook a detour.

Just as I had been a premature feminist, I had also been a civil rights activist a good ten years before the civil rights movement got under way. My commitment to the issue of racial justice was deep and long-standing. My most recent activity in this connection had occurred just prior to my entering graduate school. My husband co-produced and directed the film *Black Like Me*, based on the best-selling novel by John Howard Griffin. I had written the screenplay and worked on the production with him. After that I stopped all political and social activity for the duration of my graduate studies. But as I began to work on my research priorities, the absence of black women from history appeared to me as an urgent problem to be considered. In my antislavery research I had uncovered a number of unused sources for the history of black women. Now it seemed to me I would be making a contribution to the civil rights movement and to scholarship by continuing this line of research and publishing a source book for the history of black women. Another reason for making that decision was that there were certain questions I thought could only be answered by comparative history. Was the oppression of women universal, that is, did it go across class and race lines? Did women of different racial groups have the same history or was there a difference? I obtained permission from Bobbs-Merrill to postpone work on their book, so that I might first complete a documentary history of black women.

Essays #5–7 are outgrowths of my work on *Black Women in White America: A Documentary History*.[10] In #5, "Black Women in the United States: A Problem in Historiography and Interpretation," I tried to summarize all I had learned theoretically by my research for this documentary and to answer the questions, with which I had begun. My comparison between the history of black and white women had confirmed the thesis, that generalizations about the oppression of women are inadequate unless qualified by factors of race and class. Women of each racial group experience their historical subordination differently.

"The Community Work of Black Women" (#6) illustrates one instance of community-building work of women. It is typical of many examples of similar activities of black and white women, which can be documented. The fact that women of both races, under different circumstances and economic conditions, function in a similar manner seems to confirm that community- and institution-building is typical of women's work in the past.

"Black and White Women in Interaction and Confrontation" (#7) subjects the widely held myth of sisterhood among women of both races to a detailed analysis. I had shared that belief and had hoped to substantiate it through my research findings; instead I was forced to conclude that, historically, in the U.S. setting there is more evidence of tension than of sisterhood.

The next essay (#8) "The Political Activities of Antislavery Women," although written several years later, similarly seeks to apply the analytical tools of women's history to a concrete problem. In it I attempted to devise a methodology, which would permit me to isolate the activities of antislavery women from those of antislavery men. I also wanted to test out my thesis, that women in 19th-century America had done political work and wielded political influence apart from suffrage movement activities and prior to having the vote. While that point is sufficiently proven, much more work and research must be done to develop it fully in a book-length monograph. The essay argues and offers evidence to show that men and women approached their organizational work in different ways and with different emphasis. The historical invisibility of women is often due to the fact that we look for them in exactly the same activities as are pursued by men, and thus we cannot find them. While researching the antislavery petitions in the National Archives, I found, by pure serendipity, evidence that the lecture tour of the Grimké sisters in 1837–38 resulted in a great surge of petitioning and organizing activity in the towns and villages they had visited. This should lead to an upgrading of the significance of their organizing work, which, earlier, was not possible.

"Just a Housewife" (#9) places an aspect of women's work into historical perspective, which has generally been ignored until the rise of Women's History scholarship. The essay sees women's unpaid household work as a primary causative factor in her exploitation in the work place and in her general subordinate status.

The remaining four essays, written between 1974 and 1978, mark a decisive change in my intellectual development. After my detour with *Black Women,* I returned in 1973 to the book I had under contract with Bobbs-Merrill. But "Woman in the Making of the Nation" did not progress well, although all the research was in and only the writing remained to be done. In the four years since I had first contracted for the book, the field of Women's History had grown spectacularly. The profusion of seminars, conference panels, caucus discussions, and symposia in journals characterized the emergence of new scholarship, new questions, revisionist ideas. Women scholars had begun to work collectively, experimenting with methods for sharing their knowledge, for critiquing each other's work in a supportive, non-competitive manner. I was part of that movement and had begun to learn from the many young women, who had started on this subject later than I had, but who had brought to it their own ideas and life experiences. I now was critical of the "compensatory and contribution history" framework, in which much of my own work had been cast. It took some months of work before I realized that this was what was wrong with the book. I no longer believed that I should tell the history of women under the title "Women in the Making of the Nation." I no longer thought that a chapter organization by traditional periods was adequate. But what to substitute for it? The solution came, as so often happens, in a flash of insight—I found a new title, long before I knew how well it fitted my content. The title, "The Female Experience," gave me the clue for reorganizing my research. I gave up the old chapter plan and arranged the material according to female life stages (Childhood, Youth, Marriage and the Single State, etc.) and to stages of the growth of feminist consciousness. It was amazing how all at once the same material offered new insights and a powerful illumination. The book was finished quickly; [11] with it came new theoretical perceptions and a transformation, which went far beyond the content of the book.

What I learned in the process is reflected in the three essays, which conclude this volume. "Placing Women in History" (#10) surveys the historiography of the new field over a span of five years. It describes and critiques the stages of consciousness by which historical analysis of women has progressed, from compensatory and contribution history, to the new social history, and, most recently, woman-oriented history. The essay suggests for the first time that all efforts to treat women as a sub-group—minority, class, caste— are doomed to failure. It also challenges previous attempts at building a single conceptual framework for the history of women.

Women are half of humankind, evenly distributed in all strata of society. Their culturally determined and psychologically internalized marginality seems to be what makes their historical experience essentially different from that of men. But men have defined their experience as history and left women out. For women, all history as we now know it, is pre-history.

This definition of traditional history as not only male-oriented, but male-defined, is further explored in "The Majority Finds Its Past" (#11). What is needed in order to correct the distorted picture presented by traditional history is woman-centered analysis. What would the past be like if women were placed at the center of inquiry? What would the past be like if man were regarded as woman's "Other"? Even to pose such a question only as an intellectual exercise shifts one's angle of vision. The very categories and criteria by which historians have ordered the past have become questionable. The possibility of the existence of a female culture within the dominant patriarchal culture cannot be ruled out and should be tested out in each specific case.

The final essay, "The Challenge of Women's History," summarizes the ways in which Women's History challenges traditional scholarship. It offers a radical critique of traditional history and postulates a two-stage development leading to the formulation of a new "universal history," a history in which men and women will have equal significance. First, the uncovering and interpretation of the female past; second the synthesis of it with traditional history, which would include both the development of patriarchy and the development of feminist consciousness as important aspects of the historical experience.

The changes in consciousness and historical thought which lead to the definitions in this volume are the work of an individual, yet they reflect a collective effort and owe their existence to the changes in thought and consciousness represented in the women's movement, which inspired that collective effort. Women working on Women's History have tried to bring feminist consciousness to bear not only on the content but on the method of their work. There has been a deliberate effort to foster the development of

Women's History by group work, sharing of knowledge and sources and, at times, collective research and writing. The flourishing network of Women's History study groups, conferences, and conventions, all animated by a spirit of cooperation and the enthusiasm appropriate to pioneers, has greatly accelerated the maturing of this field and of its practitioners. Collegiality has turned into sisterhood, which has for many of us become a meaningful intellectual and spiritual community. The justification for my tracing my personal intellectual growth as an introduction to this volume is that it has significance beyond that of one woman thinking about the past of women. My thinking took place at a time when many other women began to ask questions similar to my own and began to act on these questions, thereby creating a new context for thought. Feminist consciousness begins with self-consciousness, an awareness of our separate needs as women; then comes the awareness of female collectivity—the reaching out toward other women, first for mutual support and then to improve our condition. Out of the recognition of communality, there emerges feminist group consciousness—a set of ideas by which women autonomously define ourselves in a male-dominated world and seek to substitute our vision and values for those of the patriarchy. The two aspects of my own consciousness, that of the citizen and that of the woman scholar, had finally fused: I am a feminist scholar.

Historians engaged in the quest for shaping autonomous definitions of self, experience, and history are, of necessity, searching for new intellectual tools for our work. We are creating the means as we are defining the goals. We have not, as yet, created the new conceptual framework for the history of women, which will be created. These essays represent my contribution to that effort. They are my working tools and the sign posts I have set up along the way on a road of discovery, which is leading both into the past and into the future.

The Majority Finds Its Past

1

New Approaches to the Study of Women in American History

The striking fact about the historiography of women is the general neglect of the subject by historians. As long as historians held to the traditional view that only the transmission and exercise of power were worthy of their interest, women were of necessity ignored. There was little room in political, diplomatic, and military history for American women, who were, longer than any other single group in the population, outside the power structure. At best their relationship to power was implicit and peripheral and could easily be passed over as insignificant. With the rise of social history and increasing concern with groups out of power, women received some attention, but interest was focused mainly on their position in the family and on their social status.[1] The number of women mentioned in textbooks of American history remains astonishingly small to this day, as does the number of biographies and monographs by professional historians dealing with women.

The literature concerning the role of women in American history is topically narrow, predominantly descriptive, and generally de-

This article first appeared in *The Journal for Social History*, vol. III, #1 (Fall 1969), pp. 53–62. Statements about the state of the field refer to 1969, not to the present.

void of interpretation. Except for the feminist viewpoint, there
seems to be no underlying conceptual framework.†

Feminist writers, not trained historians, were the first to undertake a systematic attempt to approach the problem of women's role
in American life and history. This took the form of feminist
tracts, theoretical approaches, and compilations of woman's "contributions."[2] The early compilers attacked the subject with a missionary zeal designed, above all, to right wrong. Their tendency
was to praise anything women had done as a "contribution" and to
include any women who had gained the slightest public attention
in their numerous lists.[3] Still, much positive work was done in
simply recounting the history of the woman's rights movement and
some of its forerunners and in discussing some of the women whose
pioneering struggles opened opportunities to others. Feminist
writers were hampered by a two-fold bias. First, they shared the
middle-class, nativist, moralistic approach of the Progressives and
tended to censure out of existence anyone who did not fit into this
pattern. Thus we find that women like Frances Wright and Ernestine Rose received little attention because they were considered too
radical. "Premature feminists" such as the Grimké sisters, Maria
Weston Chapman, and Lydia Maria Child are barely mentioned.
The second bias of the feminists lies in their belief that the history
of women is important only as representing the history of an oppressed group and its struggle against its oppressors.

This latter concept underlies the somewhat heroic, collectively
authored *History of Woman Suffrage*. This work, probably because it
represents an easily available though disorganized collection of
primary sources, has had a pervasive influence on later historians.
Following the lead and interpretation of the feminists, professional
historians have been preoccupied with the woman's rights movement in its legal and political aspects. Modern historians, too,

† The word "feminist," as here used, refers to the second wave of feminism, that of the 20th-century woman's rights and woman's suffrage
movement.

think that what is important to know about women is how they got the ballot.[4]

The only serious challenge to this conceptual framework was offered by Mary Beard in the form of a vigorous though often fuzzy polemic against the feminists.[5] What is important about women, said Mary Beard, is not that they were an oppressed group—she denied that they ever were—but that they have made a continuous and impressive contribution to society throughout all of history. It is a contribution, however, which does not fit into the value system generally accepted by historians when they make decisions as to who is or is not important to history. Mary Beard undertook in several of her books to trace the positive achievements of women, their social role, and their contributions to community life. Her concepts are most successfully reflected in *The Rise of American Civilization,* which she co-authored with her husband Charles Beard. In it the position of women is treated throughout in an integrated way with great attention to the economic contributions made by women.[6] But the Beards' approach to the subject of women had little influence on the historical profession. Perhaps this was due to the fact that in the 1930s and 1940s both the general public and historians became somewhat disenchanted with the woman's rights movement.

The winning of suffrage had made only a slight change in the actual status of women, and other factors—technological and economic changes, access to higher education, changing sexual mores—now loomed a great deal larger. The impact of Freudianism and psychology had made reformers in general somewhat suspect. Feminism was not infrequently treated with the same humorous condescension as that other successful failure: temperance.

Women have received serious attention from economic historians. There is a good deal of excellent literature dealing with the problem of women workers. Women as contributors to the economy from colonial times on, the laws affecting them, their wages and working conditions, and their struggle for protective legislation have been fully described.[7] Although female labor leaders have not generally been given much attention, their activities are on record. Excellent collections of material pertaining to women at Radcliffe and Smith College are available, but remain insufficiently explored.

Modern historians of the reform movements have done much to restore a sane balance to female achievement in reform; yet one still finds excluded from notice certain women who would have been included as a matter of course had they been men. Sophie Loeb, Grace Dodge, and Mary Anderson could be cited as examples.[8]

The historical literature on the family in America is quite scanty, but there seems to be a revival of interest in the subject. Several interesting monographs have begun to deal with the family role of women in its various aspects. This approach is promising and should be pursued by other historians.[9]

A new conceptual framework for dealing with the subject of women in American history is needed. The woman's rights movement frame of reference has become archaic and fairly useless. The 20th-century revolution in technology, morality, education, and employment patterns has brought enormous changes in the status and role of American women; these changes demand a historical perspective and understanding. The emergence of a recent "new feminism" is a social phenomenon requiring interpretation. Most importantly, women themselves are as entitled as minority group members are to having "their" history fully recorded.

Yet the subject is complex. It is difficult to conceptualize women as a group, since they are dispersed throughout the population. Except for special-interest organizations, they do not combine together. The subject is full of paradoxes which elude precise definitions and defy synthesis.

Women at various times and places were a majority of the population, yet their status was that of an oppressed minority, deprived of the rights men enjoyed. Women have for centuries been excluded from positions of power, both political and economic, yet as members of families, as daughters and wives, they often were closer to actual power than many a man. If women were among the most exploited of workers, they were also among the exploiters. If some women were dissatisfied with their limited opportunities, most women were adjusted to their position in society and resisted efforts at changing it. Women generally played a conservative role as individuals and in their communities, the role of conserving tradition, law, order, and the status quo. Yet women in their organizations were frequently allied with the most radical and even revolutionary causes and entered alliances with the very groups threatening the status quo.

If women themselves acted paradoxically, so did society in formulating its values for women. The rationale for women's peculiar position in society has always been that their function as mothers is essential to the survival of the group and that the home is the essential nucleus of society as we know it. Yet the millions of housewives and homemakers have throughout our history been deprived of the one tangible reward our society ranks highest: an income of their own. Neither custom, law, nor changes of technology, education, or politics have touched this sacred tradition. The unpaid housewife-and-mother has affected attitudes toward the women who perform homemaking services for strangers. Traditionally women in the service trades have been the lowest paid among all workers. Nor has this pattern been restricted to the unskilled groups. When women have entered an occupation in large numbers, this occupation has come to be regarded as low status and has been rewarded by low pay. Examples for this are readily found in the teaching and nursing fields. Even intellectual work has been treated with the same double standard. Creative fields in which women excel—poetry, the short story—have been those carrying the lowest rewards in money and esteem. Only in the performing arts has individual female talent had the same opportunity as male talent. Yet a cursory glance at the composition of any major symphony orchestra even today will reveal that in this field, too, opportunities for women have been restricted.

In dealing with the subject of women, studies frequently use other distinctive groups in our society as models for comparison.

Women's position has variously been likened to that of the slaves, oppressed ethnic or racial minorities, or economically deprived groups. But these comparisons quickly prove inadequate. The slave comparison obviously was a rhetorical device rather than a factual statement even at the time when Harriet Martineau first made it. [10] While the law denied women equal citizenship and for certain purposes classed them with "Indians and imbeciles," it never denied them physical freedom nor did it regard them as "chattel personnel." In fact, even within the slavery system, women were oppressed differently from men. The "minority group model" is also unsatisfactory. All members of a minority group which suffers discrimination share, with a very few exceptions, in the low-status position of the entire group. But women may be the wives of Cabinet members, the daughters of Congressmen, the sisters of business leaders, and yet, seen simply as persons, they may be disfranchised and suffer from economic and educational discrimination. On the other hand, a lower-class woman may advance to a position of economic or social power simply by marriage, a route which is generally not open to members of racial minority groups. In one particular respect the minority group comparison is illuminating: like Negroes, women suffer from "high visibility"; they remain more readily identifiable for their group characteristics than for their personal attainments. [11]

Modern psychology, which has offered various conflicting theories about the role and place of women, has further complicated the task of the historian. If a social historian wishes to study a particular ethnic or religious minority, he can study its location and economy, its culture, leadership, adjustment to American society, and contributions. The question of psychology would only arise in dealing with personal biographies. But the historian of women is at once faced with the necessity of making psychological judgments. Is it not a basic fact that the psychology as well as the physiology of women is different from that of men? Therefore they must of necessity have different expectations, needs, demands, and roles. If so, is the difference in "rights" not simply natural, a reflection of reality? The problems become more vexing when dealing with individual women. The biographer feels obliged first of all to concern himself with his subject's sexual role. Was she married? A mother? If she was not, this indicates that whatever she achieved was the result of sexual frustration. If she was married, one is under an obligation to explain that she did not neglect her children or perhaps that she did. And always there is the crucial question: "What was her relationship to her father?" This is not intended to disparage the efforts of those biographers who wish to enlist the aid of modern psychology for their work. But it should be pointed out that a great deal of excellent history about men has been written without the author's feeling compelled to discuss his subject's sex life or relationship to his mother in explaining his historical significance. In dealing with women, biographers are impeded by the necessity of dealing first with sex, then with the person. This is an approach which must be examined in each case for its applicability: where it is useful, it should be retained; where it is not, it should be discarded without apology.†

In order to broaden the study of women in American history, it is not really necessary to suggest new sources. Primary research material is readily available, not only in the several manuscript collections devoted to the subject, but in the usual primary sources for social historians: local historical records, letters, diaries, the organizational records of women's clubs, religious and charitable or-

†The comments in the above paragraph reflect my then current irritation with the constraints and pressures to which I had been subject on the part of publishers. Several major publishing houses had rejected the manuscript of my biography of the Grimké sisters (*The Grimké Sisters from South Carolina: Rebels Against Slavery* (Boston: Houghton Mifflin, 1967) because I refused to ascribe the sisters' feminism to their "frustrations," failure to find sexual satisfaction (in Sarah's case), and "father-fixation." This was the heyday of instant, pop-culture Freudian psychology in fiction, biographies, films. When writing about women, the refusal to use sexual stereotypes as a frame of reference lessened one's chances for publication and for critical acclaim.

ganizations, labor unions in fields employing women workers. There are numerous magazines, especially written for women, which provide good source material. Archives of Congress and of state governments contain petitions and statements made at hearings which can yield valuable information about the activities and interests of women. Many of these readily available sources remain neglected.

A fresh approach to known material and to available sources could provide valuable new insights. The following suggestion might make a useful beginning:

First, the subject "Women" is too vast and diffuse to serve as a valid point of departure. Women are members of families, citizens of different regions, economic producers, just as men are, but their emphasis on these various roles is different. The economic role of men predominates in their lives, but women shift readily from one role to another at different periods in their lives. It is in this that their function is different from men and it is this which must form the basis for any conceptual framework. In modern society the only statement about women in general which can be made with validity concerns their political status. Therefore the subject should be subsumed under several categories, and any inquiry, description, and generalization should be limited to a narrower field. It is useful to deal with the *status* of women at any given time—to distinguish their economic status, family status, and political-legal status. There must also be a consideration of class position, as has been usefully proven in recent studies of the feminist movement.[12]

Second, we should look at different aspects of women's role in American history. We must certainly be concerned with the woman's rights movement, but only as part of the total story. Historians must painstakingly restore the actual record of women's contributions at any given period in history. It is interesting that the history of women before the advent of the feminist movement has been more fully recorded and in a more balanced way than it has afterward, so that the story of colonial women can be quite fully traced through secondary literature.[13] But when we deal with the period after 1800, it often proves difficult to establish even descriptive facts. During the early national period, women organized elaborate welfare and relief systems which they staffed and administered. This story should be part of the history of the period; it is not now. Women were the teachers in most of the nation's public schools during the 19th century; this is worth recording and exploring. Women made a significant contribution to the growth and development of frontier communities. These are but a few of the many areas in which more research and uncovering of factual information are needed.

Third, we might well discard the "oppressed group model" when discussing women's role in the political life of the nation. Instead, we might start with the fact that one generalization about women which holds up is that they were, longer than any other group in the nation, deprived of political and economic power. Did this mean they actually wielded no power or did they wield power in different forms? My research has led me to believe that they wielded considerable power—in the middle of the 19th century even political power. They found a way to make their power felt through organizations, through pressure tactics, through petitioning, and various other means; these later became models for other mass movements for reform.

Fourth, another important fact is that women as a group were, for a considerable period of history, deprived of equal access to education. While they were not illiterate, their education was limited, usually to below the high school level. This was true of the majority of women until the end of the 19th century. It might be very useful to investigate what impact this had on female behavior and, more specifically, women's performance as a group in terms of outstanding achievement. To put it another way, how many generations of educated women are necessary to produce a significant number of outstanding women academicians? How many generations of college-trained women are necessary before women in sizable numbers make contributions in the sciences? When do women begin to move from the small-scale, home-centered creative forms, the fiction, poetry, and article-writing, to the larger-scale work within the framework of cultural institutions? Is the proverbial dearth of female philosophers really a result of some innate distinctiveness of female mental function or rather the product of centuries of environmental and institutional deprivation? This type of inquiry lends itself to a comparative cross-cultural approach. A comparison between the educational deprivation of women and that suffered by certain minority groups might lead us to a demonstrable correlation between educational deprivation and a gap of several generations before adequate and competitive performance is possible. This could explain a great deal about some of our problems with minority groups, public schooling, and academic achievement.†

Fifth, it would be worthwhile to distinguish the ideas society held at any given moment in regard to woman's proper "place" from what was actually woman's status at that time. The two do not necessarily overlap. On the contrary, there seems to be a considerable gap between the popular myth and reality. Social historians might legitimately be concerned with the significance of this gap, how to account for it, and whether it fits any distinguishable pattern. It would also be important to understand the function of ideas about women in the general ordering of society. Was the fact that colonial women were idealized as thrifty housewives and able helpmeets cause or effect of the labor shortage in the colonies? Are the idealized suburban housewife, the fashion-conscious teenager,

† It is interesting that in approaching my subject in the traditional, patriarchal mindset in which I was trained, I seek to justify the study of women by stressing what it might teach us about "important" subjects, such as the problems of minority groups. I was not then able to justify the study of women and their history as intrinsically valid or proceed from the firmer assumption that it required no justification. Today, I would add to this paragraph: "Such a comparison would also demonstrate in what ways the subordination of women is of longer duration and more profoundly damaging in effect than that experienced by any other subordinate group."

the sex-symbol model, causes or effects of our consumer-oriented society? And what effect does the socially held concept of woman's role have on the development of female talent, on woman's contribution to the society? †

Finally, we come back to the initial problem of how to judge the contribution of women. Are women noteworthy when their achievement falls exactly in a category of achievement set up for men? Obviously not, for this is how they have been kept out of the history books up to now. Are women noteworthy then, as the early feminists tended to think, if they do anything at all? Not likely. The fact remains that women are different from men and that their role in society and history is different from that of men. Different, but equal in importance. Obviously their achievements must also be measured on a different scale. To define and devise such a scale is difficult until the gaps in our historical knowledge about the actual contributions of women have been filled. This work remains to be done.

But we already know enough about the subject to conclude that the roles women played at different times in our history have been changing. The patterns and significance of these changes, the con-

† The research questions I suggested as major priorities in the above paragraphs remain valid and unanswered. Except for the last question—the distinction between values, prescriptive and actual behavior (myth and reality of women's lives)—researchers have ignored them. The major work in women's history has followed questions such as: How did women fight against oppression and improve their condition? Under what conditions and how did working women live and organize? What reform movements did women influence? How did women function in radical movements? A host of newer questions has been added by the introduction of the subjects of "sexuality" and "gender." Female bonding and the way in which women related to other women have received considerable attention. Despite a few fine studies of women's work in one or another community organization, the larger study of women as a force in community development and in the maintenance of community institutions has yet to be undertaken. A study of the impact and consequences of long-range female educational deprivation has yet to be made.

tinuities and discontinuities, the expectations and strivings of the pioneers, and the realities of the social scene—all these await study and new interpretations. One would hope at once for a wider framework and a narrower focus—a discarding of old categories and a painstaking search of known sources for unknown meanings. It is an endeavor that should enlist the best talents of the profession and, at long last, not primarily female talent.†

†The last sentence clearly demonstrates the limitations of my perspective at that time. Only a few years out of graduate school, I still believed that the only way women's history would gain respectability and acceptance was by winning over male historians to its practice. The growth of Women's Studies still lay ahead, and in my stance of "lone voice crying in the wilderness" I had no inkling of the force, dynamism, and self-confidence academic women would bring to bear on their fields. I still welcome male historians to the field and hope for their increasing awareness and understanding of its interpretations, but it is already clear that women historians are playing and must continue to play a primary role in restoring and interpreting the female past.

2

The Lady and the Mill Girl: Changes in the Status of Women in the Age of Jackson

The period 1800 1840 is one in which decisive changes occurred in the status of American women. It has remained surprisingly unexplored. With the exception of a recent, unpublished dissertation by Keith Melder and the distinctive work of Elisabeth Dexter, there is a dearth of descriptive material and an almost total absence of interpretation.[1] Yet the period offers essential clues to an understanding of later institutional developments, particularly the shape and nature of the woman's rights movement. This analysis will

This article first appeared in *American Studies*, Vol. 10, No. 1, Spring 1969, © 1969. Research for this article was facilitated by a research grant provided by Long Island University, Brooklyn, N.Y., which is gratefully acknowledged.

The generalizations in this article are based on extensive research in primary sources, including letters and manuscripts of the following women: Elizabeth Cady Stanton, Susan B. Anthony, Abby Kelley, Lucretia Mott, Lucy Stone, Sarah and Angelina Grimké, Maria Weston Chapman, Lydia Maria Child, and Betsey Cowles. Among the organizational records consulted were those of the Boston Female Anti-Slavery Society, the Philadelphia Female Anti-Slavery Society, Anti-Slavery Conventions of American Women, all the Woman's Rights Conventions prior to 1870, and the records of various female charitable organizations.

consider the economic, political, and social status of women and examine the changes in each area. It will also attempt an interpretation of the ideological shifts which occurred in American society concerning the "proper" role for women.

Periodization always offers difficulties. It seemed useful here, for purposes of comparison, to group women's status before 1800 roughly under the "colonial" heading and ignore the transitional and possibly atypical shifts which occurred during the American Revolution and the early period of nationhood. Also, regional differences were largely ignored. The South was left out of consideration entirely because its industrial development occurred later.

The status of colonial women has been well studied and described and can briefly be summarized for comparison with the later period. Throughout the colonial period there was a marked shortage of women, which varied with the regions and always was greatest in the frontier areas.[2] This (from the point of view of women) favorable sex ratio enhanced their status and position. The Puritan world view regarded idleness as sin; life in an underdeveloped country made it absolutely necessary that each member of the community perform an economic function. Thus work for women, married or single, was not only approved, it was regarded as a civic duty. Puritan town councils expected single girls, widows, and unattached women to be self-supporting and for a long time provided needy spinsters with parcels of land. There was no social sanction against married women working; on the contrary, wives were expected to help their husbands in their trade and won social approval for doing extra work in or out of the home. Needy children, girls as well as boys, were indentured or apprenticed and were expected to work for their keep.

The vast majority of women worked within their homes, where their labor produced most articles needed for the family. The entire colonial production of cloth and clothing and in part that of shoes was in the hands of women. In addition to these occupations, women were found in many different kinds of employment. They were butchers, silversmiths, gunsmiths, upholsterers. They ran mills, plantations, tan yards, shipyards, and every kind of shop, tavern and boarding house. They were gate keepers, jail keepers, sextons, journalists, printers, "doctoresses," apothecaries, midwives, nurses, and teachers. Women acquired their skills the same way as did the men, through apprenticeship training, frequently within their own families.[3]

Absence of a dowry, ease of marriage and remarriage, and a more lenient attitude of the law with regard to women's property rights were manifestations of the improved position of wives in the colonies. Under British common law, marriage destroyed a woman's contractual capacity; she could not sign a contract even with the consent of her husband. But colonial authorities were more lenient toward the wife's property rights by protecting her dower rights in her husband's property, granting her personal clothing, and upholding pre-nuptial contracts between husband and wife. In the absence of the husband, colonial courts granted women "femme sole" rights, which enabled them to conduct their husband's business, sign contracts, and sue. The relative social freedom of women and the esteem in which they were held was commented upon by most early foreign travelers in America.[4]

But economic, legal, and social status tells only part of the story. Colonial society as a whole was hierarchical, and rank and standing in society depended on the position of the men. Women did not play a determining role in the ranking pattern; they took their position in society through the men of their own family or the men they married. In other words, they participated in the hierarchy only as daughters and wives, not as individuals. Similarly, their occupations were, by and large, merely auxiliary, designed to contribute to family income, enhance their husbands' business or continue it in case of widowhood. The self-supporting spinsters were certainly the exception. The underlying assumption of colonial society was that women ought to occupy an inferior and subordinate position. The settlers had brought this assumption with them from Europe; it was reflected in their legal concepts, their willingness to exclude women from political life, their discriminatory educational practices. What is remarkable is the extent to which this felt inferiority of women was constantly challenged and modified under the impact of environment, frontier conditions, and a favorable sex ratio.

By 1840 all of American society had changed. The Revolution had substituted an egalitarian ideology for the hierarchical concepts of colonial life. Privilege based on ability rather than inherited status, upward mobility for all groups of society, and unlimited opportunities for individual self-fulfillment had become ideological goals, if not always realities. For men, that is; women were, by tacit concensus, excluded from the new democracy. Indeed their actual situation had in many respects deteriorated. While, as wives, they had benefitted from increasing wealth, urbanization, and industrialization, their role as economic producers and as political members of society differed sharply from that of men. Women's work outside of the home no longer met with social approval; on the contrary, with two notable exceptions, it was condemned. Many business and professional occupations formerly open to women were now closed, many others restricted as to training and advancement. The entry of large numbers of women into low status, low pay, and low skill industrial work had fixed such work by definition as "woman's work." Women's political status, while legally unchanged, had deteriorated relative to the advances made by men. At the same time the genteel lady of fashion had become a model of American femininity, and the definition of "woman's proper sphere" seemed narrower and more confined than ever.

Within the scope of this essay only a few of these changes can be more fully explained. The professionalization of medicine and its impact on women may serve as a typical example of what occurred in all the professions.

In colonial America there were no medical schools, no medical journals, few hospitals, and few laws pertaining to the practice of the healing arts. Clergymen and governors, barbers, quacks, apprentices, and women practiced medicine. Most practitioners acquired their credentials by reading Paracelsus and Galen and serv-

ing an apprenticeship with an established practitioner. Among the
semi-trained "physics," surgeons, and healers the occasional "doc-
toress" was fully accepted and frequently well rewarded. County
records of all the colonies contain references to the work of the
female physicians. There was even a female Army surgeon, a Mrs.
Allyn, who served during King Philip's war. Plantation records
mention by name several slave women who were granted special
privileges because of their useful service as midwives and "doctoresses." [5]

The period of the professionalization of American medicine dates
from 1765, when Dr. William Shippen began his lectures on
midwifery in Philadelphia. The founding of medical faculties in
several colleges, the standardization of training requirements, and
the proliferation of medical societies intensified during the last
quarter of the 18th century. The American Revolution dramatized
the need for trained medical personnel, afforded first-hand battle-
field experience to a number of surgeons and brought increasing
numbers of semi-trained practitioners in contact with the handful
of European-trained surgeons working in the military hospitals.
This was an experience from which women were excluded. The
resulting interest in improved medical training, the gradual appearance of graduates of medical colleges, and the efforts of medical societies led to licensing legislation. In 1801 Maryland required
all medical practitioners to be licensed; in 1806 New York enacted
a similar law, followed by all but three states. [6] This trend was
reversed in the 1830s and 40s when most states repealed their
licensure requirements. This was due to pressure from eclectic,
homeopathic practitioners, the public's dissatisfaction with the
"heroic medicine" then practiced by licensed physicians, and to the
distrust of state regulation, which was widespread during the Age
of Jackson. Licensure as prime proof of qualification for the practice
of medicine was reinstituted in the 1870s.

In the middle of the 19th century it was not so much a license
or an M.D. which marked the professional physician as it was
graduation from an approved medical college, admission to hospi-

tal practice and to a network of referrals through other physicians. In 1800 there were four medical schools, in 1850, forty-two. Almost all of them excluded women from admission. Not surprisingly, women turned to eclectic schools for training. Harriot Hunt, a Boston physician, was trained by apprenticeship with a husband and wife team of homeopathic physicians. After more than twenty years of practice she attempted to enter Harvard Medical school and was repeatedly rebuffed. Elizabeth Blackwell received her M.D. from Geneva (New York) Medical College, an eclectic school. Sarah Adamson found all regular medical schools closed against her and earned an M.D. in 1851 from Central College at Syracuse, an eclectic institution. Clemence Lozier graduated from the same school two years later and went on to found the New York Medical College and Hospital for women in 1863, a homeopathic institution which was later absorbed into the Flower-Fifth Avenue Hospital.

Another way in which professionalization worked to the detriment of women can be seen in the cases of Drs. Elizabeth and Emily Blackwell, Marie Zakrzewska, and Ann Preston, who despite their M.D.s and excellent training were denied access to hospitals, were refused recognition by county medical societies, and were denied customary referrals by male colleagues. Their experiences were similar to those of most of the pioneer women physicians. Such discrimination caused the formation of alternate institutions for the training of women physicians and for hospitals in which they might treat their patients.[7] The point here is not so much that any one aspect of the process of professionalization excluded women but that the process, which took place over the span of almost a century, proceeded in such a way as to institutionalize an exclusion of women, which had earlier been accomplished irregularly, inconsistently, and mostly by means of social pressure. The end result was an *absolute* lowering of status for all women in the medical profession and a *relative* loss. As the professional status of all physicians advanced, the status differential between male and female practitioners was more obviously disadvantageous and underscored women's marginality. Their virtual exclusion from the most prestigious and lucrative branches of the profession and their concentration in specializations relating to women and children made such disadvantaging more obvious by the end of the 19th century.

This process of pre-emption of knowledge, of institutionalization of the profession, and of legitimation of its claims by law and public acceptance is standard for the professionalization of the sciences, as George Daniels has pointed out.[8] It inevitably results in the elimination of fringe elements from the profession. It is interesting to note that women had been pushed out of the medical profession in 16th-century Europe by a similar process.[9] Once the public had come to accept licensing and college training as guarantees of up-to-date practice, the outsider, no matter how well qualified by years of experience, stood no chance in the competition. Women were the casualties of medical professionalization.

In the field of midwifery the results were similar, but the process was more complicated. Women had held a virtual monopoly in the profession in colonial America. In 1646 a man was prosecuted in Maine for practicing as a midwife.[10] There are many records of well-trained midwives with diplomas from European institutions working in the colonies. In most of the colonies midwives were licensed, registered, and required to pass an examination before a board. When Dr. Shippen announced his pioneering lectures on midwifery, he did it to "combat the widespread popular prejudice against the man-midwife" and because he considered most midwives ignorant and improperly trained.[11]

Yet he invited "those women who love virtue enough, to own their Ignorance, and apply for instruction" to attend his lectures, offering as an inducement the assurance that female pupils would be taught privately. It is not known if any midwives availed themselves of the opportunity.[12]

Technological advances, as well as scientific, worked against the interests of female midwives. In 16th-century Europe the invention and use of obstetrical forceps had for three generations been the well-kept secret of the Chamberlen family and had greatly enhanced their medical practice. Hugh Chamberlen was forced by circumstances to sell the secret to the Medical College in Amsterdam, which in turn transmitted the precious knowledge to licensed physicians only. By the time the use of the instrument became widespread it had become associated with male physicians and male midwives. Similarly in America, introduction of the obstetrical forceps was associated with the practice of male midwives and served to their advantage. By the end of the 18th century a number of male physicians advertised their practice of midwifery. Shortly thereafter female midwives also resorted to advertising, probably in an effort to meet the competition. By the early 19th century male physicians had virtually monopolized the practice of midwifery on the Eastern seaboard. True to the generally delayed economic development in the Western frontier regions, female midwives continued to work on the frontier until a much later period. It is interesting to note that the concepts of "propriety" shifted with the prevalent practice. In 17th-century Maine the attempt of a man to act as a midwife was considered outrageous and illegal; in mid-19th-century America the suggestion that women should train as midwives and physicians was considered equally outrageous and improper.[13]

Professionalization, similar to that in medicine with the elimination of women from the upgraded profession, occurred in the field of law. Before 1750, when law suits were commonly brought to the courts by the plaintiffs themselves or by deputies without specialized legal training, women as well as men could and did act as "attorneys-in-fact." When the law became a paid profession and trained lawyers took over litigation, women disappeared from the court scene for over a century.[14]

A similar process of shrinking opportunities for women developed in business and in the retail trades. There were fewer female storekeepers and business women in the 1830s than there had been in colonial days. There was also a noticeable shift in the kind of merchandise handled by them. Where previously women could be found running almost every kind of retail shop, after 1830 they were mostly found in businesses which served women only.[15]

The only fields in which professionalization did not result in the elimination of women from the upgraded profession were nursing and teaching. Both were characterized by a severe shortage of labor. Nursing lies outside the field of this inquiry since it did not become an organized profession until after the Civil War. Before then it was regarded peculiarly as a woman's occupation, although some of the hospitals and the Army during wars employed male nurses. These bore the stigma of low skill, low status, and low pay. Generally, nursing was regarded as simply an extension of the unpaid services performed by the housewife—a characteristic attitude that haunts the profession to this day.

Education seems, at first glance, to offer an entirely opposite pattern from that of the other professions. In colonial days women had taught "Dame schools" and grade schools during summer sessions. Gradually, as educational opportunities for girls expanded, they advanced just a step ahead of their students. Professionalization of teaching occurred between 1820 and 1860, a period marked by a sharp increase in the number of women teachers. The spread of female seminaries, academies, and normal schools provided new opportunities for the training and employment of female teachers.

This trend, which runs counter to that found in the other professions, can be accounted for by the fact that women filled a desperate need created by the challenge of the common schools, the ever-increasing size of the student body, and the westward growth of the nation. America was committed to educating its children in public schools, but it was insistent on doing so as cheaply as possible. Women were available in great numbers, and they were willing to work cheaply. The result was another ideological adaptation: in the very period when the gospel of the home as woman's only proper sphere was preached most loudly, it was discovered that women were the natural teachers of youth, could do the job better than men, and were to be preferred for such employment.

This was always provided, of course, that they would work at the proper wage differential—30 to 50 per cent of the wages paid male teachers was considered appropriate. The result was that in 1888 in the country as a whole 63 per cent of all teachers were women, while the figure for the cities only was 90.04 per cent.[16]

It appeared in the teaching field, as it would in industry, that role expectations were adaptable provided the inferior status group filled a social need. The inconsistent and peculiar patterns of employment of black labor in the present-day market bear out the validity of this generalization.

There was another field in which the labor of women was appreciated and which they were urged to enter—industry. From Alexander Hamilton to Matthew Carey and Tench Coxe, advocates of industrialization sang the praises of the working girl and advanced arguments in favor of her employment. The social benefits of female labor particularly stressed were those bestowed upon her family, who now no longer had to support her. Working girls were "thus happily preserved from idleness and its attendant vices and crimes," and the whole community benefitted from their increased purchasing power.[17]

American industrialization, which occurred in an underdeveloped economy with a shortage of labor, depended on the labor of women and children. Men were occupied with agricultural work and were not available or were unwilling to enter the factories. This accounts for the special features of the early development of the New England textile industry: the relatively high wages, the respectability of the job and relatively high status of the mill girls, the patriarchal character of the model factory towns, and the temporary mobility of women workers from farm to factory and back again to farm. All this was characteristic only of a limited area and of a period of about two decades. By the late 1830s the romance had worn off: immigration had supplied a strongly competitive, permanent work force willing to work for subsistence wages; early efforts at trade union organization had been shattered, and mechanization had turned semi-skilled factory labor into unskilled labor. The process led to the replacement of the New England-born farm girls by immigrants in the mills and was accompanied by a loss of status and respectability for female workers.

The lack of organized social services during periods of depression drove ever greater numbers of women into the labor market. At first, inside the factories distinctions between men's and women's jobs were blurred. Men and women were assigned to machinery on the basis of local need. But as more women entered industry the limited number of occupations open to them tended to increase competition among them, thus lowering pay standards. Generally, women regarded their work as temporary and hesitated to invest in apprenticeship training, because they expected to marry and raise families. Thus they remained untrained, casual labor and were soon, by custom, relegated to the lowest paid, least skilled jobs. Long hours, overwork, and poor working conditions would characterize women's work in industry for almost a century.[18]

Another result of industrialization was in increasing differences in life styles between women of different classes. When female occupations, such as carding, spinning, and weaving, were transferred from home to factory, the poorer women followed their traditional work and became industrial workers. The women of the middle and upper classes could use their newly gained time for leisure pursuits: they became ladies. And a small but significant group among them chose to prepare themselves for professional careers by advanced education. This group would prove to be the most vocal and troublesome in the near future.

As class distinctions sharpened, social attitudes toward women became polarized. The image of "the lady" was elevated to the accepted ideal of femininity toward which all women would strive. In this formulation of values lower-class women were simply ignored. The actual lady was, of course, nothing new on the American scene; she had been present ever since colonial days. What was new in the 1830s was the cult of the lady, her elevation to a status symbol. The advancing prosperity of the early 19th century made it possible for middle-class women to aspire to the status formerly reserved for upper-class women. The "cult of true womanhood" of the 1830s became a vehicle for such aspirations. Mass circulation newspapers and magazines made it possible to teach every woman how to elevate the status of her family by setting "proper" standards of behavior, dress, and literary tastes. *Godey's Lady's Book* and innumerable gift books and tracts of the period all preach the same gospel of "true womanhood"—piety, purity, domesticity.[19] Those unable to reach the goal of becoming ladies were to be satisfied with the lesser goal—acceptance of their "proper place" in the home.

It is no accident that the slogan "woman's place is in the home" took on a certain aggressiveness and shrillness precisely at the time when increasing numbers of poorer women *left* their homes to become factory workers. Working women were not a fit subject for the concern of publishers and mass media writers. Idleness, once a disgrace in the eyes of society, had become a status symbol. Thorstein Veblen, one of the earliest and sharpest commentators on the subject, observed that it had become almost the sole social function of the lady "to put in evidence her economic unit's ability to pay." She was "a means of conspicuously unproductive expenditure," devoted to displaying her husband's wealth.[20] Just as the cult of white womanhood in the South served to preserve a labor and social system based on race distinctions, so did the cult of the lady in an egalitarian society serve as a means of preserving class distinctions. Where class distinctions were not so great, as on the frontier, the position of women was closer to what it had been in colonial days; their economic contribution was more highly valued, their opportunities were less restricted, and their positive participation in community life was taken for granted.

In the urbanized and industrialized Northeast the life experience of middle-class women was different in almost every respect from that of the lower-class women. But there was one thing the society lady and the mill girl had in common—they were equally disfranchised and isolated from the vital centers of power. Yet the political status of women had not actually deteriorated. With very few exceptions women had neither voted nor stood for office during the colonial period. Yet the spread of the franchise to ever wider groups of white males during the Jacksonian age, the removal of property restrictions, the increasing numbers of immigrants who acquired access to the franchise, made the gap between these new enfranchised voters and the disfranchised women more obvious. Quite naturally, educated and propertied women felt this deprivation more keenly. Their own career expectations had been encouraged by widening educational opportunities; their consciousness off their own abilities and of their potential for power had been enhanced by their activities in the reform movements of the 1830s; the general spirit of upward mobility and venturesome entrepreneurship that pervaded the Jacksonian era was infectious. But in the late 1840s a sense of acute frustration enveloped these educated and highly spirited women. Their rising expectations had met with frustration, their hopes had been shattered; they were bitterly conscious of a relative lowering of status and a loss of position. This sense of frustration led them to action; it was one of the main factors in the rise of the woman's rights movement.[21]

The women, who at the first woman's rights convention at Seneca Falls, New York, in 1848 declared boldly and with considerable exaggeration that "the history of mankind is a history of repeated injuries and usurpations on the part of man toward woman, having in direct object the establishment of an absolute tyranny over her," did not speak for the truly exploited and abused working woman.[22] As a matter of fact, they were largely ignorant of her condition and, with the notable exception of Susan B. Anthony, indifferent to her fate. But they judged from the realities of their own life experience. Like most revolutionaries, they were not the most downtrodden but rather the most status-deprived group. Their frustrations and traditional isolation from political power funneled their discontent into fairly utopian declarations and immature organizational means. They would learn better in the long, hard decades of practical struggle. Yet it is their initial emphasis on the legal and political "disabilities" of women which has pro-

vided the framework for most of the historical work on women.†
For almost a hundred years sympathetic historians have told the
story of women in America by deriving from the position of
middle-class women a generalization concerning all American
women. To avoid distortion, any valid generalization concerning
American women after the 1830s should reflect a recognition of
class stratification.

For lower-class women the changes brought by industrialization
were actually advantageous, offering income and advancement opportunities, however limited, and a chance for participation in the
ranks of organized labor.‡ They, by and large, tended to join men
in their struggle for economic advancement and became increasingly concerned with economic gains and protective labor legislation. Middle- and upper-class women, on the other hand, reacted
to actual and fancied status deprivation by increasing militancy and
the formation of organizations for woman's rights, by which they
meant especially legal and property rights.

The four decades preceding the Seneca Falls Convention were
decisive in the history of American women. They brought an actual deterioration in the economic opportunities open to women, a
relative deterioration in their political status, and a rising level of
expectation and subsequent frustration in a privileged elite group
of educated women. It was in these decades that the values and
beliefs that clustered around the assertion "Woman's place is in the
home" changed from being descriptive of an existing reality to
becoming an ideology. "The cult of true womanhood" extolled
woman's predominance in the domestic sphere, while it tried to
justify women's exclusion from the public domain, from equal education and from participation in the political process by claims to
tradition, universality, and a history dating back to antiquity, or
at least to the *Mayflower*. In a century of modernization and industrialization women alone were to remain unchanging, embodying

†To the date of the first printing of this article (1969).

‡In 1979, I would not agree with this optimistic generalization.

in their behavior and attitudes the longing of men and women caught in rapid social change for a mythical archaic past of agrarian family self-sufficiency. In pre-industrial America the home was indeed the workplace for both men and women, although the self-sufficiency of the American yeoman, whose economic well-being depended on a network of international trade and mercantilism, was even then more apparent than real. In the 19th and 20th centuries the home was turned into the realm of woman, while the workplace became the public domain of men. The ideology of "woman's sphere" sought to upgrade women's domestic function by elaborating the role of mother, turning the domestic drudge into a "homemaker" and charging her with elevating her family's status by her exercise of consumer functions and by her display of her own and her family's social graces. These prescribed roles never *were* a reality. In the 1950s Betty Friedan would describe this ideology and rename it "the feminine mystique," but it was no other than the myth of "woman's proper sphere" created in the 1840s and updated by consumerism and the misunderstood dicta of Freudian psychology.[23]

The decades 1800–1840 also provide the clues to an understanding of the institutional shape of the later women's organizations. These would be led by middle-class women whose self-image, life experience, and ideology had largely been fashioned and influenced by these early, transitional years. The concerns of middle-class women—property rights, the franchise, and moral uplift—would dominate the woman's rights movement. But side by side with it, and at times cooperating with it, would grow a number of organizations serving the needs of working women.

American women were the largest disfranchised group in the nation's history, and they retained this position longer than any other group. Although they found ways of making their influence felt continuously, not only as individuals but as organized groups, power eluded them. The mill girl and the lady, both born in the age of Jackson, would not gain access to power until they learned to cooperate, each for her own separate interests. It would take al-

most six decades before they would find common ground. The
issue around which they finally would unite and push their movement to victory was the "impractical and utopian" demand raised
at Seneca Falls—the means to power in American society—female
suffrage.

3

The Feminists: A Second Look

I ask no favors for my sex. All I ask our brethren is that they
will take their feet from off our necks and permit us to stand
upright on the ground which God designed us to occupy.

SARAH GRIMKÉ, 1838

Women are the best helpers of one another. Let them think; let
them act; till they know what they need. . . . But if you ask
me what offices they may fill, I reply—any. . . . Let them be
sea-captains if you will.

MARGARET FULLER, 1845

Between 1967 and 1970 a new feminism appeared in American political life as a vigorous, controversial, and somewhat baffling phenomenon. Any attempt to synthesize this diffuse and dynamic
movement is beset with difficulties, but it might be useful to view
it in historical perspective and to attempt an evaluation of its
ideology and tactics on the basis of the literature it has produced.

Feminist groups represent a wide spectrum of political views and
organizational approaches, divided generally into two broad cat-

This essay was first published in *The Columbia Forum,* XIII, #3 (Fall
1970), 24–30.

egories: the reform movement and the more radical Women's Liberation groups. The first is exemplified by NOW (National Organization of Women), an activist, civil rights organization, which uses traditional democratic methods for the winning of legal and economic rights, attacks mass media stereotypes, and features the slogan "equal rights in partnership with men." Reform feminists cooperate with the more radical groups in coalition activities, accept the radicals' rhetoric, and adopt some of their confrontation tactics; yet essentially they are an updated version of the old feminist movement, appealing to a similar constituency of women.

Small, proliferating, independent Women's Liberation groups, with their mostly youthful membership, make up a qualitatively different movement, which is significant far beyond its size. They support most of the reform feminist goals with vigorous and at times unorthodox means, but they are essentially dedicated to radical changes in all institutions of society. They use guerrilla theater, publicity stunts, and confrontation tactics, as well as the standard political techniques. Within these groups there is a strong emphasis on the re-education and psychological reorientation of the members and on fostering a supportive spirit of sisterhood.

What all new feminists have in common is a vehement impatience with the continuance of second-class citizenship and economic handicaps for women, a determination to bring our legal and value systems into line with current sexual mores, an awareness of the psychological damage to women of their subordinate position, and a conviction that changes must embrace not only laws and institutions, but also the minds, emotions, and sexual habits of men and women.

An important parallel exists between the new feminism and its 19th-century counterpart. Both movements resulted from an advance in the actual condition of women. Both were "revolutions of rising expectations" by groups who felt themselves deprived of status and frustrated in their expectations. Education, even up to the unequal level permitted women in the 1830s, was a luxury for the advantaged few, who found upon graduation that, except for school-teaching, no professions were open to them. At the same time, their inferior status was made even more obvious when the franchise, from which they were excluded, was extended to propertyless males and recent immigrants.

The existence of the early feminist movement depended on a class of educated women with leisure. The women who met in 1848 at Seneca Falls, New York, did not speak for the two truly exploited and oppressed groups of women of their day: factory workers and black women. Mill girls and middle-class women were organizing large women's organizations during the same decade, but there was little contact between them. Their life experiences, their needs and interests, were totally different. The only thing they had in common was that they were equally disfranchised.† This fact was of minor concern to working women, whose most urgent needs were economic. The long working day and the burdens of domestic work and motherhood in conditions of poverty gave them not enough leisure for organizing around anything but the most immediate economic issues. Except for a short period during the abolition movement, the interests of black women were ignored by the woman's rights movement. Black women had to organize separately and, of necessity, they put their race interests before their interests as women.

Unlike European women's rights organizations, which were from their inception allied to strong socialist-oriented labor movements, the American feminist movement grew in isolation from the most downtrodden and needy groups of women. William O'Neill, in his insightful study *The Woman Movement: Feminism in the United States and England,*[1] describes the way the absence of such an alliance decisively affected the composition, class orientation, and ideology of the American woman's rights movement. Al-

† In the light of recent scholarship it would be more accurate to add that all women were also educationally disadvantaged (though with sharp differences between women of different classes) and that all women were regulated and subordinated in their sexual behavior by men, groups of men, or by the state.

though there were brief, sporadic periods of cooperation between suffragists and working women, the feminists' concentration on the ballot as the cure-all for the ills of society inevitably influenced their tactics. Despite their occasional advocacy of unpopular radical causes, they never departed from a strictly mainstream, Christian, Victorian approach toward marriage and morality. By the turn of the century feminist leadership, like the male leadership of the Progressives, was nativist, racist, and generally indifferent to the needs of working women. Aileen Kraditor demonstrates in *The Ideas of the Women Suffrage Movement: 1890–1920*[2] that suffrage leaders relied on tactics of expediency. "Give us the vote to double your political power," was their appeal to reformers of every kind. They believed that, once enacted, female suffrage would promote the separate class interests, since women, as an oppressed group, would surely vote their common good. Opportunist arguments were used to persuade males and hostile females that the new voters would be respectable and generally inoffensive. A 1915 suffrage banner read:

> For the safety of the nation to
> Women give the vote
> For the hand that rocks the cradle
> Will never rock the boat

Not surprisingly, after suffrage was won, the woman's rights movement became even more conservative. But the promised block-voting of female voters failed to materialize. Class, race, and ethnic, rather than sex, divisions proved to be more decisive in motivating voting behavior. As more lower-class women entered the labor market and participated in trade-union struggles with men, they benefited, though to a lesser extent, where men did. Middle-class women, who now had free access to education at all levels, failed to take significant advantage of it, succumbing to the pressure of societal values that had remained unaffected by the narrow suffrage struggle. Economic advantages proved illusory as well, and consisted for most women in access to low-paid, low-

status occupations. The winning of suffrage had failed to emancipate women.

Still, the struggles of the early feminists had lessened legal and
institutional restrictions against women, had given women entry
into politics at all levels, and had taught them how to organize effectively. There was no slump in women's activities in the 1920s,
but there was a shift in emphasis, from the single-issue suffrage
campaign to a broad-spectrum attack on various issues related to
the welfare of women and children—the Sheppard-Towner Act,
world peace, and end to child labor; minimum wage and maximum hours legislation, aid to mothers of dependent children, and
the highly controversial issue of an Equal Rights Amendment. The
Great Depression, which made economic survival the primary concern for individuals of both sexes, affected women especially by
depriving them of some of the gains of earlier struggles.

If the new feminism did not appear on the scene in the 1930s or
40s, this was because the war economy had created new job opportunities for women. But at the end of World War II, returning
veterans quickly reclaimed their "rightful places" in the economy,
displacing female workers, and millions of women voluntarily took
up domesticity and war-deferred motherhood. The young women
of the 40s and 50s were living out the social phenomenon that
Betty Friedan called the "feminine mystique" and Andrew Sinclair
the "new Victorianism." Essentially it amounted to a cultural com-
mand to women, which they seemed to accept with enthusiasm, to
return to their homes, have large families, lead the cultivated
suburban life of status-seeking through domestic attainments, and
find self-expression in a variety of avocations. This tendency was
bolstered by Freudian psychology as adapted in America and
vulgarized through the mass media.[3]

It was left to the college-age daughters born of the World War
II generation to furnish the woman-power for the new feminist revolution. Like their forerunners, the new feminists were, with few
exceptions, white, middle class, and well educated. Raised in economic security—an experience quite different from that of their

Depression-scarred mothers—they had acquired an attitude toward work that demanded more from a job than security. They reacted with dismay to the discovery that their expensive college educations led mostly to the boring, routine jobs reserved for women. They felt personally cheated by the unfulfilled promises of legal and economic equality.

Moreover, they were the first generation of women raised entirely in the era of the sexual revolution. Shifting moral standards (especially among urban professionals), increased personal mobility, and the easy availability of birth control methods afforded these young women unprecedented sexual freedom. Yet this very freedom led to frustration and a sense of being exploited.

Many of these young women had participated, with high hopes and idealism, in the civil rights and student movements of the 50s and 60s. But they discovered that there, also, they were expected to do the dull jobs—typing, filing, housekeeping—while leadership remained a male prerogative. This discovery fueled much of the rage that characterized the Women's Liberation stance and turned many of these young women to active concern with their identity and place in society.

They continued in the 19th-century tradition by emphasizing equal rights and accepting the general concept of the oppression of women. The reformists have adopted, also, the earlier conviction that what is good for middle-class women is good for all women. Both branches, reform and radical, learned from the past the pitfalls of casting out the radicals in order to make the movement more respectable. Until now, they have valiantly striven for unity and flexibility. They have jointly campaigned for child-care centers, the Equal Rights Amendment, and the abolition of abortion legislation. They have organized congresses to unite women and a women's strike, and they have shown their desire for unity by accepting homosexual groups into the movement on the basis of full equality. But the radicals in Women's Liberation have gone far beyond their Victorian predecessors.

Radical feminism combines the ideology of classical feminism with the class-oppression concept of Marxism, the rhetoric and tactics of the Black Power movement, and the organizational structure of the radical student movement. Its own contribution to this rich amalgam is to apply class-struggle concepts to sex and family relations, and this they have fashioned into a world view. On the assumption that the traditional reformist demands of the new feminist are eminently justified, long overdue, and possible of fulfillment, the following analysis will focus on the more controversial, innovative aspects of radical theory and practice.[4]

The oppression of women is a central theoretical point for all feminists. But the radicals do not use this term simply to describe second-class citizenship and discrimination against women, conditions that can be ameliorated by a variety of reforms. The essence of their concept is that all women are oppressed and have been throughout all history. A typical statement reads:

> Women are an oppressed class. Our oppression is total, affecting every facet of our lives. . . . We identify the agents of our oppression as men. Male supremacy is the oldest, most basic form of domination. All other forms of oppression (racism, capitalism, imperialism, etc.) are extensions of male supremacy: men dominate women, a few men dominate the rest. . . . *All men* receive economic, sexual, and psychological benefits from male supremacy. *All men* have oppressed women.[5]

Actually opinions as to the source of the oppression vary. Some blame capitalism and its institutions, and look to a socialist revolution for liberation, while others believe that all women are oppressed by all men. Where socialist governments have failed to alter decisively the status of women, the socialists say, it is because of the absence of strong indigenous Women's Liberation movements.

If what they mean by oppression is the suffering of discrimination, inferior rights, indignities, economic exploitation, then one must agree, undeniably, that all women are oppressed. But this does not mean that they are an oppressed class, since in fact they are dispersed among all classes of the population. And to state that "women have always been oppressed" is unhistorical and politically counterproductive, since it lends the authority of time and tradition to the practice of treating women as inferiors.

In fact, in the American experience, the low status and economic oppression of women developed during the first three decades of the 19th century and was a function of industrialization. It was only *after* economic and technological advances made housework an obsolete occupation, only *after* technological and medical advances made all work physically easier and childbearing no longer an inevitable yearly burden on women, that the emancipation of women could begin. The antiquated and obsolete value system under which American women are raised and live today can best be fought by recognizing that it is historically determined. It can therefore be ended by political and economic means.

The argument used by radical feminists that the essential oppression of women occurs in the home and consists in their services as housewives is equally vague and unhistorical.† The economic importance of housework and the status accorded the housewife depend on complex social, demographic, and economic factors. The colonial housewife, who could be a property-holding freeholder in her own right and who had access to any occupation she wished to pursue since she lived in a labor-scarce, underdeveloped country with a shortage of women, had a correspondingly high status, considerable freedom, and the knowledge that she was per-

---

† My criticism of the radical feminists' ahistorical approach still holds. I would not, today, react so unsympathetically as I did then to their flat assertion that "all men receive economic, sexual and psychological benefits from male supremacy." It is typical of the intellectual progression of many women toward feminism that we at first accept the most obvious legal and political rights demands, while denying staunchly the pervasiveness, universality, and extent of the subordination of women. I was no exception.

forming essential work. A similar situation prevailed on the Western frontier well into the 19th century.

The movement's oversimplified concept of class oppression may hamper its ability to deal with the diverse interests of women of all classes and racial groups. No doubt all women are oppressed in some ways, but some are distinctly more oppressed than others. The slaveholder's wife suffered the "disabilities of her sex" in being denied legal rights and educational opportunities and in her husband's habitual infidelities, but she participated in the oppression of her slaves. To equate her oppression with that of the slave woman is to ignore the real plight of the slave. Similarly, to equate the oppression of the suburban housewife of today with that of the tenant farmer's wife is to ignore the more urgent problems of the latter.

New feminists frequently use the race analogy to explain the nature of the oppression of women. A collectively written pamphlet defines this position:

> For most of us, our race and our sex are unequivocal, objective facts, immediately recognizable to new acquaintances. . . . Self-hatred in both groups derives not from anything intrinsically inferior about us, but from the treatment we are accustomed to. . . . Women and Blacks have been alienated from their own culture; they have no historical sense of themselves because study of their condition has been suppressed. . . . Both women and Blacks are expected to perform our economic function as service workers. Thus members of both groups have been taught to be passive and to please white male masters in order to get what we want.[6]

This analogy between Blacks and women is valid and useful as long as it is confined to the psychological effect of inferior status, but not when it is extended to a general comparison between the two groups. Black women are discriminated against more severely than any other group in our society: as Blacks, as women, and frequently as low-paid workers. So far, radical feminists have failed to deal adequately with the complex issues concerning black women, and the movement has generally failed to attract them.†

There is a segment of the radical feminist movement that sees all men as oppressors of all women and thinks of women as a caste. The minority group or caste analogy was first developed by Helen Hacker in 1951 and has greatly influenced Women's Liberation thinking.[7] Hacker posited that women, although numerically a majority, are in effect an oppressed caste in society and show the characteristics of such a caste: ascribed attributes, attitudes of accommodation to their inferior status, internalization of the social values that oppress them.

This analogy has since been augmented by a number of psychological experiments and attitude studies, which seem to confirm that women, like men, are socially and culturally prepared from early childhood for the roles society expects them to play. Social control through indoctrination, rewards, punishments, and social pressure leads to the internalization of cultural norms by the individual. Women are "brainwashed" to accept their inferior status in society as being in the natural order of things. It is, in fact, what they come to define as their femininity. There is increasing experimental evidence that it is their acceptance of this view of their femininity that causes women to fall behind in achievement during their high school years and to lack the necessary incentives for success in difficult professions.[8] And this acceptance creates conflicts in the women who do succeed in business and the professions. Mass media, literature, academia, and especially Freudian psychology, all contribute to reinforce the stereotype of femininity and to convince women who feel dissatisfied with it that they are neurotic or deviant. It is a process in which women themselves learn to participate.

Radical feminists see this system as being constantly reinforced by all-pervasive male supremacist attitudes. They regard male supremacy, or sexism—a term the movement coined—as the main enemy. They claim that, like racism, sexism pervades the con-

†True in 1970, the time of the first publication of this article.

sciousness of every man (and many women) and is firmly en-
trenched in the value system, institutions, and mores of our society. Attitudes toward this adversary vary. Some wish to change
institutionalized sexism; others believe that all men are primarily
sexist and have *personal* vested interests in remaining so; still others
see a power struggle against men as inevitable and advocate man-
hating as essential for the indoctrination of the revolutionists.

In viewing the oppression of women as caste or minority group
oppression, one encounters certain conceptual difficulties. Women
have been at various times and places a majority of the population,
yet they have shared in the treatment accorded minorities. Paradoxically, their status is highest when they are actually a minority,
as they were in colonial New England. Caste comes closest to
defining the position of women, but it fails to take into account
their uniqueness, as the only members of a low-ranking group who
live in more intimate association with the higher-ranking group
than they do with their own. Women take their status and privilege from the males in their family. Their low status is not maintained or bolstered by the threat of force, as is that of other subordinate castes. These facts would seem to limit severely the
propaganda appeal of those radical feminists who envision feminine
liberation in terms of anti-male power struggles. The ultimate
battle of the sexes, which such a view takes for granted, is surely as
unattractive a prospect to most women as it is to men. This particular theoretical analysis entraps its advocates in a self-limiting,
utopian counterculture, which may at best appeal to a small group
of alienated women but which can do little to alter the basic conditions of the majority of women.

The attack on sexism, however, is inseparable from the aims of
Women's Liberation; in it means and ends are perfectly fused. It
serves to uncover the myriad injuries casually inflicted on every
woman in our culture, and in the process women change themselves, as they are attempting to change others. Male supremacy
has had a devastating effect on the self-consciousness of women; it
has imbued them with a deep sense of inferiority, which has

stunted their development and achievements. In fighting sexism, women fight to gain self-respect.

In attempting to define the nature of the oppression of women, radical feminism reveals little advance over traditional feminist theories. All analogies—class, minority group, caste—approximate the position of women but fail to define it adequately. Women are a category unto themselves; an adequate analysis of their position in society demands new conceptual tools. It is to be hoped that feminist intellectuals will be able to develop a more adequate theoretical foundation for the new movement. Otherwise there is a danger that the weaknesses and limitations of the earlier feminist movement might be repeated.

Largely under the influence of the Black Power movement, Women's Liberation groups have developed new approaches to the organizing of women that include sex-segregated meetings and consciousness-raising groups. Various forms of separatist tactics are used: all-female meetings in which men are ignored; female caucuses that challenge male domination of organizations; outright anti-male power struggles in which males are eventually excluded from formerly mixed organizations; deliberate casting of men in roles contrary to stereotype, such as having men staff child-care centers while women attend meetings, and refusing to perform the expected female services of cooking, serving food, typing.

These tactics are designed to force men to face their sexist attitudes. More important still is their effect on women: an increase in group solidarity, a lessening of self-depreciation, a feeling of potential strength. In weekly "rap" sessions members engage in consciousness-raising discussions. Great care is taken to allow each woman to participate equally and to see that there are no leaders. Shyness, reticence, and the inability to speak out soon vanish in such a supportive atmosphere. Members freely share their experiences and thoughts with one another, learn to reveal themselves, and develop feelings of trust and love for women. The discovery that what they considered personal problems are in fact social phenomena has a liberating effect. From a growing awareness of how their inferior status has affected them, they explore the meaning of their femininity and, gradually, develop a new definition of womanliness, one they can accept with pride. Women in these groups try to deal with their sense of being weak, and of being manipulated and programmed by others. Being an emancipated woman means being independent, self-confident, strong, no longer mainly a sex object, valued for one's appearance.

The effect of the group is to free the energies of its members and channel them into action. This may largely account for the dynamic of the movement. A significant development is that the group has become a *community*, a substitute family. It provides a noncompetitive, supportive environment of like-minded sisters. Many see in it a model for the good society of the future, which would conceivably include enlightened men. It is interesting that feminists have unwittingly revitalized the mode of cooperation by which American women have traditionally lightened their burdens and improved their lives, from quilting bees to literary societies and cooperative child-care centers.

From this consciousness-raising work have come demands for changes in the content of school and college curricula. Psychology, sociology, history have been developed and taught, it is claimed, from a viewpoint that takes male supremacy for granted. Like Blacks, women grow up without models from the past with whom they can identify. New feminists are demanding a reorientation in the social sciences and history; they are clamoring for a variety of courses and innovations, including departments of feminist studies. They are asking scholars to re-examine their fields of knowledge and find out to what extent women and their viewpoints are included, to sharpen their methods and guard against built-in male supremacist assumptions, and to avoid making generalizations about men and women when in fact they are generalizing about men only. Feminists are confident that once this is done serious scholarly work regarding women will be forthcoming. Although

one may expect considerable resistance from educators and administrators, these demands will undoubtedly effect reforms that
should ultimately enrich our knowledge. In time, these reforms
could be more decisive than legal reforms in affecting societal values. They are a necessary precondition to making the full emancipation of women a reality.†

Radical feminists have added new goals to traditional feminist
demands: an end to the patriarchal family, new sexual standards, a
re-evaluation of male and female sex roles. Their novel views
regarding sex and the family are a direct outgrowth of the life experiences and life styles of the younger, or "pill," generation, the
first generation of young women to have control over their reproductive functions, independent of and without the need for cooperation from the male. This has led them to examine with detach-
ment the sexual roles women play. One statement reads:

> The role accorded to women in the sexual act is inseparable
> from the values taught to people about how to treat one an-
> other. . . . Woman is the object; man is the subject. . . .
> Men see sex as conquest; women as surrender. Such a value sys-
> tem in the most personal and potentially meaningful act of
> communication between men and women cannot but result in
> the inability of both the one who conquers and the one who
> surrenders to have genuine love and understanding between
> them.
> The question of sexual liberation for both men and women is
> fundamental to both the liberation of women and to the devel-
> opment of human relationships between people, since the ca-

† This was an early definition of what would later be known as Women's
Studies. My detached and disassociated tone in speaking of "the feminists" as "they" and not "we" indicates the limits of my then carefully
defined commitment. I made a sharp distinction between myself, the
scholar interested in the history of women, and the feminist interested in
certain political and social demands for change. I then saw such a separation as a necessity and a virtue. Obviously, I no longer do.

pacity for meaningful sexual experience is both an indication
and an actualization of the capacity for love which this society
stifles so successfully.[9]

Female frigidity is challenged as a male-invented myth by at
least one feminist author, Anne Koedt.[10] She explains that the
woman's role in the sexual act has been defined by men in such a
way as to offer *men* the maximum gratification. She exposes the way
in which women fake sexual pleasure in order to bolster the male
ego. It is a theme frequently confirmed in consciousness-raising
groups.

Radical feminists speak openly about sex and their "hang-ups"
in regard to it. This in itself has a liberating effect. Although they
take sexual freedom for granted, they challenge it as illusory and
expose the strong elements of exploitation and power struggle inherent in most sexual relationships. They are demanding instead a
new morality based on mutual respect and mutual satisfaction.
This may seem utopian to some men, threatening to others—it is
certainly new as raw material for a revolutionary movement.

In America, femininity is a commodity in the marketplace.
Women's bodies and smiling faces are used to sell anything from
deodorants to automobiles. In rejecting this, radical feminists are
insisting on self-determination in every aspect of their lives. The
concept that a woman has the right to use her own body without
interference and legislative intervention by one man, groups of
men, or the state, has already proved its dynamic potential in the
campaign to abolish abortion legislation.

But it is in their rejection of the traditional American family
that radical women are challenging our institutions most profoundly. They consider the patriarchal family, even in its fairly
democratic American form, oppressive of women because it institutionalizes their economic dependence on men in exchange for sexual and housekeeping services. They challenge the concept that
children are best raised in small, nuclear families that demand the
full- or part-time services of the mother as housekeeper, cook, and
drudge. They point to the kibbutzim of Israel, the institutional

child-care facilities of socialist countries, and the extended families
of other cultures as alternatives. Some are experimenting with het-
erosexual communal living; communes of women and children
only, "extended families" made up of like-minded couples and
their children, and various other innovations. They face with equa-
nimity the prospect of many women deliberately choosing to live
without marriage or motherhood. The population explosion, they
say, may soon make these choices socially desirable. Some feminists
practice voluntary celibacy or homosexuality; many insist that homosexuality should be available to men and women as a realistic
choice.

Not all radical feminists are ready to go that far in their sexual
revolution. There are those who have strong binding ties to one
man, and many are exploring, together with newly formed male
discussion groups, the possibilities of a new androgynous way of
life. But all challenge the definitions of masculinity and femininity in American culture. Nobody knows, they say, what men and
women would be like or what their relations might be in a society
that allowed free rein to human potential regardless of sex. The
new feminists are convinced that the needed societal changes will
benefit men as well as women. Men will be free from the economic
and psychic burdens of maintaining dependent and psychologically
crippled women. No longer will they be constantly obliged to test
and prove their masculinity. Inevitably, relations between the sexes
will be richer and more fulfilling for both.

What is the long-range significance of the new feminist movement? Judging from the support the feminists have been able to
mobilize for their various campaigns, it is quite likely that significant changes in American society will result from their efforts. In
line with the traditional role of American radical movements, their
agitation may result in the enactment of a wide range of legal and
economic reforms, such as equal rights and job opportunities,
vastly expanded child-care facilities, and equal representation in institutions and governing bodies. These reforms will, by their very
nature, be of greatest benefit to middle- and upper-class women

and will bring women into "the establishment" on a more nearly egalitarian basis.

The revolutionary potential of the movement lies in its attacks on the sexual values and mores of our society and in its impact on the psychology of those women who come within its influence. Changes in sexual expectations and role definitions and an end to "sexual politics," the use of sex as a weapon in a hidden power struggle, could indeed make a decisive difference in interpersonal relations, the functioning of the family, and the values of our society. Most important, the new feminists may be offering us a vision for the future: a truly androgynous society, in which sexual attributes will confer neither power nor stigma upon the individual—one in which both sexes will be free to develop and contribute to their full potential.

4

Women's Rights and American Feminism

Recent years have seen a surge of interest in the history of women, a field previously long neglected. Scholars in the field have not yet solved the problem of how to conceptualize women's role in history. They are also hampered by semantic confusion. The terms "woman's rights," "women's emancipation," "feminism" and, lately, "women's liberation" are frequently used interchangeably. A more precise semantic definition may clarify some of the basic assumptions with which historians approach this subject.

Just as the abolition movement is a specific phase, in time and scope, of the broader and more general antislavery movement, so the woman's rights movement is a phase, specific and limited in time and scope, of the broader American feminist movement. American feminism embraces all aspects of the emancipation of American women, that is, any struggle designed to elevate their status, socially, politically, economically, and in respect to their self-concepts. The woman's rights movement, on the other hand, has more narrowly defined the emancipation of women as the winning of legal rights. For seventy-two years it overlapped and was

This article was first published in *The American Scholar,* Vol. 40, No. 2 (Spring 1971).

synonymous with the woman's suffrage movement. It was therefore a specific aspect of the broader movement, just as the civil rights movement was but an aspect of the movement for black emancipation. Of the current scene, one can say that the woman's rights movement is defined by those organizations and individuals who see the question of women's emancipation largely as one of legal changes, whereas the feminist movement embraces the new feminism of women's liberation and a variety of other groups and causes.

What are women's rights? Essentially, they are civil rights—the right to vote, to hold office, to have access to power at every level on an equal basis with men, and to use the same channels for upward mobility as men do. They are also property rights—the right to contract, the right to hold and dispose of property, the right to one's earnings. All of these rights are based on the acceptance of the status quo, and the groups advocating them act like "out" groups wanting "in." Their demands are essentially reformist, based on appeals to justice and equity. Needless to say, their fulfillment is long overdue.

What is women's emancipation? It is freedom from oppressive restrictions imposed by sex; self-determination and autonomy. Freedom from oppressive restrictions means freedom from natural, biological restrictions due to sex as well as from societally imposed ones. Self-determination means being free to decide one's own destiny, being free to define one's own social role. Autonomy means earning one's own status, not being born to it or marrying it. It means financial and cultural independence, freedom to choose one's own life-style regardless of sex. In order for women to have autonomy, the handicap of male orientation and male domination in social institutions must first be removed.

Obviously, society must reach a certain level of development before such emancipation can take place. The preconditions for women's emancipation are: urbanization; industrialization with technology permitting society to remove food preparation and care of the sick from the home; the mechanization of heating and laundry; spread of health and medical care sufficient to lower infant mortality and protect maternal health; birth control; the development of transportation sufficient to permit physical mobility to all groups of the population, with its accessory freedom from parental and communal restraints; and availability of education on all levels to all children without discrimination. Clearly, women's full emancipation has nowhere on earth been accomplished. This is not so much the result of a male conspiracy as of shifting historic circumstances. The fact is that women do indeed live under disabilities of sex in societies where maternal health care is poor and infant mortality high, offset only by a high birth rate. Such societies require for their survival that as many women as possible bear and rear as many children as possible. In such societies, women are not "free" to engage in the same work as men do, nor are they able to conceptualize the possibility of doing so. Such primitive agrarian societies have existed everywhere on earth at various times and are marked by a division of labor between the sexes, in which biology is indeed destiny.†

In the United States these conditions prevailed generally in the colonies, except for a few cities, and later in the frontier regions. It is noteworthy that during this period there was no woman's rights movement, because none was possible or conceivable, but there was feminist activity and self-conscious effort on the part of a few individuals to strive for women's emancipation. In 1647, Margaret Brent asked for the right to cast two votes in the Maryland assembly—one as Lord Baltimore's attorney, another as a landholder and "court baron." The fact that she was granted one vote as an at-

---

† It is noteworthy that in pre-agrarian societies, among hunting and gathering people, there is a far greater range of variation in the tasks assigned to the sexes, especially in regard to child-rearing. There is good evidence that the sexual division of labor we take for granted as "natural" and "universal" is in fact the product of historic development, originating with the agrarian revolution. For detailed evidence see M. K. Martin and B. Voorhis, *The Female of the Species* (New York, Columbia University Press, 1975).

torney tells us a good deal about the position of women in the colony. Similarly, one might cite Anne Hutchinson's assertion of the right of women to interpret scripture to other women, or the case of Mary Dyer, whose nonviolent resistance campaign against religious intolerance ended on the scaffold in 1660, and who, with other Quaker women, asserted by voluntary death the right of women to engage in such political-religious work. Mercy Otis Warren, Abigail Adams, and Judith Sargent Murray are other early feminists who in various ways advanced arguments for women's emancipation. It is significant that all of these were wealthy or well-to-do women.

Under conditions of a shortage of labor and—as in colonial New England and on the frontier—a shortage of women, a sex-based division of labor did not imply differentiation in status. All work was essential for the survival of the community, hence all work had dignity. But when the community was wealthy enough to make luxuries, such as a prolonged education, available to some, but not to others, role differentiation based on sex began to be felt as oppressive and unequal. As long as all children shared in the primitive educational opportunities, and as long as most education was carried on in the home or by private tutors, boys and girls enjoyed nearly equal educational opportunity. But when education began to be institutionalized, the exclusion of girls from higher education was an actual deprivation and implied lower status. Similarly, the access to a variety of occupations enjoyed earlier by colonial women became limited as soon as American society had advanced to a point where professionalization could take place. Professional status was restricted to those who had followed a prescribed course of education within established institutions. Since women were excluded from such institutions, they were automatically excluded from the rising professions, such as law and medicine. In the American setting, this shrinking of opportunities for women occurred in the early 19th century. Combined with increased opportunities for males, resulting from the spread of the franchise and from upward mobility based on entrepreneurship, this status loss, both actual and perceived by women, was very obvious. It was this deprivation that gave rise to a sense of status displacement in an educated, white, middle-class elite, and that led to the emergence of the organized woman's rights movement.

It is true all over the world that woman's rights movements are dependent on a class of educated women with leisure. But the nature of the movement depends on historic circumstances. A number of historians have wondered why the American woman's rights movement placed so much emphasis on the ballot, to the neglect of other reforms. The explanation has been offered that this was in some way connected with the attitude of suffragists toward morality and their total acceptance of Victorian morality. This essentially conservative attitude toward sexual reform was seen, especially by Aileen Kraditor and William O'Neill, as having a seriously crippling effect on the movement. No doubt, but one is entitled to ask why this was so.[1]

The explanation may be that the woman's rights movement, due to its composition, was in the mainstream of American reform. Like other such movements, it tended to stress legal and constitutional reform rather than more radical changes. To cite a few examples:

The United States labor movement was decisively affected by the fact that American labor had citizenship and voting rights before it formed a mass trade-union movement. This development is significantly different from the European and British patterns, in which working-class, socialist-oriented parties became a permanent feature of the political system. American women and American Negroes did not have voting rights when they organized movements for their emancipation, but they lived in a nation in which the right to vote was constitutionally guaranteed to all citizens. At the time when both of these movements were launched, voting rights had recently been extended to propertyless white males. Therefore, it was only natural that both of these movements focused on the ballot as the solution to their problems. The antislavery campaign saw its triumph in the passage of the civil rights amendments. All other needed reforms, including land distribution, were presumably to follow upon this magic enactment. Ironically, a hundred years later, the civil rights movement was offered yet another Civil Rights Act and kindred legal reforms as a substitute for the organizational, societal, institutional changes that are needed to render such laws meaningful and effective. The woman's rights movement operated within the same tradition and suffered from the same limitations—despite the fact that alternatives existed from the start. As early as 1825 American working girls had organized in trade unions for economic demands and, briefly, used political as well as economic means to advance these demands. But their movement remained generally isolated from the woman's rights movement.

Among the advocates of other forgotten alternatives to the woman's rights movement were Frances Wright, Robert Dale Owen, Ernestine Rose, John Humphrey Noyes, Henry C. Wright, and later Charlotte Gilman, Victoria Woodhull, Emma Goldman, and Margaret Sanger. These radicals had in common the convictions that the institutions of society were as oppressive to women as were its laws, that the patriarchal family was a questionable institution, and that sexual morality as hitherto defined would have to change. Their methods for attack and their specific programs varied, but they made the connection between religion, the family, sexual mores, and the social status of women. They pointed out, even if not always in specific terms, that merely constitutional changes would not basically alter the position of women.

Frances Wright, the first woman to engage in public lecturing in America, scandalized her contemporaries in a variety of ways. Not only did she advocate birth control, easy divorce and free love, but she allowed the latter to be practiced, even on an interracial basis, in the utopian community she had founded in Tennessee. Nashoba was to demonstrate the feasibility of the gradual emancipation of slaves, who earned their purchase price by manual labor in the community, while being educated for freedom. Frances Wright believed that these former slaves should be accorded the same sexual rights as other members of the community and she

refused to disavow her fellow-utopians' actions, when a community
diary, published in a reform journal during her absence, revealed
incidents of interracial free love relationships, which deeply
shocked abolitionist reformers outside the community. Moreover,
she was actively involved in organizing the first labor party in the
United States, the Workingman's Association—and promoted
within that group, during the 1828 and 1830 state election campaigns, the principle of public education for all children, starting
at age two and in boarding schools. While women's liberation was
not specifically listed as one of the expected benefits, she did mention that this scheme would equalize educational opportunities for
workers' children, imbuing children of all classes with the egalitarian spirit that she regarded as the essential principle of American democracy. That the public education issue split the Workingman's Party in 1830, causing it serious electoral losses and
probably contributing to its early demise, is not surprising.[2]
Frances Wright appeared on the scene too soon to influence the
first generation of feminists directly, although some of them had
certainly heard of her activities. It is noteworthy that the first volume of *History of Woman Suffrage* features a tribute to Frances
Wright, though only in her role as a public speaker.[3] Latter-day
feminists ignored her advanced ideas for sexual, moral, and educational reform.

Both the first and second generation of activists in the woman's
rights movement had direct acquaintance with and exposure to the
practices and ideas of other utopians. The Fourierists allowed
women to wear a costume somewhat similar to the Bloomer costume, with ballooning pants tied at the ankles, which was certainly an improvement over the whaleboned, corsetted and bustled
monstrosities, weighing upward of fifteen pounds, in which 19th-
century women attempted to pursue their daily activities. The
Fourierists collectivized housekeeping chores, but divided the work
tasks in the conventional manner among men and women. But
since women had full voting rights in their communes, Fourierists
could certainly have served as models for possible alternatives to

the Victorian family. The same holds true for other communarians, such as those at Oneida, whose moving spirit, John Humphrey Noyes, advocated free love, equality of the sexes, and male continence as a method of birth control.[4]

Ernestine Rose, Frances Wright, and Robert Dale Owen were freethinkers or opponents of established religion, who wrote and spoke extensively and exposed the connection between the subordinate position of women and the teachings of orthodox religion. Henry C. Wright advocated greater equality in marital and sex relations, sex education and family planning. Charlotte Gilman, Victoria Woodhull, Emma Goldman, Margaret Sanger, all had unorthodox life-styles—each was divorced; Charlotte Gilman voluntarily renounced custody and care of her only child in favor of her husband and his second wife, with whom she remained on the friendliest terms for years after her divorce; Victoria Woodhull, who led a notoriously scandalous life without any effort at dissimulation, attacked the double standard by her printed revelations of a sexual scandal involving the highly respected clergyman and reformer, Henry Ward Beecher, and one of his parishioners, Elizabeth Tilton, a married woman. Emma Goldman openly acknowledged her love affairs and widely publicized her advocacy of "free love."[5]

Charlotte Gilman's major theoretical contribution was a fully developed theory of women's emancipation, based not so much on legal changes as on an economic revolution and basic changes in the institution of marriage.[6] Margaret Sanger's single-minded pursuit of birth control as the cure-all for the "disabilities of sex" was perhaps the most significant alternative to the woman's rights approach. It is interesting that Sanger carried her lonely and at first quite unsuccessful campaign so far as deliberately to become a fugitive from the law and leave the country in order to avoid arrest for violating an obscenity law. Her justification was entirely political: she would be arrested only at a time of her choosing, when her case would advance her cause by testing the Comstock law's provision forbidding the distribution of contraceptive information and devices. While she was in Europe, she arranged for 100,000 copies of her magazine, carrying birth control information, to be distributed in the United States. Having thus created a clear test case, Sanger returned to New York and peacefully submitted to her arrest. This action was at least as radical and political as was the much more publicized picketing of the White House by the Woman's Party, and accomplished a good deal more for the emancipation of women.[7]

Recent scholarship has brought to light the important role played by Emma Goldman and other feminist women in the socialist and anarchist movement. Goldman lectured widely on birth control from 1910 on and served sixty days in jail for distributing pamphlets which offered advice on birth control methods and devices. She was one of the earliest influences on Margaret Sanger, who later sought to deny the socialist roots of her inspiration.[8] The list of early practitioners and theorists of women's emancipation could be extended, but the point is made: they were continuously in evidence on the American scene; they provided useful radical alternatives to the Victorian family and to the strictly Constitutional approach taken by suffragists—but they were not able to influence significantly the organized woman's rights movement.

The distinction between women's rights and women's emancipation becomes crucial in dealing with women of different social classes. It is a common fallacy to proceed on the assumption that what is true for middle-class women is true for all women. The fact is that, for members of the working class and for the poor, women's rights are essentially meaningless. In the absence of property, inheritance and other property rights are irrelevant. The right to contract means only the right to contract one's labor, and here the working-class woman must, out of need, take what the market offers, regardless of the law. In fact, equal rights and standards regulated by law often deprive the poorest women of the chance to work at all—since work is available to them only at substandard wages. To lower-class children of both sexes—and this applies to the period from the Civil War to World War I—access to education is significant only insofar as it opens doors to upward mobility, which is in their case limited by various other restraints and prejudices. For the working-class girl, spinsterhood is not synonymous with independence, since, with her low wages and in the crowded housing conditions of the poor, spinsterhood means staying in her parents' house as an adult, which is hardly freedom. In fact, marriage and other sexual liaisons offer much more chance of upward mobility for the lower-class girl than does education. Working-class standards of morality take such facts into consideration and are far less restrictive and retributive than are upper-class standards, especially regarding premarital sex and illegitimate children. Historians who make generalizations about the impact of Victorian morality on American women would do well to remember that Victorian morality applied to the "better" classes only. It was taken for granted during that period and well into the 20th century that working-class women—and especially black women—were freely available for sexual use by upper-class males.

The proverbial immorality of factory girls caused much concern to Victorian ladies, who expended prodigious energies in useless efforts at amelioration. The racist myth that most black women were immoral persisted and proved to be the greatest stumbling block to the interracial activity of women. It took decades of patient educational work by black club-women to dispel it and to prove that middle-class black women shared the moral standards of white middle-class women. Class differences in marriage patterns were undeniable, although frequently ignored. Lower-class families freely separated without benefit of the law before divorce was legalized, and entered common-law marriages when they could not legally remarry. After divorce was legalized, they divorced at a greater rate than their middle-class counterparts. Even today, the values, sexual mores, life-styles, and life expectations of women of the blue-collar class are dramatically different from those of the middle class.[9] In fact, the life-styles of working-class women are much closer to those of the majority of 19th century women than to those of our own time.

The case is still different for black women, who have been doubly oppressed, as Blacks and as women. Race oppression has been
experienced as the primary burden, and it is a particular aspect of
this burden that a far greater percentage of black women than
white are poor working mothers in menial service occupations.
Race, caste, class, and sex discrimination fall upon them with particular severity. Historically, they have organized in separate
groups as women and, for the advancement of their racial interests,
have joined organizations with their men.

There is yet another difference between the status and perceived
problems of middle-class women and those of lower-class women.
Their position as housewives is quite different. It is obvious that
historically the family has undergone important changes in structure and function, bringing about essential changes in the position
of women. What Betty Friedan has described as the "feminine
mystique" is essentially the symptom of a cultural lag, in which
our societal and personal values are adapted to a family pattern that
has long ceased to exist.[10] The large, rural family—jointly producing most of the products for its own consumption, living self-suf-
ficiently outside of the cash economy, training its young in the
home, caring for its old, and providing both men and women with
lifelong activity and work, which had the dignity of being essential
to the group—needed the housewife and provided her with satisfying work.

A few decades after the Civil War this family had ceased to be
the prototype of the American family. But it was not until the
20th century that the full effect of urbanization, better medical
care, and longer life expectancy, combined with a lower birth rate,
was fully felt. The modern urban family, which has removed all
productive and most educational and welfare functions from the
home and which requires the full-time services of the housewife-
mother for a relatively brief span of time—five to eight years,
while the children are pre-schoolers—has made the lifelong occupation of housewife archaic. As Betty Friedan pointed out, no
amount of glamorizing, advertising, and verbal upgrading can

make homemaking anything more than a part-time job stretched out into a full-time, supposedly life-filling occupation. Since upper- and middle-class families have fewer children, employ domestic help, and can afford the various services available to lighten household chores, it is not surprising that middle-class women feel more discontented and restless in their empty, socially prescribed role. . . .

All of this is quite different for the lower-class family. Among the eleven million poor families (those with an annual income under $4000), the housewife still performs an essential function. Even the economically more privileged blue-collar worker's family could not survive, if the mother did not contribute her unpaid labor, which directly supplements the wages paid to her husband. This does not lessen her burden or exploitation, but it does make a difference in her subjective attitude toward her role. It also explains her general indifference to women's rights organizations.†

If these women find little appeal in women's rights as such, their emancipation is nevertheless progressing. Labor-protective legislation, welfare-state measures, improvements in medical and health care, the availability of birth control information—these are all reforms that advance the status of lower-class women. Working women have traditionally perceived that the trade-union movement, despite its predominant insensitivity to the problems of women, still offers their best chance for advancement. In those unions where women have been able to organize as separate entities, such as in the United Automobile Workers, considerations of their special needs could be secured, and important advances, such as job protection after maternity leaves, could be written into

† At the time this article first appeared, working-class women had not yet begun to participate in an organized way in the women's liberation movement. Since then, working women have organized along feminist lines in the Congress of Labor Union Women (CLUW), and working-class housewives have organized in the National Congress of Neighborhood Women. These are just two among a number of feminist groups comprised mainly of working-class women.

union contracts. This parallels the European pattern, where the major legislative gains for working women were won through the pressure of strongly feminist-oriented organizations of working-class women within or without the trade-union movement. This has been the exception in the United States, however, not the rule.

The preconditions for the emancipation of American women prevailed throughout most of the country for the upper and middle classes by the time of World War I. Women of all classes had by then experienced some very tangible improvements over their previous condition, which they would soon take for granted as "natural": freedom to dress so as to enjoy unhampered movement; freedom to move outside the family and escape familial or communal taboos and ostracism for deviant behavior; the right and possibility not to have one's procreative functions dominate all one's life; the right to divorce without social stigma. To middle-class women, the attainment of suffrage, and of those legal-constitutional changes they expected would inevitably follow upon suffrage, seemed adequate. This explains the waning interest in the woman's rights movement after 1920.

World War II, as had previous wars, exposed working-class women to the possibilities of well-paying jobs, free child-care centers, training opportunities for skilled employment. But, after the war, "Rosie, the Riveter" was told to go home where she belonged and produce babies, not ships. She did just that, with disastrous effects on our overcrowded schools and other institutions. One might have expected, then, that pressures for female advancement would at last come from these lower-class women.[11]

That this did not happen is due to a familiar paradox: the women who most need reforms are helpless to enact them: the women who are most able to work for reforms are not in great need of them. The results are as one might expect: middle-class women support the more far-reaching demands of working-class women up to a point, then they relax their efforts. In this country, during the Progressive period, the interests of women of all classes briefly coincided. Suffragists needed the support of trade unionists and labor in general in order to secure their goal; working women hoped that female suffrage would serve to enact the reforms they needed—this overlapping of interests held the alliance together. After 1920, having won their "rights," middle-class women succumbed to the negative pressures of society, which earlier they had been able to withstand. Working-class women, who usually bear the triple burden of work, housework, and child care, without benefit of those replacement services available for money, are too weak as a group to organize and struggle in their own behalf, except for the most immediate economic gains. Still, there has been a continuous thread of organizational effort on the community level from the New Deal to the present day. Such movements as meat boycotts during World War II, consumer strikes, rent struggles, and, more recently, organization around school issues, in which lower-class women have played a significant role, deserve to be studied and interpreted by social historians.

The women's emancipation movement has experienced a sudden resurgence in the past five years. The current movement has followed the traditional pattern of concentrating on constitutional-legal reforms that most benefit middle-class women, such as the Equal Rights Amendment. But the women's liberation movement has infused feminism with a new spirit. The more youthful and radical wing of the new feminist movement has been innovative and experimental and has striven hard to escape the historical pattern of reform and failure.

Technology and science have provided, for the first time in human history, the conditions for the potential eradication of sex-based differences among humans. Overpopulation on a world scale has raised moral questions that affect the most personal human relations. Excessive reproduction, like excessive consumption, may soon be considered against the best interests of society, if not outright immoral. With the lessening importance of their reproductive role, with altered conditions for their social functioning, women need to have oppressive institutional restraints lifted from them. There is no longer any justification for their existence.

This means, practically speaking, the kind of change in role expectations and psychological orientation women's liberationists have been talking about. It does not mean only women's rights. It means the emancipation of both men and women from a sex-dominated archaic division of labor and from the values that sustain it.

5

Black Women in the United States:
A Problem in Historiography
and Interpretation

The outstanding fact about the history of black women is that as a group they have experienced double oppression: that oppression shared by all Blacks in a racist society and that peculiar to women. One mark of such oppression is a denial or neglect of their history. This long neglect has only recently begun to be corrected by an upsurge of interest in Black history, its acceptance by the historical profession into the body of American history, and its reinterpretation by white and black scholars. Yet black women have not shared in this black renaissance. This is so because as women they suffer the general invisibility of women in American history. Black women belonging to two groups which have traditionally been treated as inferior by American society have been doubly neglected: as Blacks and as women. Their records lie buried, seldom read, rarely interpreted. Their names and achievements are known to only a few specialists. When they do appear in history textbooks at all it is merely as victims, as helpless sufferers of conditions imposed upon them by others.

This essay was first given as a paper at the Annual Meeting of the Organization of American Historians (Chicago, 1973).

I am grateful to Professor Phyllis Vine for her technical advice and helpful criticism of this article.

This is reflected in the historiography of the subject. It is difficult to find black women in primary sources. Only a very few libraries have arranged their resources in such a way as to make material on black women easily accessible to the researcher. The card catalogues of most manuscript collections do not keep a listing for "Negro women," although they sometimes may list a few of the Negro women's clubs. The papers of outstanding figures such as Mary McLeod Bethune, Charlotte Hawkins Brown, Nannie Burroughs, and Ida B. Wells are scattered in various libraries and have never been edited or even partially published. There is no collection of the records of Negro women's clubs comparable to the club movement records of white women contained in the Sophia Smith Collection and those at the Schlesinger Library at Radcliffe.

Many libraries have primary sources on black women hidden among family papers, general organizational records, and educational and religious organization files. Much invaluable source material has simply not been collected and undoubtedly is lost to history. The few notable exceptions, such as the Mary Church Terrell papers at the Library of Congress, the women's history sources at the Schomburg Collection of the New York Public Library and those at Howard University and Fisk University, merely illustrate the wealth of material awaiting the work of archivists, librarians, and scholars.

The modern historian is dependent on the availability of primary sources. The kinds of sources collected depend to a large extent on the predilections, interests, prejudices, and values of the collectors and historians of an earlier day, which in this case reflect the indifferent attention given to women in history. It is therefore not surprising that there have been few scholarly biographies of black women of the past, fewer monographs, no scholarly interpretive works.[1] Black women are mentioned, usually briefly and peripherally, in most Black History texts. A recent rash of biographical works and anthologies reflecting current interest has been mostly on the journalistic level. Anthologies and biographical compilations, which prove the existence of a history of black women, suffer from the usual defects of compensatory historiography: they are unreliable as to the evidence and uncritical as to interpretation. Most of these were compiled by writers, educators, and journalists, not by historians.[2] Yet there is a rich and accessible history of black women. Those wishing to write and interpret that history share with those writing women's history the conceptual problems of interpreting known materials from a new point of view, a different angle of vision. But first they must do the job which the early compilers and collectors of women's history, the early feminists, did for their field—they must unearth, compile, and organize the raw materials on which interpretations can be based. The men who did similar groundwork for the field of Black history— Carter Woodson, Monroe Work, W. E. B. DuBois, Charles Johnson—amassed a great wealth of source material pertaining to women. It lies unorganized and largely unused among their papers and awaits the use of the modern historian.

What are the sources for a history of black women? Obviously, they are to be found among the sources for Black history, as well as among the women's history sources. Organizational records, both of women's organizations and of black or inter-racial organizations, offer much material, provided the researcher is willing to put in a good deal of time and effort. Neither the takers of minutes, the compilers of organizational files, nor their collectors have singled out women for attention, so that the researcher must constantly be on the alert for finding references to women and about women among a mass of other material. Autobiographies, manuscripts, letters, and diaries are invaluable, but the researcher will also be well rewarded by searching in official records, local history sources, church records. John Blassingame and Angela Davis have demonstrated what a sensitive reinterpretation of existing and well-known sources can reveal. Dorothy Porter has done pioneering work in interpreting little-known local records.[3] Local and regional histories of black women remain to be written. Studies of the Negro wom-

en's club movement, both nationally and more especially region-
ally, can yield much information about neglected aspects of black
community structure and experience, in which women played an
important part.[4] The economic contribution of black women and
the history of working women deserve a full and scholarly study.
The many black women of achievement deserve to have biographers and some, at least, merit collections of their speeches, letters, and writings. The themes are many; the sources are available.
Interpreting them, both separately and in the context of general
social history, is the challenging task before present and future historians.

The following generalizations are intended to suggest some of
the questions and problems which will have to be answered by historians in dealing with the problem of black women in history.

The first question to be asked of all subjects which have suffered
historical neglect are compensatory: What did black women actually do, experience, and achieve in the past? What is their special
historical contribution?

The second set of questions is comparative and concerns the
duality of their group definition: In what way was their historical
experience similar to that of black men? In what way was it similar
to that of white women?

Finally, assuming the premise of their double oppression as
members of two low-status groups, what useful generalizations can
be derived from comparing different subordinate or oppressed
groups within one culture? How much does the fact of their womanhood or of their blackness affect the collective history of black
women? How useful is the concept of "women-as-an-oppressed-
group" for analyzing the history of women? What methodological
conclusions, if any, can one draw for women's history by comparing black and white women?

What did black women actually do, experience, and achieve in
the past?[5] By and large, the record shows, as a group they fully
shared in the experience of their race. As individuals they did and
achieved what black men did. Black people in general, and black

women in particular, were far from being merely passive victims of oppression. The moral and spiritual contribution of black women to the survival of their families under harsh and repressive conditions was significant. As workers, they not only helped in the support of their families but provided essential, though poorly rewarded, services for the white community. They were active participants in the social struggles of their day, provided leadership, and, most importantly, helped build and maintain welfare and educational institutions in their communities. A few historical examples of institution-building by black women can illustrate the range of their efforts.

Black women always played an important role in furthering black education. Even during slavery times slave women ran underground schools and found ways of imparting the precious tools of literacy to some children.[6] The contributions of the Northern "school marm" to the education of freedmen children have been noted, but far less is known about the extensive contribution of black women teachers who sustained rural schools under the most primitive and impoverished conditions in the Jim Crow South at the turn of the century. Emma J. Wilson, a graduate of Scotia Seminary, opened a school in her native Mayesville, South Carolina, with ten pupils in an abandoned cotton-gin house, accepting eggs and chickens as tuition, and built this school into one serving 500 students and caring for fifty orphans. Similar feats were performed in other Southern states. While the contribution of Booker T. Washington in founding and building up Tuskegee Institute has been justly celebrated, that of women who did the same work is hardly known. Thus Lucy Lainey founded Haines Normal Institute in Atlanta, starting with 75 pupils in 1886. By 1940 the school had over 1000 students. Charlotte Hawkins Brown founded Palmer Memorial Institute in Sedalia, North Carolina, in 1902 and built this finishing school for black girls into one of the leading Southern schools, with fourteen modern buildings and a plant valued at over a million dollars. Nannie Burroughs, under the slogan "We Specialize in the Wholly Impossible," performed a similar feat of entrepreneurship and educational pioneering in her National Training School for Girls in Washington, D.C. In Daytona Beach, Florida, Mary McLeod Bethune literally started a school on a garbage dump in 1904, earning money for beds, groceries, and the packing boxes which served as desks by daily baking pies with her pupils and selling these to railroad workers. Today, Bethune-Cookman College stands as a monument to the organizational genius and indomitable spirit of this great woman.[7]

Throughout their history, black women always defined themselves first and foremost as members of an oppressed race, feeling their oppression as members of that race more keenly than their oppression as women. Expressions by black women concerning the priority of race oppression are numerous. A few characterize the trend: "After all whether they encourage or discourage me, I belong to this race," Frances Ellen Watkins Harper wrote in 1870 from the Reconstruction South, "and when it is down I belong to a down race; when it is up I belong to a risen race." And she continued: "Oh, if some more of our young women would only consecrate their lives to the work of upbuilding the race!" Earlier, during a discussion of the Fourteenth and Fifteenth Amendments and the continued exclusion of *women* from the ballot, she had remarked that "when it was a question of race, she let the lesser question go. But the white women all go for sex, letting race occupy a minor position."[8] Commenting on the social scene in the Harlem of the 1920s, a young black social worker observed: "In this matter of sex equality, Negro women have contributed few outstanding militants. Their feminist efforts are directed chiefly toward the realization of the equality of the races, the sex struggle assuming a subordinate place."[9]

Historically, black women built community organizations and welfare institutions which, once completed or well launched, would generally be headed by black men.[10] Similarly, antilynching campaigns, which were initially powered by black women and were central to the concern of the Negro women's club movement, were always seen as a means of protecting the black community as a whole and protecting black men, rather than of defending black women. Ida B. Wells, a national leader of the Negro women's club movement and an active suffragist, always gave priority to a militant defense of her race in her activities. Specifically, she repeatedly jeopardized her political standing and influence in order to expose the horror of a lynching or to expose the collusion of respected politicians in exonerating the lynchers.[11] Over and over again the defense of the family is seen as the primary concern of black women; their understanding of the defense of the family always includes the elevation of the black man. "We are here to work side by side with the black man in trying to bring liberation to all people," is the way Fannie Lou Hamer, the 20th-century Mississippi grassroots leader, summarized a long tradition.[12]

The above leads naturally to the next sets of questions: in what way was the historical experience of black women similar to that of black men? In what ways was it similar to that of white women?

As members of a subordinate racial caste, black women shared the low status, the economic exploitation, and the educational, legal and social restrictions based on race discrimination experienced by their group.

Educated black women enjoyed a small advantage in economic status and employability over black men, which will be discussed below as "the sex loophole in race discrimination." On the other hand, black women always have higher unemployment rates than either black men or white men and women. In no area of life have black women ever been permitted to attain higher status than white women.

What has disadvantaged black women additionally is that they have been, ever since slavery days, objects of exploitative sex by white men.[13] This single feature of their condition as women of a lower caste group distinguishes them at once from both white women and black men. Another way of stating this is to say that the oppression peculiar to women is experienced differently by women of a subject caste or subject race than it is by women of the dominant race. This can best be illustrated by comparing the position of black and white women in slave society. The very existence of the white woman and of her family was founded on the economic and physical exploitation of slaves and yet within the plantation household black and white women lived in close daily contact, companionship, and often intimacy. In a sense they were both victims of a system they neither shaped nor controlled. The life of the white upper-class woman was strictly circumscribed by tradition and custom: she was denied higher education; her activities were restricted to the domestic circle; she was totally removed from public life and political power and from any economic activity not centered in the home. Sexually she was expected to live in chastity before marriage; once married, to submit unquestioningly to her husband's desires and to bear his children as frequently as her biology decreed. She was to live in absolute marital fidelity and to endure with forbearance the customary infidelities of her husband with slave women. Although here and there a woman of the planter class bitterly resented a situation in which she lived, as one of them expressed it, in "a harem in which she was the favorite wife," most of them accepted conditions as they were. Some vented their frustrated feeings on the hapless victims of their husbands' sexual exploitation or on the children of those unions. Unaware of their own inferior status and the restrictions placed upon them, they accepted with gratitude the chivalry and outward deference of their men, shared in their men's status privileges, and generally accepted their racist attitudes.[14]

The oppression of the slave woman was more direct, more brutal, and without redeeming features. The black woman was exploited as a worker, as a breeder of slaves, and as a sex object for white men. Her exploitation as a worker was the same as that of the male slave. Her exploitation as a breeder did not usually consist of forced mating; it rather meant that her life was so patterned that early marriage was insisted upon, frequent childbirth was unavoidable and childless marriages were dissolved at the behest of the master. One of the few ways in which slave women might expect to enhance their status was to have borne "many niggers for

Massa," as her husband's slaves explained to Frances Kemble. Her children were the property of her master; it was on such property that her white mistress' status and fortune rested. Since the slave woman customarily also relieved her white mistress of the drudgery of child care of the white woman's children, it becomes evident that many of the privileges white women enjoyed were at the expense of black women.[15]

White lower-class women were also expected by society to produce children as often as nature provided, reliable birth control information not being available, but they were not penalized if they remained sterile. Other than the benefit accruing to families with many children in an agricultural society, the status of white lower-class women was not enhanced by their producing many children. Certainly, their capacity for motherhood did not provide financial profit for anyone other than perhaps the mother and father themselves, who might hope to increase their family's welfare by having many children. Women of both races and all classes were excluded from available educational opportunities, deprived of the right to participate in the political system, and hedged in by legal restraints peculiar to their sex.

The sexual availability of black slave women to any white man who cared to use them was a decisive differentiating feature of their oppression as members of the race. In so far as it served simply the sexual pleasure of the master, this practice continued in the tradition of the feudal class oppression of lower-class women: the lord of the manor availing himself of his female servants prior to their marriage, according to the first-night rights—*droit du seigneur*—and the ready use by members of the ruling elite of lower-class women. One can cite as examples the practices prevalent in French society before the Revolution; use by men of the Russian nobility of women of the serf class; and reflections of such practices in the plays of Ibsen and Strindberg in even such democratic societies as those of the Scandinavian countries at the end of the 19th century. The sexual exploitation of women of a subservient class is as old as class society and can be found in every culture without regard to race. It is, in fact, one of the very definitions of female enslavement.

But there was an added element in the sexual exploitation of slave women, which was based on a quite different tradition, namely, the use of the women of a conquered group by the conquerer as a means of humiliating the males of the conquered group. The occurrence of this practice during slavery and after the formal end of slavery during race riots and periods of terror against Blacks affirms the colonial nature of the oppression of black people in the United States.[16] Black men, like all conquered foes, were symbolically castrated and effectively humiliated by being prevented from defending their wives and daughters from the sexual abuse of white men. Slave narratives and oral history testimony of ex-slaves abound in incidents of black men being severely punished for attempting to defend their wives, mothers, or sisters from the sexual abuse of white men. There is evidence of isolated instances of successful resistance by black women to such forced sexual liaison with white men.[17] The bulk of the evidence suggests that, once forced into such liaisons, black women often attempted to utilize their position in order to protect their children and the black men with whom they shared their lives.

That the sexual exploitation of black women by white men is an essential feature of race-caste oppression in the United States has been attested to by a wide-ranging group of writers, such as W. J. Cash, Lillian Smith, Eldridge Cleaver, Richard Wright, Winthrop Jordan, Gunnar Myrdal, and many others.[18] The essential aspects of this expression of white male sexual dominance over black women have long survived the existence of slavery. It continued until very recently, when the militancy of the black nationalist movement could put an end to it. White male sexual dominance was upheld by laws forbidding intermarriage, enforced by terror against black men and women, and, though frowned upon by white community opinion, tolerated both in its clandestine and open manifestations. It is reflected in the monotonous one-sidedness of rape-conviction statistics, especially in the Southern states, which reveal the essential double standard: the rape of black women by white men goes unpunished; the rape of white women by black men is severely punished. Historical records of the anti-lynching movement and especially the unique contribution to this movement of Ida B. Wells point out the use of lynching as a weapon of terror to uphold this sexual double standard.[19] This issue became a crucial motivating force for the organization of the national Negro women's club movement. The issue of sexual oppression, more than any other issue, differentiates the history of black women from that of black men and of white women.

Comparison of the history of black and white women shows other illuminating differences. Historically, feminist organization does not appear until there exists a group of educated middle-class women. Due to race discrimination the development of a sizable black middle class did not occur until the latter part of the 19th century. Even then, much of what was considered black middle class would be considered lower class among whites; that is, families of stably employed skilled workers, artisans, with a sprinkling of intelligentsia. White women began to organize on a large scale in clubs and welfare and reform organizations in the late 1840s, with the full development of the women's club movement taking place in the early 1870s. The same development occurred for Blacks with a lag of approximately thirty years. It was only after the development of the Negro women's club movement that feminist consciousness first appeared among black women, and here, too, it is an exceptional attitude rather than a pervasive one. One must note here the single exception, the strong feminism of Sojourner Truth, who was distinctly a forerunner and whose ideas were not shared by black women of her day. Black women always expressed a closer solidarity with their men than did white women, and were relatively late in organizing sex-separated organizations. Even when they recognized the special role that must be played by black women in order to strengthen the general struggle of their people, they did not perceive black men as being antagonistic to them or as being their oppressors. This is quite different from the self-conscious feminism of white women during the early decades of the 20th century.

Race oppression of black people in the United States has deeply affected the patterns of black family life. The economic marginality of Blacks in general, the mass migrations from rural South to city ghetto, and above all the economic restrictions on black males forced black family life into patterns somewhat different from the predominantly male-dominated nuclear family of white society. Although from the late 19th century to today at least 75 per cent of all black families always *were* nuclear families headed by a male, there also developed another black family pattern, that of the extended family consisting of women, their children, and their adult male relatives. This family structure, in which all children, regardless of the marital or economic status of their families, are ensured a modicum of security, represents a useful adaptation for group survival by an economically depressed community.[20]

Ever since slavery days black women have had to work for their own support and for the support of their families. Rigid discrimination bars against black men and the low and insecure wages they could earn forced the majority of black married women, even mothers of small children, to work for pay outside the home. In this they differed from white married women, who entered the labor force in large numbers only in the 20th century.[21] One of the adaptations black families made to this reality was to educate their daughters to self-dependency.

Until very recently—and for a majority of Blacks to this day—educational achievement for black men did not mean the opening up of economic opportunities. But it did mean that for black girls. Since there were few semi-skilled or middle-range jobs available to black women due to discrimination bars, the only hope a black girl had to escape the unskilled-job trap was in getting a professional education. Thus, black families, who expected their daughters to work most of their lives, would make greater sacrifices to educate their daughters than their sons. In this, they ran counter to the general American pattern of educationally depriving daughters for the sake of sons.[22]

Advanced education was longer denied to black women than to white, due to race discrimination. Although the first black women physicians were graduated in the 1860s, it was only in the 20th century that black women began to enter the field in greater numbers. Interestingly, the first female physicians in the South were black. Dr. Matilda Arabelle Evans practiced in Columbia, South Carolina, at the turn of the century, and Dr. Hallie Tanner Johnson was the first woman to practice medicine in the state of Alabama. Although earlier there had been several black women graduates of law schools, the first black woman lawyer admitted to the bar was Lutie A. Lyttle of Topeka, Kansas in 1887. This black pioneer did not have many successors, for it would be several decades before a significant number of black women would follow her into the profession.

It was only with the emergence of a sizable black middle class that black women began to enter professional and skilled occupations in greater numbers. The civil rights movement of the 1950s played a significant role in opening up greater educational opportunities for Blacks of both sexes. It was only then that the difference between black and white family expectations in regard to women began to show up in the statistics. The 1960 census shows that black female physicians represented 9.7 per cent of all black physicians, while white female physicians were 6.4 per cent of all white physicians. Black women lawyers were 9.1 per cent of all Blacks in the profession, as against white women lawyers who constituted 3.3 per cent of the profession. Similar patterns appear in the figures for schoolteachers. They show, above all, that women of both races are grossly under-represented in the professions, but that black women are *somewhat better* represented than white.

Race discrimination bars operate more rigidly against black men than against black women, so that there is a "sex loophole" in race discrimination.[23] When educational and employment opportu-

Table 3. Unemployment rates by age, race, and sex: 1964, 1974[27]

	White men 20 yrs. and over	Black men 20 yrs. and over	White women 20 yrs. and over	Black women 20 yrs. and over	Both sexes White	16–19 Black
1964	3.4	NA (not available)	4.6	NA	14.8	NA
1974	3.5	7.3	5.0	8.7	14.0	34.9

Source: U.S. Census

both sexes. The worsening unemployment for Blacks in the period since 1974, not covered by Table 3, has not altered this pattern. It should be noted that in the availability and structuring of youth job-training programs, black girls have been consistently disadvantaged.

The decade 1964–74 brought some income gains to black families with husbands and wives working, but simultaneously there was a sharp increase in the number of black families headed by a woman. Such families are economically in a precarious position. Of 1.5 million female-headed families, 53 per cent fell below the poverty line income of $3800 in 1974.

Life expectancy figures (Table 4) and maternal and infant mortality rates (Table 5) provide a good index for comparisons of the economic well-being of different groups. Here, too, there are some gains for black women relative to white women, especially if viewed over a longer time span, but, overall, black women remain more disadvantaged than white women.

Table 4. Life expectancy at birth, by sex, age, and race, 1959–61, 1973[28]

	Men			Women		
	White	Black	Diff. between Wh. & Bl.	White	Black	Diff. between Wh. & Bl.
1959–61	67.6	61.5	6.1	74.2	66.5	7.7
1973	68.4	61.9	6.5	76.1	70.1	6.0
Net gain	0.8	0.4	0.4	1.9	3.6	

Source: U.S. Census

Table 4 shows that black men have lost more ground than black women on the index of life expectancy, both in comparison with women of their own race and with men of the white race.

Table 5. Maternal and infant mortality rates: 1940, 1970, 1973
(per 1000 live births)

	Black and other races		White	
	Maternal	Infants 1 year and under	Maternal	Infants 1 year and under
1940	7.6	73.8	3.2	43.2
1970	0.6	30.9	0.1	17.8
1973	0.3	26.2	0.0	15.8

Source: U.S. Dept. of Health, Education and Welfare, National Center for Health Statistics.

The reduction in maternal and infant mortality rates is dramatic over previous decades, but Table 5 shows that the discrepancy between white and black rates remains high.

However one chooses to interpret these figures, they show that the vast majority of black women are at the bottom of the earning-prestige-opportunity-status ladder in the United States. This fact might be interpreted by some as indicating that black men oppress black women in the same manner in which white men oppress white women. This interpretation falters on the fact that black men have historically been as totally removed from the control and decision-making level of economic and political institutions as have women. Powerless black men may individually vent their own frustrations on their women, which may place additional burdens upon these women. Abandoned mothers, existing on welfare or doing menial work for a living without the aid of husbands, are not matriarchs but are doubly victimized.

Matriarchy, by definition, means power by women: decision-making power; power over their own lives; power over the lives of others; power in their communities. To speak of black matriarchy in contemporary society is a cruel hoax. White society, through the enormous racist pressures applied to the black community and

to black men, has immensely added to the burdens borne by black
women, many of whom do not even enjoy the relative economic security marriage can afford white women in exchange for dependency.[29]

But the status of black women can be viewed from two different
viewpoints: one, as members of the larger society; two, within
their own group. When they are considered as Blacks among
Blacks, they have higher status within their own group than do
white women in white society. Their life expectation includes self-
support and economic independence, and their role models are
women who—out of necessity—have combined motherhood and
work. Independent, self-reliant, and adapted to survival, the black
woman in America has also mediated between two cultures. While
she has for many long periods been forced to socialize her children
to a pretended acceptance of discriminatory patterns, she has also
managed to imbue them with race pride and a desire for full equality. This dual role has resulted in the unusual resiliency and flexibility of black women and in their stance of dignified resistance
to oppression. All of this has made a decisive difference in the
way the black woman perceives herself. "Liberated in her own
mind," she realizes that her own emancipation cannot be separated from the liberation of the race and from the improvement
of the life of the black community.

A comparative approach to the history of black and white American women can help in validating some generalizations. The similar pattern of development of the Negro and white women's club
movement, which occurs at different time periods for the two
groups, strongly suggests that the chief factor in the emergence of
such organized activity is the existence of a group of educated,
middle-class women with some leisure. Since such a group develops later in the black community than in the white, one would
expect to find the development of the Negro women's club movement to be later in time. This is exactly what does occur.

Another theoretical problem of women's history, in which a comparative approach offers some insights, concerns the concept of women as an oppressed group. Feminists have claimed the universality and priority of sexual oppression as an experience common to all women. However useful that concept may be as an agitational tool, it does not work as a tool for historical analysis. The study of black women in American history illustrates that generalizations about sex oppression *as universal* are invalid. The nature of sex oppression differs for women of the dominant and the oppressed race. It also differs for women of different classes. Working-class women of all races have always expressed their oppression in class terms rather than in sex terms, and have organized around their work; but black working-class women experienced their oppression as *black* workers much more seriously than as women workers.

Another methodological point to be made is that women's status cannot simply be defined in legal or economic terms. It is possible for a group of women to have high status in one aspect of their lives—within the family, for example—and very low status in another—their economic position. It is obvious that some of the adaptations made by black families for survival have led to different role expectations and to different family status for black women than for white. If one is to judge from the model of black women's history, status within the family is more important in forming the self-consciousness of women than is their status in society.

Lastly, there is much to be learned concerning the relationship between the ideology of woman's place and the reality of woman's place by examining the history of black women. The way in which a slight weakening of male dominance in the black family is perceived as "female dominance," even matriarchy, despite the overwhelming evidence of the oppression of black women, indicates how important status perceptions are for the formation of political consciousness. Women, as all oppressed groups, perceive their status *relatively,* in comparison with their own group, with previously known conditions, with their own expectations. White society has long decreed that, while "woman's place is in the home," black woman's place is in the white woman's kitchen. No wonder that many black women define their own "liberation" as being free to take care of their own homes and their own children, supported by a man with a job.

The history of black women should be an integral part of all American history. It certainly is essential to the full development of Black history. It is indispensable to the study of the history of American women, not only because of its intrinsic value and interest but as a corrective to class- and race-based generalizations.

6

Community Work
of Black Club Women

Black women organized, throughout the 19th century, at first on a
local level, to undertake educational philanthropic and welfare activities. In the 1890s local clubs in a number of different cities
began to form federations. In 1896 the newly formed National Association of Colored Women (NACW) united the three largest of
these and over a hundred local women's clubs.[1]

The activities of the black women's club movement were recorded by the pioneering black historians.[2] However, the continuity and extent of this work and its significance have largely escaped
the notice of historians. There is as yet no adequate history of the
black women's club movement and no interpretative literature
available.[3] Because of the widely scattered affiliated organizations,
the fluid structure of the NACW, and the succession of its publications, it has been difficult even to trace its actual strength and to
follow its development.

Close study of women's clubs in several communities suggests
that the importance of their work has been seriously underesti-

This essay was presented as a paper at the annual meeting of the American Historical Association, New Orleans, Louisiana, December 1972. It
was first published in *The Journal of Negro History,* Vol. LIX, No. 2 (April
1974), 158–67.

mated. Contrary to widely held racist myths, black communities have a continuous record of self-help, institution building, and strong organization to which black women have made continuous contributions.

The impulse for organizing arose wherever an urgent social need remained unmet. Most frequently, women's clubs were formed in order to provide kindergartens, nursery schools, or day-care centers for black children. The virtual absence of social welfare institutions in many Southern communities and the frequent exclusion of Blacks from those that existed, led black women to found orphanages, old folks' homes, and similar institutions. The founding and support of educational institutions had been a continuous activity in the black community since the days of slavery, but the extent to which women contributed and often sustained this effort has yet to be recorded. Since Reconstruction days the schoolteacher in her one-room schoolhouse was sustained by fund-raising committees of black church ladies' auxiliaries long before she was the beneficiary of white philanthropy. In the case of the most important female founders of black educational institutions—Emma J. Wilson, Cornelia Bowen, Lucy Lainey, Charlotte Hawkins Brown, Nannie Burroughs, and Mary McLeod Bethune—the schools became centers for community organizations, women's activities, and a network of supporting institutions.[4]

Margaret Murray Washington, director of Girls' Industries and later dean of women at Tuskegee Institute, organized the Tuskegee Women's Club and was its president from its inception in 1895. This club can serve as a prototype for dozens of its kind. Composed of a relatively small membership of educated women—from thirty-five to nearly a hundred—it offered social and recreational programs, literary discussions, guest lecturers, and self-study circles whose interests ranged from health and hygiene topics to Afro-American history.

Membership in the club denoted a certain social standing in the community and was not infrequently used to enforce the snobbish and restrictive attitudes of the leadership. The welfare activities, as reported in club records, show strong class prejudices on the part of the club women and reflect a patronizing, missionary attitude in dealing with the poor. These shortcomings were characteristic of the women's club movement of both races, but they should not overshadow the large amount of socially useful work done by these clubs.

Mothers' meetings provided uplifting educational discussions, advice on child care, home economics, vegetable gardening, and sewing. Missionary, temperance, and welfare activities, and work at the local jail and settlement house was carried on in a regular way. Added to this variety of services were the running of a Sunday school, Bible teaching and—in many cases—of a kindergarten. The Tuskegee Club also ran a small library and took part in some suffrage and political activities. Similar work was carried on in hundreds of black communities and in conjunction with many schools and colleges.[5]

In the 1890s the long tradition of women's organized effort in support of some local charitable or educational institution was transformed into something new and different by the emergence of multipurpose women's clubs, embracing a broad range of activities and interests. The immediate stimulus for their formation was po litical: the defense of the race against lynchings. In 1892, Ida B. Wells, the intrepid Memphis, Tennessee, journalist and newspaper editor, exposed the economic motives for the brutal lynching of three black businessmen, urged resistance, boycott, and emigration as a weapon for black survival. As a result of her stand, her newspaper office and equipment were destroyed, and her life was threatened, should she dare return to the city. Ida B. Wells responded by organizing a nationwide anti-lynching crusade. Her constant theme was to expose lynching as an integral part of the system of racial oppression, the motives for which were usually economic or political. She hit hard at the commonly used alibi for lynchings, the charge of "rape," and dared bring out into the open the most taboo subject of all in Victorian America—the habitual sexual abuse of black women by white men. Thus, she expressed what was to become the ideological direction of the organized movement of black women—a defense of black womanhood as part of a defense of the race from terror and abuse.[6]

On the eve of her departure for England, where she would inspire the organization of the British Anti-Lynching Society, Ida B. Wells spoke at a fund-raising rally in her support, organized by a group of prominent New York women. This 1892 meeting, which brought together Mrs. Josephine St. Pierre Ruffin of Boston, Victoria Earle Matthews of New York, and Dr. Susan McKinney of Brooklyn, inspired the formation of the first two black women's clubs. The New York and Brooklyn women formed the Women's Loyal Union and, somewhat later, Mrs. St. Pierre Ruffin organized the Woman's Era Club of Boston. On her return from England Mrs. Ida B. Wells helped to organize the first women's club in Chicago in 1893. The Ida B. Wells Club met weekly on "Ladies' Day" in the club house of the all-male Tourgee Club. Its members did charitable work, operated a kindergarten, brought prominent cultural and political leaders to town for lectures, and were politically active in defense of the race against lynchings, police brutality, and discrimination.[7] Following shortly upon the organization of the first club in Chicago, the Phillis Wheatley Club was organized in 1896 to work for neighborhood improvements. It began to operate a day nursery in 1904, and in 1908 set up a home for girls. Within a decade there were seven colored women's clubs active in the city of Chicago.[8]

Several of the leaders of this organizing effort—Ida B. Wells, Josephine St. Pierre Ruffin, Mary Church Terrell—freely acknowledged that they had been influenced by the success of the white women's club movement. The general encouragement of voluntary efforts to solve social ills, which prevailed in the Progressive period, may have contributed to the "spirit of organization" which seemed to take hold of many minds at once during the decade. The example of successful effort in one place immediately fired enthusiasts in another to solve their problems by way of a women's club.

The move toward a national organization was actively promoted by Josephine St. Pierre Ruffin, who organized the First National Conference of Colored Women in Boston in 1895. The National Federation of Afro-American Women was founded the same year with Mrs. Margaret Murray Washington as president. It united thirty-six women's clubs in twelve states, including the New Era Club. Meanwhile a similar movement toward national unity had taken place under the leadership of the Washington Women's Club and led to the formation of the National League of Colored Women under Mrs. Mary Church Terrell's leadership. There ensued a brief rivalry for leadership of the national organization, which was resolved when the two groups united in 1896 and drew large numbers of new affiliates into the National Association of Colored Women.

The national federation movement greatly spurred organizational activity and put it on a more business-like basis. The reporting of club activities in the various women's journals lent dignity and a sense of direction to the small groups of local women, taught them more sophisticated methods of organization, and provided channels for the training of leadership. It is notable that these activities seemed to cluster around colleges or urban centers.

A great many women's clubs responded specifically to the needs of migrants to urban centers. Victoria Earle Matthews, founder and president of the Women's Loyal Union, perceived the need for social work among black girls who had recently arrived in New York City from the South seeking employment. She founded the White Rose Mission in 1897 as a shelter and rescue home and set up branches in various cities. Typically, the White Rose Mission expanded its work to that of a settlement house, offering recreation, literary and cultural events, and classes on Negro History. Jane Edna Hunter founded the Working Girls' Home Association (renamed the Phillis Wheatley Association) in Cleveland in 1911. Originally designed to serve as a shelter for black girls denied admission to the city's YWCA, it soon became a settlement house, offering a full range of social and educational activities, an employment agency, and a summer camp. Under Jane Hunter's guidance similar institutions sprang up in a number of cities and several states. An example of a women's club first concerned with national goals and later with local work is the Colored Woman's League of Washington, D.C. Created in 1892, it helped to organize the first national organization of black women. Its local work consisted of establishing a training center for kindergarten teachers and then setting up and maintaining seven free kindergartens and several day nurseries. As was the case in many of these pioneering efforts, the kindergartens, orphanages, and old people's homes were taken over by local or state authorities as soon as they had proven themselves successful. The Washington kindergartens were incorporated into the public school system of the city, most of the black teachers employed in them being graduates of the League's training school.[9]

The Atlanta Neighborhood Union is remarkable among all these successful institutions for its continuity of service from 1908 to the present, for the sophisticated level of organization sustaining it, and for the wide range and scope of its services. Like Hull House in Chicago, with which it can adequately be compared, it represents an unusual organizational achievement under the leadership of an unusual woman. Yet, as can be seen from the above brief account, the Neighborhood Union can also be viewed as a representative prototype.[10]

In 1908 faculty wives and women residing in the neighborhood of Spelman and Morehouse Colleges met in order to find some means of relieving the urgent need for play space for their children. There was in Atlanta not a single playground or park for black children. The women persuaded the administration of Morehouse College to allow the use of part of its grounds for a playground. The college insisted on adequate supervision, so the women undertook to organize it and to raise funds for necessary equipment. This involved contacting local businesses and securing donations of equipment and of workmen to install it. This venture brought the women closer together, gave them confidence in their own ability, and inspired them to look out for other community problems in need of solving. Before long, the small group of women defined its aim more ambitiously as the "moral, economic and social advancement of Negroes" in Atlanta.

Branch organizations were set up in different parts of the city, united in the Neighborhood Union; educational work was begun, and a wide range of social service projects were undertaken. Yearly carnivals and Fourth of July celebrations for children were major neighborhood events. Neighborhood home and street clean-up campaigns, gardening and improvement drives, support of anti-TB and Red Cross campaigns, and the establishment of summer Bible schools for children were among the earlier activities, which became regularly established traditions. Children's clubs combined recreation, education, and day care and, incidentally, attracted the children's mothers to further activities.

Considering the bad state of educational facilities for Blacks, a Social Improvement Committee was set up in 1913 to "better conditions of the Negro in the public schools in Atlanta." This committee undertook a six-months' fact-finding investigation in which every colored school was visited and inspected. Deplorable physical conditions, severe overcrowding, double sessions with one teacher teaching both sessions, were widely prevalent. The committee's action-oriented response to these findings is instructive: Members of the committee lobbied with the mayor and members of the City Council, and systematically visited white religious leaders and influential white women. The latter were induced to visit some of the colored schools, and their support for reform measures was secured. Public meetings were arranged, at which slide shows brought the school conditions before large audiences. Petitions were circulated and the board of education was put under constant pressure. These tactics resulted in the establishment of an additional school in temporary quarters, the raising of the salaries of black teachers, and continued pressure on politicians around school issues. However, such pressure was inadequate to alter the racist neglect of black schools. The issue was still hot in 1923; another school survey revealed "seating capacity is only 42% of total enrollment. The children are on triple sessions . . . there is an average of 72 children for each teacher employed." By then, a school survey revealed "seating capacity is only 42% of total enrollment. The children are on triple sessions . . . there is an work."

In 1915 the Neighborhood Union established a Health Center, which offered a medical clinic, health education activities, and nursing services. This work was expanded and sustained for over three decades. Thus the Health Committee reported that in 1927 nearly a thousand children "were examined in 36 health clinics, 82 mothers are enrolled in Mothers' Clubs, two new Boys' Clubs have been organized. . . . [In 1928] 27 medical clinics were held, in which more than 800 school children were examined and treated. Three health classes were organized for 78 women in the community, two new Boys' Clubs were organized with an enrollment of 112; two Girls' Clubs were organized; and almost 3000 pieces of literature were distributed." And in 1931–32, at the height of the depression, "[T]he Health Clinic at the Neighborhood Union House was enlarged to include medical and dental clinics and mothers' clinics for home care of the sick. A registered nurse, a doctor and a dentist were in attendance. Over 4000 people used the services of the Health center. 684 preschool-age children were treated, 176 families were supplied with milk, and 432 children were supplied with cod liver oil."

Annual participation in anti-tuberculosis drives and Red Cross campaigns organized by Neighborhood Union women brought the black community health services from which it had previously been excluded.

Home improvement and clean-up campaigns were oriented both toward self-help and the exerting of political pressure. Typically, housing conditions in the black ghetto were sub-standard, overcrowding severe. A 1917 housing survey organized by the Neighborhood Union revealed consistently appalling conditions: no street lights, unpaved streets; inadequate trash and garbage removal; homes lacking adequate toilet facilities; contaminated water supply. The survey was continued in 1921, when over 5000 homes were visited.

The result of that single campaign was forty houses repaired, two streets paved, lights put on one street, improvements made in twelve streets, plumbing repaired in one house, sewers put on two streets, toilets repaired in one house, and street improvements made in twenty streets.

The Neighborhood Union purchased a building in 1922, which became the center for its varied activities. It housed the health clinic, social service staff, mothers' clubs, Boy and Girl scout troops, homemaking and woodworking classes and a great many more activities. The settlement house also took an interest in the Herndon Day Nursery, the Gate City Free Kindergarten, which had been founded by Mrs. Lugenia Hope, and in the colored YWCA. In the same way in which Hull House became the focal point for a broad range of reform activities, so the Neighborhood Union serviced the various needs of the community for several generations. Women who were active in the Neighborhood Union in the 1930s had, as children, grown up in and around that settlement house.

Neighborhood Union committees functioned in a business-like manner, volunteer secretaries kept meticulous records, often written in longhand in school notebooks. An example of the way drives were organized is the "Plan of Work: of the Atlanta Colored Women's War Council," a group formed during World War I for the purpose of providing recreational facilities for colored soldiers. The Neighborhood Union was drawn into this war-time activity; its organization can be considered typical and representative of Atlanta leadership. The city was divided into nine zones, each zone subdivided into neighborhood units. In each such unit various committees were appointed, whose leaders had to report to the city-wide committee and who were responsible for engendering grassroots activity. Over 500 women were mobilized for this work within a short time, which speaks for the effectiveness of leadership.[11] Obviously, the faculty wives of Morehouse and Spelman

Colleges and of Atlanta University, many of them college-trained themselves, provided the leadership and the constant feedback with the college community. Sociologists and students were used to help with surveys, medical personnel were incorporated in the health work, and education leaders organized classes in the community. It is difficult from the available record to estimate the exact number of activists, but they cannot have exceeded 100 at any given time. Yet during the various "drives" and campaigns several hundred neighborhood women were mobilized as canvassers, petition circulators, and organizers.

The Neighborhood Union of Atlanta was for almost thirty years under the leadership of Mrs. Lugenia Hope, wife of the president of Atlanta University. This dynamic leader, characteristic of her generation, worked in a quiet, behind-the-scenes way. Yet her leadership spirit generated not only a remarkable local reform drive, but moved on to the national scene. Under her direction, Atlanta women had for some time been prodding white women in support of their cause. The first steps had been to involve white women in bettering the schools in the colored ghetto. The next, to prove that the black community supported various white community campaigns such as Red Cross and Community Chest. The World War I activities of black women raised the issue of integration in the YWCA to a new level.[12] Although the national YWCA had appointed its first "secretary for colored work," Eva Bowles, in 1913, and had, by 1920, increased its black national staff to twelve, YWCA branches in all Southern cities operated on a strictly segregated basis. Black community workers, handpicked by local white boards, and national colored secretaries from the national staff, were prevented by a tacit "hands-off" policy on racial matters from working in the South. The result was a perpetuation and reinforcement of segregation and discrimination within the YWCA. The issue came out into the open over the assignment of a black field worker to the Atlanta black community. The Atlanta club leaders asked for the replacement of this field worker to whom they objected because they considered her unresponsive to their interests. They went on to demand the right to select their own staff. As one participant in this campaign put it, "the principle involved is not one . . . of policy, but the race question, pure and simple. The question is whether or not colored women can in some communities cooperate with white women and at the same time keep their self-respect."[13] A skillfully orchestrated campaign, which was led by Mrs. Lugenia Hope, led the national board to reverse its policy and set a precedent by asking black women to submit a slate of candidates they considered suitable for appointment. In 1921, as a direct outgrowth of this controversy, the YWCA national board appointed its first black member, Mrs. Charlotte Hawkins Brown.[14]

The work of black club women contributed to the survival of the black community. Black women's clubs were, like the clubs of white women, led by educated, often by middle-class women, but unlike their white counterparts, black club women frequently successfully bridged the class barrier and concerned themselves with issues of importance to poor women, working mothers, tenant farm wives. They were concerned with education, self and community improvement, but they always strongly emphasized race pride and race advancement. Their inspiring example of self-help and persistent community service deserves to be more closely studied by historians.

7

Black and White Women in Interaction and Confrontation

The parallels in the status of women and of Blacks have been noted by social scientists and historians, and, recently, by theoreticians of the women's liberation movement. It is obvious that there are similarities in the status and history of the two groups, but these are offset by important differences. The analogy between Blacks *in general* and women is valid and useful as long as it is confined to the psychological effect of inferior status, but not when it is extended to a general comparison between the two groups.[1]

What will be attempted here is to view the contacts between black and white women, especially as expressed through their orga-

This essay was first published in *Prospects: An Annual of American Cultural Studies,* Vol. II (1976). The findings in this essay are based on extensive research in primary sources, including letters and manuscripts of feminists, antislavery women, and leaders of Negro women's clubs. Among the organizational records consulted were those of the various Female Anti-Slavery Societies, Anti-Slavery Conventions of American Women, all the Woman's Rights Conventions, New Era Club, Tuskegee Mothers' Club, YWCA, National Association of Colored Women, and others. Among the newspapers consulted were all the antislavery papers; *Frederick Douglass' Paper; Woman's Journal; Revolution; Woman's Era; Afro-American Woman; National Notes; Provincial Freeman.*

nizations, in historical perspective, and to examine the nature of this contact more closely. One will find that a similarity of interests did not always express itself in cooperation, and that the relationship between the two groups was and is quite complicated, and frequently ambivalent, if not actually hostile.

Black and white women throughout U.S. history have shared a certain common experience. As women, they were members of the one group in society holding the lowest economic position, longest denied access to equal education, faced with discriminatory practices in every aspect of life, and kept marginal to the institutional power structure. But black women were at all times discriminated against more severely than any other group in our society: as Blacks, as women, and frequently as low-paid workers. Most white women were unaware of their own inferior status in society, were treated with chivalry and with deference, and shared indirectly in the status privileges of their men. They also shared in the racist attitudes of white men. Quite frequently, many of the privileges white women enjoyed were held at the expense of black women or of lower-class white women, especially in their function as domestic workers. The vast majority of black and white women lived their separate lives in segregated spheres, and, despite their common status as women, had little awareness of and little contact with each other. And yet they were in many ways interdependent.

The ambivalent interdependence of black and white women was nowhere better symbolized than in the complex relationship of the white mistress and her black slave. The white mistress, like her husband, directly benefitted from the slave's unpaid labor. Yet, in the daily life of the plantation household, black and white women were put into close daily contact, companionship, and intimate interdependency. What bound them together was, not infrequently, their relationship to the master of the house. A white Southern woman, mistress of a large plantation and later a staunch defender of the Confederacy, described this ambivalent situation astutely:

> Under slavery we live surrounded by prostitutes. . . . God forgive us, but ours is a monstrous system. . . . Like the pa-

triarchs of old, our men live all in one house with their wives
and their concubines; and the mulattoes one sees in every family partly resemble the white children. Any lady is ready to tell
you who is the father of all the mulatto children in everybody's
household but her own. Those, she seems to think, drop from
the clouds.[2]

On the side of the black woman there was ambivalence as well;
the licentious relationship with the master was often hated, fought
against, and always degrading. It weakened the black family, poi-
soned motherhood, and served to separate sex from affection. On
the other hand, it was for many slave women the one and only avenue toward some precarious improvement in their lot and that of
their offspring. And there are sufficient cases on record of genuine
human attachment between master and slave concubine to make all
facile generalizations invalid. In such cases it was the black woman
who held the respect and affection of the man, while the white
lady, the "chief slave in the harem," had the empty shell of respectability and fancied superiority as a substitute for a genuine
marriage. There is ambivalence, too, in the role of the legendary
"Mammy" of the plantation household—substitute mother of the
white children while deprived of caring for her own, respected
domestic tyrant, often sole confidante of her mistress. A curious
psychological revenge of the black oppressed class over their white
oppressors occurred within the house of the masters; the white
lady, sexually deprived of her husband by his slave women, *allowed*
herself to be deprived of her children by their black Mammy. For
the white boy, mother love was *black* love and sexual satisfaction
was found with the black women, while the white girl learned
from early childhood that the price of respectability and wealth was
submission and acceptance of total powerlessness to affect one's
fate.[3]

In regard to law, economics, education, and political life, black
and white women were equally powerless in a society dominated by
white men. But the degree of their powerlessness was greatly different, for the slave was considered a chattel, while the white

woman was considered free. The white woman had, at all times, sufficient power to exploit and mistreat her slaves, but she seldom had enough power to protect them from abuse, should she so desire. The experiences of the British-born actress Frances Kemble, who wrecked her marriage through her efforts to ameliorate the lot of her husband's female slaves, is a case in point.[4] The South Carolina-born Grimké sisters, daughters of a planter, also tried and failed in their efforts at improving the lot of their family's slaves, and concluded that slave society would permit the elevation of neither slaves nor white women. They took the unique step, for Southern women of their station, of leaving the South and becoming abolitionists. They were radical, even among abolitionists, in their total acceptance of black women and in their emphasis on combating racism.

"They are our countrywomen," Angelina Grimké wrote of the slaves, "they are our sisters; and to us as women, they have a right to look for sympathy with their sorrows, and effort and prayer for their rescue."[5]

For roughly two decades prior to the Civil War the movements for the emancipation of Negroes and of women coincided and frequently overlapped. The close collaboration then existing between these two reform movements has obscured the much more complex and problematical relationship existing between the members of these two groups over the longer span of history.

It was not so much that black women were helped and sustained through the sympathies and organizational efforts of white women. Even from the outset, things worked in the opposite way. It was through the struggle for the rights of black people that many Northern white women first became aware of their own oppression. It is only in this sense that we can say that the antislavery movement gave birth to the woman's rights movement. In 1837, when the Grimké sisters, as agents of the American Anti-Slavery Society, toured New England, they met much opposition as the first Southern white women to lecture in public.[6] The sisters defended their right to speak and organize, and linked the cause of Blacks and of white women. "If we have no right to act, then may we well be termed 'the white slaves of the North.' " [7]

Like them, most of the early feminists came to their convictions because of their interest in abolition. Elizabeth Cady Stanton, Susan B. Anthony, Lucy Stone, Abby Kelley, and scores of others found that if they wished to work for reforms in general, they would first have to fight for their right as women to engage in public political activity.

By and large, the antislavery women showed a greater awareness of the implications of prejudice than their contemporaries; their meetings were integrated; they gave their Negro members a chance to take leadership positions in their organizations. Year after year they passed resolutions against race prejudice, such as this one:

> Resolved . . . that it is . . . the duty of abolitionists to iden-
> tify themselves with these oppressed Americans by sitting with
> them in places of worship, by appearing with them in our
> streets, by giving them our countenance in steam-boats and
> stages, by visiting them in their homes and encouraging them
> to visit us, receiving them as we do our white fellow citizens. [8]

Both the Boston and the Philadelphia Female Anti-Slavery Society were faced with mob actions because of their insistence on holding interracial public meetings; both societies met the challenge by an absolute refusal to back down from this policy. In Boston, Negro and white women linked arms as they marched out in pairs through a furious mob; similar incidents so incited public prejudice in Philadelphia that in 1838 the newly built Pennsylvania Hall was attacked by a mob while the antislavery women were meeting there and, a few hours later, was burned to the ground.

Frederick Douglass played a leading role at the first woman's rights convention in Seneca Falls, New York. Three years later, that remarkable black leader, Sojourner Truth, illuminated the connection between the two causes in her unique, dramatic way when she rose during a woman's rights convention to point to one of the clergymen who had lectured the women on the impropriety of their demands. "That man over there says dat women needs to be helped into carriages and lifted over ditches and to have the best place everywhere. Nobody ever help me into carriages or over mud puddles or gives me any best place—and aren't I a woman? I have plowed and planted and gathered into barns, and no man could head me—and aren't I a woman?" and pointing to another who had blamed the trouble of mankind on mother Eve, she declared: "If the first woman God ever made was strong enough to turn the world upside down all alone, these together ought to be able to get it right side up again, and now they're asking to do it, the men better let em." [9]

In the person of Sojourner Truth, the fusion of the abolition and woman's rights movements seemed personified.

In the abolitionist movement black and white people experienced regular personal contact and close collaboration for a common cause. It was inevitable that this should lead to an awareness of racial differences, racial tensions, at times friction, at times a friendly adjustment.

Intimate friendships between black and white women in the 19th century are rare. One example of such a relationship was the life-long friendship between Sarah and Angelina Grimké and Sarah Douglass, the Philadelphia schoolteacher. The Grimké sisters had met Sarah Douglass and her mother at Quaker meetings and had noticed that the two black women were made to sit on a separate, "colored" bench at Meeting. In protest, the sisters demonstratively seated themselves with the black women. Later, the three young women collaborated in exposing other discriminatory practices among Philadelphia Quakers. Sarah Douglass furnished factual data from her own and her mother's experience, the Grimké sisters, failing to find a publisher in the United States, transmitted the information to British Quakers, who published it in a pamphlet, in the hope of influencing American Friends. The three women worked together for years in the Philadelphia Female Anti-Slavery Society. The basis for the friendship was the white women's proven service to the antislavery cause, their willingness to identify themselves with their black sisters in action, not only in words, and their understanding that in racial matters they must and should accept the guidance of their black friends. On the other hand, there was a mutual willingness to face up to the complexities of interracial friendships. The Grimké sisters had frequently visited and been houseguests of Mrs. Douglass and her mother. When Angelina married Theodore Weld, she, her husband, and Sarah extended invitations to all their friends for visits in their new home. Sarah Douglass came, insisted on staying only for one day, and wrote a polite "Thank You" note commending them for their hospitality and "Christian conduct."

> But the sisters were not pleased with this polite gesture. "It seemed to me thy proposal 'to spend a day' with us," wrote Sarah, "was made under a little feeling something like this: 'Well, after all, I am not quite certain I shall be an acceptable visitor.' " She could well understand that her friend might feel that kind of apprehension, but hoped she could "rise above thy suspicions." Angelina put the matter more bluntly. . . . Sarah's gratitude for their "Christian conduct" had caused them pain. "In what did it consist? In receiving and treating thee as an equal. . . . Oh, how humbling to receive such thanks!" [10]

This frank exchange obviously cleared the air. Sarah Douglass' next visits to the Weld home lasted several weeks. She and Sarah Grimké remained close friends for the rest of their lives. Such intimate interracial friendships were rare.

The frictions and tensions between black and white abolitionists have received a good deal of attention from modern scholars. Best known are the bitter exchanges between Frederick Douglass and William L. Garrison, who insisted on guiding and directing the great Negro leader, as though he needed such tutelage. Douglass' letters to the abolitionist Maria Chapman, in which he complained, with justification, against the patronizing treatment he was receiving at the hand of white abolitionists, are also well known.

Another example of interracial confrontation among antislavery people in the pre-Civil War period appeared in the pages of the *Provincial Freeman,* a Canadian newspaper, then edited by a black woman, Mary Ann Shadd. On December 16, 1854, there is a column discussing the case of Mrs. Margaret Douglass of Virginia, a white woman who had kept a school for slave children. She had been indicted and tried by the state of Virginia for violating the slave code, had been found guilty and imprisoned for one month. The case commanded a good deal of attention because of the fact that the violator of the law was a white Southern woman, a species rarely found on the side of the slaves. The abolitionist press had praised Mrs. Douglass and featured her story prominently.

Mary Ann Shadd, however, found something else worth featuring. She reprinted parts of Mrs. Douglass' speech in court. Acting without counsel in her own defense, Mrs. Douglass had said that she considered amalgamation [a genteel 19th-century word for miscegenation] the cause "of the opposition to the instruction of the colored race."

> It is impossible to deny that this unnatural custom prevails to a fearful extend throughout the South. . . . It pervades the entire society . . . The white mothers and daughters of the South have suffered under it for years—have seen their dearest affections trampled upon—their hopes of domestic happiness destroyed . . . The female slave . . . knows that she is powerless beneath the whims and fancies of her master. . . . She knows that she must submit. There is no way of escape. . . . Still, she feels her degradation, and so do others with whom she is connected. . . .[11]

In these words Mrs. Douglass had described quite accurately the ambivalent bonds that tied black and white women in a common oppression under slavery. But to her, the cause lay not in the system of slavery, but in the lack of religious instruction offered the slaves. These were needed, she stated, especially in view of the sinfulness of the masters, to "instruct the negroes in their obligations to

their masters and their God. Were these instructions exemplified by the consistent lives of their masters . . . the
South would become the very garden of the Lord. There would
be no fear of insurrections, for there would be no inducement.
But when a man, black though he be, knows that at any
moment he is compelled to hand over his wife, his sister, or his
daughter to the loathsome embraces of the man whose chain he
wears, how can it be expected that he will submit without the
feelings of hatred and revenge taking possession of his
heart? . . .[12]

Obviously, these words were spoken in self-defense and designed
to reassure the court that she had acted from the highest of motives. None of the abolitionists had found anything but admiration
for this Southern white woman. But Mary Ann Shadd, while admitting that she had previously regarded the lady as a friend of the
race, now found that she had to view her as a friend of the slaveholder. Mary Ann Shadd had a keen ear for the racism hidden be-
neath this defense of the slave's humanity. She pointed out that
Mrs. Douglass regarded amalgamation

as the cause of the ignorance, degradation and crime which
hang over the sunny South; if it were not for it, the slave, having no natural aspirations to liberty, would it is presumed be
quiet, submissive, enjoy his corn, bacon, dirt and rags through
untold generations. . . . What a libel upon humanity!

She quoted Mrs. Douglass as saying that "the fathers, sons

and husbands of her southern sisters have not even the paltry
excuse . . . that their love [for their tawny mistresses] is real,
though illicit; the whole practice is plainly, unequivocally
shamelessly beastly."

"They cannot love those tawny mistresses," commented Mary Ann
Shadd,

because they are tawny or colored, if you please; therefore if
they are colored they must be a lower grade of animal than are
the southern gentlemen. . . . Mrs. Douglass then—as do all
pro-slavery people—is endeavoring to fan the flames of preju-

dice . . . at the same time that she would rivet the chains on the slave. Note the process by which they are to be riveted and the remedy for the evils, which is in the hands of the southern woman. That remedy is the instruction of the negroes in their duty to their *masters*. . . . "One good preacher among my negroes is more efficacious than a wagonload of cowhides," said a planter, and this is Mrs. Douglass' sentiment which she had plainly, unequivocally and shamefully set forth. . . . We cannot sufficiently express our abhorrence of such hollow-heartedness as this.[13]

The exchange illustrates what is obviously a recurring pattern in black and white relationships: Blacks, allied with whites in radical causes, constantly have to educate their white allies as to the realities and implications of racism. Evidently, even in 1854, such education often took the form of confrontation and sharp debate.

Another such debate occurred shortly after the Civil War. The advocates of woman's rights had worked hard for passage of the Fourteenth Amendment, fully expecting it to provide voting rights both for Negroes and for women. To their bitter disappointment, the amendment not only failed to grant suffrage to women, but actually limited suffrage to male citizens. The addition of the word "male" as a qualification for suffrage in the federal Constitution seemed to the feminists actually to worsen the legal disabilities of women, who had previously been excluded from voting by state law only. Even staunch abolitionists such as Elizabeth C. Stanton and Susan B. Anthony now wavered in their support of the Negro's cause. Frederick Douglass reproached these wavering allies by pointing to the greater urgency of his people's cause:

When women, because they are women, are dragged from their homes and hung upon lamp-posts; when their children are torn from their arms and their brains dashed upon the pavement; when they are objects of insult and outrage at every turn; when they are in danger of having their homes burnt down over their heads; when their children are not allowed to enter school; then they will have an urgency to obtain the ballot [similar to that of the Negro]. . . . Yes, it is true of the black woman, but not because she is a woman but because she is black.[14]

In retrospect, it is clear that in 1868 woman's suffrage had no chance of passage even with abolitionist support. It took the woman's rights movement several decades to recover from the shattering of the old abolitionist-feminist alliance. Organized feminists, under the leadership of a new generation of middle- and upper-class women, who shared the nativist and racist ideas of men of their class, concentrated on winning wide support for the woman's suffrage amendment. They followed the spirit of the times in turning away from the race issue, yet the consequence of this ideological shift and of the tactical turn to "expediency" and pragmatism was to push the suffrage movement into an acceptance of the status quo in race relations.

In the twentieth century, Southern suffragists made frequent use of the argument first developed by Henry Blackwell in *The Woman's Journal* that granting the vote to Southern white women would result in strengthening white rule in the South, since there were more white women in the South than there were black men and women combined.[15] The same argument was used in the North in reference to the "ignorant vote" of the immigrants. An extremist such as Kate Gordon of New Orleans, a member of the board of the National American Woman's Suffrage Association in 1901, who later resigned to build a states' rights Southern women's organization dedicated to winning suffrage for white women only, was not typical of the national leadership. Yet the constant compromise of suffrage leaders with the Southern viewpoint on the race issue inevitably led to discriminatory practices and racist incidents.[16] The few black women's suffrage clubs participated in conventions and national suffrage parades on a segregated basis. Leadership by black women was discouraged.[17] Ironically, such tactics, supposedly designed to strengthen the movement, did not serve to bring the Southern states into the pro-suffrage lineup. In fact, all the deep South states held out against the Nineteenth Amendment to the end, refusing even to ratify it. A number of racist incidents involving the Woman's Party after the winning of suffrage indicate that "expediency" had frequently served as an excuse for bigotry.

While the organized suffrage movement and the movement for Negro rights ran in separate and at times opposed directions, black and white women cooperated on other levels. Josephine Griffing, a white abolitionist, devoted herself wholeheartedly to relief and welfare work for the freedmen in Washington, D.C. and was later active in the drive for their resettlement in Kansas. Similarly, other abolitionist women expressed their support of Blacks through freedmen relief and welfare activities, supporting and adding to the work of such black women as Harriet Tubman and Sojourner Truth.† After the Civil War, many of the Northern female anti-slavery societies devoted themselves to relieving the wants of the freedmen and raising funds in support of their schools. Northern abolitionist women had begun the enormous task of educating the millions of freedmen, even while the war was still raging, by sending teachers to the Union-held areas of the South. After the war their ranks were increased by Southern women in need of employment and, gradually, by male and female black teachers. The white Southern community generally shunned these Northern teachers, refused them housing and food, and treated them as outcasts. Of necessity and often by choice they lived in the black community and shared the lives of their students. Yet the relationship of these educated white women and the illiterate poverty-stricken freedmen was not one of equals. It was of necessity tinged with paternalistic—or in this case maternalistic—attitudes and racial prejudice. A sincere dedication to social and moral uplift and a missionary approach characterized these teachers. It should be added that the few Northern black women who went south as teachers displayed a similar, somewhat patronizing attitude toward the freedmen.[18]

The pattern of paternalism continued into the postwar decades. White Northern women were instrumental in supporting the self-help efforts of black women, who founded schools and training in-

† Sojourner Truth and Josephine Griffing had earlier braved hostile crowds during their 1862 speaking tour in Kansas.

stitutes for black girls in the South. Lucy Lainey could not have succeeded without Mrs. F. E. Haines in founding and maintaining Haines School in Georgia; Charlotte Hawkins Brown was able to start her girls' school in Sedalia, North Carolina, through the help of Alice Freeman Palmer; Emma J. Wilson depended on funds raised in the North, mostly by women, to maintain Mayesville Industrial Institute in South Carolina. Later Mary McLeod Bethune and Nannie Burroughs enlisted the cooperation of wealthy whites in support of the schools they had founded and built.

Southern Blacks, living in poverty and under the most repressive political conditions, were obliged, for the time being, to accept the help of liberal-minded Northern whites, but they never stopped protesting against white paternalism in its various manifestations. White boards of trustees for black schools, incessant investigation of school management by well-meaning white donors, innumerable indignities and snubs, not to speak of indifference or often hostility on the part of local whites, were the price paid by the dedicated black women who raised the educational and cultural level of their communities by founding schools. Charlotte Hawkins Brown bore the load patiently for years, making her Palmer Memorial Institute grow from a log cabin school into a finishing school for girls worth half a million dollars in plant and equipment. Yet even her patience had limits. "Now that things are turning and many are opening their eyes to what I've tried to do," she wrote, "and desiring to have a share in the same, the question in my heart and mind, and God only knows how it hurts, is just what are they going to ask me to submit to as a negro woman to get their interest. . . . My only point is in my efforts to get money now, I don't want my friends in the North to tie my hands so I can't speak out when I'm being crushed." [19]

Frequently, black women had to prod their white friends on the racial issue and insist on raising their level of understanding. This was done very politely, and with excessive caution, but it was done. An example is to be found in Mrs. Booker T. Washington's correspondence with Mrs. Edna Dow Cheney, a wealthy Bostonian, who cooperated with black club women in Boston and supported the Tuskegee Institute Mothers' Club.

In 1896, Margaret M. Washington wrote to Mrs. Cheney:

> I am writing you now of a matter which concerns me and the rest of women of my race. I want your advice. You know as much about this separate car business in the South as I can tell you. [The reference is to segregated and inferior Jim Crow railroad facilities.] The Southern people of course make these laws. . . . The Southern women keep up this thing. They are behind the men because their education is more limited. They have little to do except nurse their prejudices. . . . I hear that the Executive Board of the National Council of Women meet in Boston this winter to prepare for their meeting next year. I thought our cause in this matter might be helped by having a colored woman to appear in this Council, to present not only this question but she might represent us in a general way. I understand that organizations of Southern white women will not enter the Federation. . . . because they are opposed to Colored organizations entering these clubs. . . . I do believe if such women as Miss Willard, Mrs. Henrotin, Mrs. Dickinson and others were to show a little less fear of their southern sisters, these conditions of which I speak would be altered.[20]

Mrs. Washington was not alone in advancing the issue of black representation in the National Women's Club movement. White women had begun to organize clubs on a national level after the Civil War. Black women launched their national club movement in 1892. Like the white club women they emphasized community betterment, education, uplift, and self-improvement. Additionally, the Negro women's clubs were dedicated to racial improvement, defense of the home, raising of the standards of education, and an end to the various discriminatory restrictions that hedged and impeded every aspect of Negro life. The establishment of social welfare agencies for black children, orphans, the aged, and the delinquent was largely the work of these women's clubs. In state after state the first welfare services available to black people were initiated by black women and only later taken over by local government.[21] It is perhaps significant of the spirit of interracial

cooperation that in 1896 the National Association of Colored
Women appealed to all of its member clubs to donate $5 per club
to support the aged and now destitute daughter of old John Brown
of Harpers Ferry.

Cooperation with white women was first established locally. In-
dividual black women were sometimes admitted to white clubs.†
Negro women's clubs were gradually admitted to state federations,
but the issue of national representation remained controversial. As
late as 1900 the General Federation of Women's Clubs, at its
Milwaukee Convention, refused the credentials of Mrs. Josephine
Ruffin, who represented the New Era Club, the oldest of the
Negro women's clubs. She also had been elected a delegate of the
New England Federation of Women's Clubs. The national organization was willing to accept her credentials from the white organization, but refused those from the black women's club. Mrs.
Ruffin refused this "compromise." The incident led to discussion
of the race issue in many clubs and in the nation's newspapers, but
the color bar in national women's organizations did not drop until
several decades later.[22]

In the South, it was in temperance societies that black and white
women took their first faltering steps toward cooperation. The first
timid contact among leaders of color-separated locals led to county
and state meetings which at times even discussed such formerly
taboo subjects as the sexual exploitation of Negro women by white
men. Since the greatest impediment to black and white cooperation was the slanderous myth that black women were morally
degraded, this issue was of considerable importance. Mere contact
with black club women dissolved the stereotyped notions of preju-
diced isolation. The white women had to learn to see a connection
between the protection of their own homes and the protection
of the honor and rights of black women. The issue around which

†Josephine St. Pierre Ruffin was a member of the New England
Women's Club. Fannie B. Williams was admitted to membership in the
Chicago Club in 1894.

this education and politicalization was effected was lynching.

In the 1890s, under the leadership of Ida B. Wells, who initiated an international crusade against lynching, Negro women's clubs launched a national campaign against this evil, and challenged white club women to support them. An early example of the now familiar pattern of the white liberal, accused of racism by black friends, grew out of this anti-lynching campaign and involved Frances Willard, the president of the Women's Christian Temperance Union, whose earlier abolitionist convictions and interracial work were a matter of record. Mrs. Willard was hesitant and equivocal on the issue of lynching and defended the Southern record against accusations made by Ida B. Wells on her English speaking-tour. Severe attacks on her in the women's press and a protracted public controversy helped to move Mrs. Willard to a cautious stand in opposition to lynching. Black women continued to agitate this issue and to confront white women with a moral challenge to their professed Christianity.[23]

Black women early perceived that lynchings were tolerated by white communities because of the rape charge against black men and the general white belief in the inherent immorality of black women. They therefore attacked lynching by exposing the falsity of the rape charge, case by case, and by trying to maximize the cooperative and friendly contacts between women of both races. Custom, tradition, institutional and legal practices made this difficult, but they persisted.

As a result of the democratic hopes raised by World War I and the shocking polarization at the end of the war, which found expression in race riots and lynchings, women of both races felt impelled to make stronger efforts than ever before to bridge the gap between the races. Eva Bowles, Mrs. Lugenia Hope, Charlotte Hawkins Brown, and Mary McLeod Bethune led black women in this effort. White church women were the first to respond. In 1919, the Women's Missionary Council Committee on Race Relations sent two white observers to a Tuskegee conference of black club women. Frank discussion and position papers were exchanged.

In 1920, through the efforts of the Commission on Inter-Racial Cooperation (CIC), four black women were invited to a conference of Southern church women. This tradition-shattering meeting ended with 105 representatives of white church and women's organizations constituting themselves the Women's Council of the CIC and pledging themselves to grassroots interracial work. Patient work on a local level and the slow integration of state and national organizations continued for several decades. By 1929, there were 805 interracial county committees functioning in the Southern states.

In 1930 the all-white Association of Southern Women for the Prevention of Lynching was formed. Its major contribution was the repudiation of the myth that lynchings were done to protect white womanhood. Over 40,000 signatures of white women leaders to a statement condemning lynchings were collected throughout the South. The organization also acted effectively on the local level to stop actual lynchings.[24] The ensuing decline of lynchings is so dramatic, that one can be justified in crediting black and white women with a major victory in this long campaign.

The winning of full equality for black women in the civic and community organizations of the South proceeded with painful slowness. As late as World War II it was considered a remarkable breakthrough for a black woman, Septima Clark, to sit on the board of the Community Chest of Charleston, South Carolina. A similarly long process of organizing, prodding, and educating on the part of a few black pioneers led to the eventual integration of the national YWCA, but this was not achieved until the 1950s. Still, the positive role of white women in combating discrimination, in helping to support black schools and welfare institutions, and in laying the groundwork in the Southern communities for an acceptance of later civil rights legislation should not be understated. Black and white women were, in regard to interracial cooperation, ahead of their communities and their men, possibly because the common concerns of women for their homes and their children prevailed over prejudice and vested interests.

All women, black and white, experienced sex discrimination in education, employment, and politics. But to most black women, the race discrimination they experienced was much more pervasive, devastating, and threatening. Black women usually put their needs as Blacks before their needs as women. Many white women, on the other hand, were made more politically sophisticated by the very process of working for their own emancipation. Inevitably, those demanding an extension of the ballot to women, attacking the low economic status of women, and even questioning the fundamental assumptions of society in regard to matrimony, divorce, and sexual mores began to challenge the established institutions of society. White women in their quest for emancipation came into conflict with the churches, the law, the political and economic establishment, and with the men in power on the local scene, inevitably white men. These were the same forces traditionally arrayed against black people. In the labor movement, too, those seeking to abolish child labor and advance the conditions of working women came up against the same forces that had so long kept black people oppressed. Thus white women were radicalized through their contacts with black women.

Despite the close linkage of the movements for Negro rights and women's emancipation in the early 19th century, which might make it appear as though white women were just "naturally" advocates of and sympathetic to the cause of Blacks, interaction between black and white women was much more ambivalent and problematical. Not infrequently there was confrontation, competition and conflict. Black and white cooperation, wherever it was effective, was based on the healthy self-interest of each of the groups involved, rather than on altruistic motives and paternalism. Although they have their womanhood in common, black and white women could not escape the confines and limitations of a society in which a person's status and power are defined not only by sex but—more importantly—by race.

8

The Political Activities
of Antislavery Women

Historians of abolitionism have paid a great deal of attention to the ideas, the personalities, the psychological and political motivation of the abolitionists, and to the outcome of four decades or more of agitation. There has been relatively little interest in an institutional analysis of the antislavery movement except for the brief periods of dramatic dissension within the movement.[1] Yet the phenomenon of a movement which began with the dedicated band of sixty-two people who formed the American Anti-Slavery Society in 1833 and went on to organize more than 1350 local societies in 1838; which in 1840 and 1844 entered politics with decisive, if negative, results and which had by 1860 so affected public opinion that a Republican could be elected President, deserves functional analysis.[2] Regardless of whether abolitionism achieved its stated goals, there is no question that it served to transform public opinion on the issue of slavery in the North and the West and that it did so by a series of organized efforts with different tactical goals.

Antislavery workers and agitators labored in groups; their soci-

This essay is based on a paper delivered at the Southern Historical Association Meeting, Atlanta, November 11, 1976. The essay has benefitted from the criticism of Professors Betty Fladeland, Eric Foner, James McPherson, Anne Firor Scott, Ronald Walters, and Peter Wood.

eties were local organizations and county and state networks; the anniversaries and conventions served organizational, educational, and public relations functions. To change public opinion, antislavery organizations had to be visible locally, have continuity and a recognizable public face, and had to carry on some form of propaganda and organizing work. Such work formed the basis for fund-raising, recruitment of forces, political campaigning, even the bringing of law suits. The important groundwork out of which political antislavery would grow was laid in the years 1836–43. Antislavery petition campaigns were an important aspect of this work. Women, who played a crucial role in antislavery petitioning, had far more importance in transforming public opinion and thereby influencing political life than has hitherto been recognized.

Quite in keeping with the general neglect of the history of women, the antislavery activities of women have been slighted by historians. In so far as women abolitionists were singled out for closer scrutiny, interest focused on a few individual "leaders," their biographies and especially their psychology, with emphasis on their supposed deviance. Where organized female activity has been interpreted at all, historians have taken for granted the supposedly negative effect of the "woman question" in splitting the American Anti-Slavery Society in 1840.[3] Even historians of women have been more interested in the effect of antislavery activities on the rise of feminism than in the activities themselves.[4]

Men and women in the antislavery movement did not necessarily engage in the same activities nor approach their work in the same way. Thus the questions historians traditionally ask of their sources frequently fail to elicit material pertaining to the activities of women. Much antislavery historiography has been focused on leadership. Who were the antislavery leaders? Why and how did they come to the movement? How effective were they? Yet, three separate studies of antislavery leaders have defined leadership in such a way that it would be difficult for women to be included.[5] Among criteria for leadership were: representation at antislavery conventions (only male conventions were considered), political candidacy, frequent mention in the press, and membership in community organizations. Given the social restraints on women, only the latter is applicable to women, and so it is no wonder that no woman appears among antislavery leaders in these books.

Yet in each community where there were antislavery societies there were women known as leaders. It is generally recognized that, except for a few wealthy contributors, women provided most of the financial support of the antislavery movement. Women sold and distributed literature: less noted is the fact that they also wrote such literature and served as editors for many of the antislavery papers.[6]

Dwight L. Dumond and Gilbert Barnes were the first historians to call attention to the pivotal effect of the 1837–39 petition campaign and to the role of women in it. But they regarded women's activities as merely auxiliary to those of men and failed to take into consideration the dynamic effect of the campaign in bringing large groups of women into policial activity for the first time. This view of the subject has prevailed.[7]

A more recent study of women's antislavery petitions focuses on petitions from one small New York township and uses the signatures in combination with census data to construct a "profile" of the female antislavery activists—an interesting and useful analysis but one which tells us nothing about the impact of this activity on women and on the community.[8]

Disfranchised groups in a democracy can hope to influence those holding political power only by persuasion, by educational activity, and by exerting pressure in a variety of forms. Their peculiar relationship to political power, as the group longest disfranchised, caused women to use various methods of pressure and persuasion. Slaves, women, and some members of reform societies had petitioned since colonial days. Petitions and memorials against slavery had been used in the 18th century, but mass petitioning first occurred in the 1820s as part of the work of missionary societies. By 1830 petitions reached the House of Representatives in large numbers on such varied issues as the tariff, currency reform, the

10-hour day, abolition of Sunday mail, abolition of slavery, and opposition to the removal of the Cherokee Indians. The American Anti-Slavery Society took up petitioning in 1835–36 as an important means of educating Congress and the public.

Antislavery petitions began to flood Congress and were met in 1836 in the House by enactment of the "gag rule," which provided for tabling without further action all petitions on the subject of slavery. The "gag rules" passed by succeeding Congresses at the insistence of Southern Congressmen broadened the abolition campaign into a defense of free speech. The political effect was to widen the base of the antislavery movement.

The striving of women to organize separate societies and take part in antislavery activities was greatly spurred by British influence and example. British women had worked for passage of the 1833 Emancipation Act by petitioning activities starting in the early 1820s. The reformers Elizabeth Heyrick and the Quaker Elizabeth Fry, both active in public work for emancipation, were known and respected models for American women. The 1835 visit by the popular antislavery lecturer George Thompson, which had been financed by Scottish and British women's organizations, also had considerable impact. But in the frontier and rural regions these influences were not as significant in encouraging women to organize as was the actual petitioning experience of antislavery men and women.

As early as 1836, in her *Appeal to the Christian Women of the Southern States,* Angelina Grimké had pointed out that petitions were a particularly apt means of political expression for women, who were excluded from other means of influencing politics. She urged Southern women to take up petitioning and cautioned them not to be disappointed if progress was slow. "If you could obtain but six signatures to such a petition in only one state, I would say, send up that petition, and be not in the least discouraged." [9]

In May 1837 when the first Anti-Slavery Convention of American women met in New York City, female antislavery societies were clustered in only a few regions. In Massachusetts there were female antislavery societies as early as March 1833 in Reading, Boston, Groton, Amesbury, and Lowell. In 1834 female societies were formed in Salem, Newburyport, and Haverhill. In 1835 such groups organized in South Weymouth, Weymouth, Braintree, Dorchester, Lynn, Fall River, and New Bedford. The second cluster of organizations was in Pennsylvania, centering on Philadelphia. New York City had two active female societies of white women and one of colored women. After the convention societies were organized in scattered towns in Maine, New Hampshire, Rhode Island, Pennsylvania, Michigan, Connecticut, and upstate New York.[10]

The convention made petitioning the focus of their activities, but women first had to overcome traditional indoctrination and fear of disapproval. The convention addressed itself to the subject in a variety of ways. A resolution offered by Angelina Grimké stated that the right of petition was "natural and inalienable, derived immediately from God . . . whether it be exercised by man or woman. . . ." It urged "every woman . . . annually to petition Congress with the faith of an Esther. . . ."[11] Apparently the appeal to divine and biblical sanction for petitioning did not convince all women present of the propriety of this activity. The convention engaged in spirited debate and a resolutions battle over the rationale for women's participation in what was clearly understood to be political activity. The radical position urging women to regard slavery as a "national sin because Congress has the power to abolish it" lost out to a more moderate resolution appealing to mothers to pray for the abolition of slavery for the welfare of their children.[12] Nevertheless, the convention proceeded in a businesslike way to organize its petition activity by taking pledges from delegates to send petitions for the abolition of slavery and the slave trade in the District of Columbia to each town in their several states in the course of the present season. Undertaking also to petition the various churches to take an antislavery stand and commending Rep. John Quincy Adams for his defense of the "right of petition for women and for slaves," the convention adjourned.[13]

In order to carry out the convention resolutions women had to organize in their communities, to set up a network of petition gatherers, letter writers, agents, and lecturers. The Anti-Slavery Conventions of American Women held in 1838 and in 1839 further intensified this campaign. Women sent hundreds of petitions to the Congress and thereby precipitated a political crisis in the fight against the gag rule and for the right of petition. In October 1837 the *Congressional Globe* reports Senator Wm. C. Preston of South Carolina as saying that 28,000 memorialists had subscribed to abolition petitions. Robert Walker, the Senator from Mississippi, found a majority were signed by females and children. He believed, "if the ladies and Sunday school children would let us alone, there would be but a few abolition petitions."[14] Mr. Walker underestimated the zeal of male petitioners, but he correctly perceived the importance of petitioning for the mobilization of abolition sentiment among women. By the end of 1838 these petitions were so numerous as to create a storage problem. A number of them were kept and are now in the National Archives, but most of those sent after 1840 were apparently destroyed.[15]

What follows is based on a hand count and analysis of 402 antislavery petitions sent to the 25th Congress in its three sessions in 1837–38.[16] These petitions in the National Archives are filed in the order in which they were received, which makes it possible to get a sense of the organizational sequence of the campaign. They are arranged by region and by the object of their appeal. During this period the major objects of the petitioners were: abolition of slavery in the District of Columbia; opposition to the annexation of Texas; and outlawing the internal slave trade. Most of the petition-signers signed all three petitions.[17]

Most of the petitions have a notation on the outside specifying the number of signatures, whether male or female; the name of the petition-gatherer (sometimes, and not so frequently, if female), and the place of origin.[18]

From areas where abolition societies made up of males predominated, the petitions came in, usually one from each town or county, with mostly the signatures of men. From Vermont came 24 petitions with 1792 male signatures and 671 female signatures: from Michigan three with 535 male and 120 female signatures: from Illinois five signed by 266 males and 66 females. (See Table 1.) It is evident from these petitions that women got involved in the campaign first through the encouragement of men, who asked their wives and daughters to sign petitions and help circulate them. Here and there female names appeared next to the names of male family members, indicating that they had been solicited by the male petition gatherer within the family circle. Another way was to have the female names on a separate sheet or on a petition divided in half vertically, with all the male names on one side, the female names on the other. This may indicate that males gave the petition to women to circulate among their friends or possibly their sewing circle or church group. The names of men and women never appear randomly mixed.

The old centers of antislavery activity, where strong female societies had flourished since 1833, provided most of the petitions. Pennsylvania and Massachusetts sent 280 petitions out of a total of 402.

It is not only absolute numbers but the pattern of distribution of female and male signatures which can inform us about the role played by women in the petition campagins. For purposes of comparison, the petitions have been grouped into those with more male signatures (Table 1) and those with more female signatures (Table 2). Table 3 provides a summary of all the petitions, regardless of gender distribution.

When comparing Table 1 and Table 2, what is most remarkable is the ratio of male to female petition signers. In Table 1 the ratio is 3.3 male to 1 female signer; in Table 2 the ratio is almost exactly reversed—3.5 female to 1 male. In Table 1 female signers appear mostly on "mixed" petitions. In Table 2 female signers appear in great numbers on petitions circulated by women, while "mixed" petitions are relatively unimportant in accounting for the total. This reflects the organized activity of separate female antislavery

Table 1. Antislavery petitions sent to the 25th Congress
(1–3 sessions, 1837–38, identifiable by sex of signer)

			Number of petitions			Signatures		
Origin	To	Total	Male signers only	Female signers only	Male/Fem. signers	Male	Female	Total
New York	House	15	8	3	4	2088	852	2940
Vermont	House	26	15	3	8	1792	671	2463
Ohio	House	50	30	4	16	4074	942	5016
	Senate	18	8	2	8	1463	247	1710
Illinois	Senate	5	3	2	—	266	66	332
Michigan	Senate	3	2	1	—	535	120	655
Totals		117	66	15	36	10,218	2898	13,116

Table 2. Antislavery petitions sent to the 25th Congress
(1–3 sessions, 1837–39, identifiable by sex of signer)

		Number of petitions			Signatures		
Origin	Total number of petitions	Male signers only	Female signers only	Male/Fem. signers	Male	Female	Total
Massachusetts to House	173	78	83	12	8340	14,285	22,625
Massachusetts to Senate	54	1	53	—	29	20,951	20,980
Connecticut to Senate	5	—	—	5	625	908	1533
Pennsylvania to House	49	29	12	8	3020	4133	7153
Pennsylvania to Senate	4	1	2	1	41	1754	1795
Totals	285	109	150	26	12,055	42,031	54,086

organizations and can be seen most clearly in the 54 petitions sent
to the Senate from Massachusetts: 53 petitions circulated by
women account for 20,951 signatures, and one circulated by a man
accounts for 29. A similar pattern can be seen in the four Pennsylvania petitions to the Senate, with 41 male signatures and 1754
female ones. As Table 3 shows, in the total number of signatures

on 402 petitions, women signers outnumber men by better than two to one.

If we look at the origin of the petitions, it becomes obvious that female petitioning activity was correlated to the spread of female societies. Vermont, Illinois, and Michigan had few female societies: in New York City, where most of the New York petitions originated, there were only three small and relatively inactive women's societies. Ohio is interesting, in that antislavery organiza-

Table 3. Antislavery petitions sent to the 25th Congress
(1–3 sessions, 1837–38, identifiable by sex of signer)
Summary of petitions, by sex of signer

Total number of petitions	Total number of petitions by sex			Signatures		
	Male signers only	Female signers only	Male/Fem. signers	Male	Female	Total
Table 1 117	66	15	36	10,218	2898	13,116
Table 2 285	109	150	26	12,055	42,031	54,086
Total 402	175	165	62	22,273	44,929	67,202

Source: For all three tables: Petitions to the 25th Congress, 1–3 Sessions, House Records HR-25 A and Senate Records 25-H-H1, National Archives.

tion was strong, as can be seen by the large number of petitions; but it was unevenly distributed among Garrisonians in the Western Reserve and adherents of the American Anti-Slavery Society in other areas. The bulk of the petitions and those with the most signatures came from the Western Reserve and reflect the strength of Garrisonian abolitionism, which encouraged women to take an active and independent part in antislavery work.[19]

The petitions also reveal some interesting aspects of the way in which men and women carried on this work. It is not possible to say with absolute certainty who the petition circulators were in each case. Frequently the name of the petition gatherer is listed on the back of the petition and often the person is the first signator. Clearly, petitions with female signatures only were circulated by women. Given the prejudice against women's participation in public affairs, which permeated antislavery circles as it did society in general, one can assume that males would seldom solicit the signatures of females. If they did, they would do so within the family circle, as was indicated by one petition which was headed "5 women from Ashtabula County, Ohio—these signers are my wife, my son's wife and daughter of lawful age," indicating that this procedure was considered exceptional. Table 3 shows that men and women circulated sex-separated petitions in almost equal numbers (175 male; 165 female). Considering the overwhelming predominance of female signatures, it seems reasonable to assume that most of the 62 "mixed" petitions were also circulated by women.

There were a number of petitions which came from the same town, one circulated by a man, one by a woman. I made a separate count of the signatures in each case and found that the women's petitions always had more names than those of men. In comparing the way family names appeared on the petitions, a curious pattern emerged: the names of men of the same family would be randomly scattered among the signers on petitions circulated by a man, indicating that men circulated their petitions at the workplace or perhaps at meetings and only later—if at all—included male *family members*. The women's petitions would always show a cluster of family members, which indicates that women first gathered the signatures of all their female relatives and then moved on, probably house to house, to gather other women's signatures. One such petition was particularly moving—it showed the names of 24 women of the same family, headed by Lois Packard, who obviously was the matriarch—94 years old. Clearly, men and women, engaged in the same activity, went about it in different ways.

Analysis of antislavery petitions combined with a study of church affiliation, census data, and property records can reveal much about the women who engaged in the petitioning. Two recent studies have used this method to determine the religious affiliation and property standing of men and women who signed antislavery petitions. In articles analyzing two petitions from Sandwich, New Hampshire, Patricia Heard and Ellen Henle additionally find the same pattern I found in the petitions I analyzed:

more women than men signers (260 women; 222 men). They also noticed that at least 23 wives signed, while their husbands did not, which may indicate the exercise of female autonomy or it may simply mean the absence of husbands. They also analyzed the route taken through the village by the petition gatherers and found that men and women followed approximately the same route.[20]

A more elaborate study by Judith Wellman of 304 upstate New York antislavery petitions sent in 1838–39 shows that 14.5 per cent of the petitions were signed by women alone (44) and 54.9 per cent were signed by men and women together. Wellman reasons that "women, either alone or with men, signed almost 70% (69.4%) of the petitions." This would support the findings in my sample.[21]

The predominance of women among petition signers shows that women sought to exert what political influence they could in the cause of antislavery. But what of the effect of petitioning on women? Is there evidence that it became an instrument of organizing and helped to draw women into greater involvement in antislavery? Was petitioning a one-time activity or did it lead women toward other reforms and broader political activities?

The sudden spurt of petitioning fervor growing out of the first Female Anti-Slavery Convention is obvious in the number and size of the petitions. When women begin to petition on their own we first see huge petitions such as "remonstrance of Lydia Maria Child and 3028 others, women of Boston, Mass." or "Sarah G. Buffum and 2832 women of Bristol County, Mass." or "H. Huntington and 1400 others, women of Lowell, Mass."

It was then also that petitions came in clusters, several from one town, or several towns in one county bundled together. This was the result of an organized drive with responsible coordinators in towns and counties, who gathered various petitions together before forwarding them to Washington. It reflected the level of organization, region by region, of female societies.

The Massachusetts petitions were particularly interesting. They began with a mammoth petition of 4054 women of Boston. On October 12, 1837, Daniel Webster presented petitions of the women of 39 towns of Massachusetts and ten more petitions of "citizens" (which must be taken to be male and female, since male petitions almost always state "male" or "voters").[22]

When one checks the list of Massachusetts towns from which petitions were received against the list of female antislavery societies in the state, it appears that almost every such society sent at least one petition; many sent more than one. There were petitions also from a number of towns that did not have societies; one can assume these were circulated by sympathetic individuals. When one checks the list of towns from which the petitions were signed against the list of towns in which the Grimké sisters had lectured during their 1837–38 lecture tour, the correlation is striking: out of 44 Massachusetts petitions, 34 came from towns in which the sisters had lectured. Conversely, out of 67 towns in which the sisters had spoken, 34 sent petitions to Congress within six months of their visit.[23]

The Grimké sisters' tour offers an interesting example of the way in which educational work, organizing, and petitioning were interconnected. The fourteen Massachusetts antislavery societies represented at the 1837 women's convention were probably the strongest of the state's female societies. Sarah and Angelina Grimké lectured in every town where there were female societies and in many others, speaking to at least 40,500 persons. As a direct result of their trip new female societies were formed in eight towns within six months of their tour: Concord, W. Bradford, W. Amesbury, Holliston, Andover, W. Newbury, Brookline, and Worcester, where they had been invited with the express purpose of helping to form a new society.[24] The old societies and the new were spurred in their petitioning activity by these lectures. The gathering of petitions, in turn, led to a growth in membership and local influence.† Women who signed petitions once did not neces-

† The sisters kept accurate records of the first two weeks of their tour, recording the new members recruited at their meetings. At six meetings in the Boston area they reported 154 new members had been recruited. If anywhere near this level of recruitment was sustained during their other

sarily become active antislavery workers, but they would be likely
to attend the annual antislavery fair or to contribute to it, thus
spreading the financial base of the movement.

That petitioning immediately led to a widening of political influence can be seen in Massachusetts. In March 1838 Angelina
Grimké brought a women's antislavery petition with 20,000 signatures before a committee of the Massachusetts legislature, and for-
mally addressed the politicians. The importance of her presentation
did not so much lie in the fact that she was the first woman ever to
speak to an American legislature, as in the fact that she represented
an organized network of female antislavery societies. Here was
indeed a new force on the political scene, one which politicians had
been forced to recognize as a pressure group. Massachusetts women
continued to petition Congress, but the main force of their effort
was directed to their state legislature. Early in 1839, petitions
signed by more than 1400 women were presented to the Massachusetts House of Representatives, asking the repeal of all state
laws which discriminated against Blacks and which outlawed interracial marriage. The petitions were met with scorn and ridicule,
but provoked a lengthy debate in the House on the right and propriety of women petitioners. This debate only served to spur petitioning activity by women, and, although the ban on interracial
marriages was not rescinded during that session, abolitionist pressure with active female participation continued, until the law was
repealed in 1843.

Petition gathering was arduous work in which women had to
brave opposition, ridicule, attack, and the disapproval of friends
and neighbors. Juliana Tappan wrote about her experience:

> I have left many houses ashamed of my sex . . . Ladies sitting
> on splendid sofas looked at us as if they had never heard of the
> word Texas and I presume some of them would have been un-
> able to say . . . whether or not it belonged to the U.S.[25]

---

82 meetings, Wendell Phillips was right in regarding their tour as an
organizing success.

Another woman wrote of the apathy that met her efforts to form a female antislavery society in Connecticut:

> Women have been taught to depend on the men for their opinions. We had occasion to observe this in our efforts to obtain signatures to petitions; my daughter visited almost every house in this town for the purpose and found that it was the men generally, who needed free discussion, for the women would not act contrary to the ideas of the male part of their family.[26]

A Massachusetts woman who had circulated the petition against the ban on interracial marriages reported opposition but was less disturbed by it:

> I suppose you heard of our *heretical* position. Many of its signers seemed troubled by the ridicule consequent upon it, but it strikes me as a nail which hit . . . There is nothing like shocking people's prejudices sometimes. It reveals their extent and power and oft times works much good.[27]

Though the particular responses of individual women varied, petition gathering engendered self-confidence and assertiveness. It led many women toward increased participation in the public sphere. From petitioning their representative to canvassing the opinions of candidates prior to election was only a small step, one which women in New England and in Ohio took in the 1840 and 1842 elections. Some women campaigned for Whig candidates in 1840. Antoinette Brown and Lucy Stone took part in Gerrit Smith's campaign for Congress in 1852 and "had the pleasure of helping to bring about a successful issue of his campaign."[28]

Many abolitionist women supported antislavery candidates and took an active part in political campaigns. But the majority did not. After the 1840 split in the antislavery movement it is striking to note the decline in female participation in the Western & Foreign Anti-Slavery Society, which denied full participation to women. The New York City female societies virtually disappeared.[29] Judith Wellman in her study of antislavery petitioning activities in Oneida County, New York, has also noted a sharp drop-off in female participation in that region after 1840. While petitioning activity nearly doubled in 1850–51 (over 1838–39), the percentage of female signatures shrank dramatically: from 70 per cent of all signatures in 1838 to 2.3 per cent in 1850. In other words women had provided the bulk of the petition signers and circulators in 1838, but were a tiny minority of signers in 1850. Judith Wellman reasons that this is due to the fact that antislavery had shifted from a moral reform movement to a political one, a shift which by definition excluded women.[30] It is certainly true that the shift to political abolitionism discouraged female participation, as can be seen by looking at the regions in which the Garrisonian movement remained strong—Massachusetts, Pennsylvania, and Ohio. In those areas women continued to be publicly active and increasingly visible as petitioners, lecturers, and speakers. There is also good evidence, however, that many women, once they had become habituated to political activity through petitioning, transferred this activity to causes more directly connected with their self-interest. There were mass petitioning campaigns for women for equal property rights legislation in New York, Massachusetts, and Ohio in the 1840s and 1850s. With the convening of the first woman's rights convention at Seneca Falls in 1848 and with the subsequent biannual conventions in many states, women's political activity began to focus on woman's rights issues. The ancient method of trying to influence legislators and change public opinion by means of memorials was raised to new levels of significance. The resolutions, memorials, and appeals which issued from local, state, and national woman's rights conventions for more than seven decades became instruments of propaganda, education, and pressure. Equal in importance was their significance in helping to mould an ideology of feminism around which women's political activities could be rallied.

The final surge of women's antislavery political activity came in 1863 when the Women's Loyal National League was formed for the purpose of collecting one million signatures for a petition asking for passage of the 13th Amendment. That goal was not reached, but Senator Charles Sumner presented a roll of petitions with 300,000 signatures, all of them collected by women.

One more aspect of women's petitioning activity needs to be considered: its functions as a builder of antislavery strength in communities. Petitioning itself led to strengthened organization; fund-raising and distribution of literature followed from petitioning.

There is a good reason to believe that abolition sentiment and activity were carried out to a large extent by family groups. Abolitionist families were the base for support of the antislavery newspapers; they were the mainstay of the underground railroad; they provided continuity of ideas and beliefs, regardless of shifting tactics and organizational emphasis at various times. Members of antislavery families from New England furnished the core of abolitionist organizers and supporters in the Western Reserve of Ohio. Hicksite Quaker families spearheaded antislavery organization in Rhode Island and eastern Pennsylvania. Since women, in order to overcome the inhibitions and strictures against political activity, needed the support of their female relatives, it is not surprising to find family clusters among antislavery women. Judith Wellman found that of the female petition signers in 1836 in Paris township, Oneida County, New York, 42 per cent had other family members who also signed petitions.[31] The membership list of the Ohio Ashtabula County Female Antislavery Society in 1835–37 also shows a high percentage of family groups. Out of 245 names checked, 89 (over 36 per cent) were in family groups of 2–6 (counting only those with the same surname).[32] If one counted those actually related by family of birth, including married sisters with different surnames, the percentage would undoubtedly be higher. There can be little doubt that families in which the women were so strongly organized provided a strong supportive base for the antislavery politics of men. In Ohio and perhaps elsewhere these kinds of antislavery activities had considerable significance in building a reform tradition in certain families and localities which gave continuity to the reform impulse.

In summary, the petitioning activities of antislavery women in the 1830s and 40s were of far greater significance to the building of the antislavery movement than has been previously recognized. Moreover, these activities contributed directly to the development of a contingent of local and regional women leaders, many of whom were to transfer their political concerns to feminist activities after 1848. Further investigation of this aspect of reform should lead to a re-evaluation of antislavery history, which would give to women a less marginal place and see their work as an integral aspect of the antislavery movement.

9

Just a Housewife

If there is one valid generalization to be made about American women it is that the overwhelming majority of them have been and are engaged in domestic food preparation, maintenance of the home and clothing, and—if they are mothers—in child-rearing. Single, married, or divorced, regardless of whether she holds a paid job or not, a woman is a housewife, at least part of her life. Even if she can afford to hire another woman to do her housework, the responsibility of running the household is hers. The housewife's job is gender-linked—by definition and history, a housewife is a woman and every woman is a housewife—and it is therefore crucial to any analysis of the position of women in society.

The manner in which housework is done has changed considerably, but the essential demands of the job and the working conditions have changed relatively little over the course of 250 years. Work previously done by hand is now done by machines; many jobs formerly performed in the home are now done out of it,

This essay, in an earlier version, was delivered as a paper at the Sarah Lawrence College Conference "Feminist Perspectives on Housework and Childcare," held October 22, 1977, and published in the transcript, Amy Swerdlow (ed.), *Feminist Perspectives on Housework and Childcare* (Bronxville, N.Y., 1978), pp. 22–34.

requiring the modern housewife to spend more time in fetching, carrying, and ordering than in making the product herself. Technological innovations have eased the physical strains and labor involved in some of the housewife's tasks, but modernization has had little effect on making the kind of structural changes which would transform the job into an occupation like any other in industrialized society. As did generations of her predecessors, the housewife still performs a routine service job, creating products which are daily consumed. No matter how well cooked the meals, the family will require more the next day. The product vanishes, and its value is ephemeral. The housewife works in isolation, constantly tied to house and children, performing a job which demands her 24-hour-a-day, 7-day-a-week availability. And, yet, what she does is seldom considered as "work" by her family; legally and economically she is not considered as belonging to the work force; her services are not counted as part of the Gross National Product (GNP), and they confer neither rights nor benefits upon her. In a money economy, housework is the only job offering not pay but, like indentured servitude, support in exchange for services.

The housewife's status has changed over time. In pre-industrial society—in colonial America and in the frontier regions throughout the 19th century—the work of the housewife was an essential part of the family economy and provided subsistence as much as did the work of the men. On farms and plantations, men and women worked in the same location. The work for both was compensated for in support and with some small cash payment (women had their egg and vegetable money). The work of women was as highly regarded as that of men; it was also complex work involving a large variety of manufacturing and processing skills. However, work assignments were gender-linked even then—men did not perform domestic or child-rearing tasks, although many women performed all kinds of farm labor.

The pre-industrial housewife was the teacher of her own and, possibly, of her neighbors' children, the nurse of the sick and the

old, and an active and respected force in the church and community. As the family changed from a unit of production to a unit of
consumption, the housewife changed from being primarily a pro-
ducer of goods to being a shopper and maintainer of goods. With
this came loss of skills and work satisfaction. As education, welfare, and health services moved out of the home, the most satisfying and challenging tasks of the housewife were taken over by society, leaving her with the unskilled drudge jobs. And the gap
between men and women and their societally assigned functions
widened. Man, the breadwinner, now working outside the home
and bringing not bread but cash into the home, had entered the
marketplace as an active and valued participant in its function.
Woman, continuing to work in the home as she always had, was
now separated from those activities most esteemed by a society
which measured value in cash. Woman's work and, by inference,
woman herself became devalued.

Modernization had yet another impact on the status of the
housewife. As the death rate dropped and men and women lived
longer, as infant mortality rates dropped, family patterns began to
change.

In 17th- and 18th-century America the average married couple
lived alone for only a year or two before their first child was born.
After that, a woman lived in a household, in which there were
young children, until the time her husband died. The median
length of time a woman spent between marriage and the end of the
child-bearing stage of life was 17.4 years. Eighteenth-century
women were of a median age of 60.2, when their last child married
and left home; they spent 39.7 years in child-rearing. Due to high
mortality, the median duration of marriage was 30.4 years; thus
most marriages were cut short by death of one of the spouses nine
years before the last child left home. While the basic family unit
consisted of husband, wife, and their children, relatives frequently
lived within walking distance. Single female relatives often lived
within the household, so that the household chores were accomplished in a social setting.

Throughout the 19th and early 20th century, women had fewer children and spent less of their life time in child-rearing. Due to greater longevity, couples could look forward to a marriage duration of 35.4 years and at least one year of old age together, after the last child left home. But it was only in the 1920s and after that marriage became focused not so much on child-rearing as on the couple's relationship to one another, with child-bearing occupying only 9.7 years of a woman's life, child-rearing only 31.2. The median duration of marriages in 1920–29 was 43.6 years. Fewer children spending fewer years at home left more than a decade in the average marriage, when husband and wife lived alone, and many more years, when the widowed wife was alone.[1] In the small households in city apartments or in suburbia, modern housewifes performed their tasks in isolation from relatives, close neighbors and, for much of the day, without children. While this lightened their tasks, it also lessened their function. Seen in historical perspective, the housewife's position in society has deteriorated. The housewife now performs her monotonous, repetitious cycle of activities in the service of fewer and fewer people and in ever greater isolation for many more years than did women in previous centuries.

The home, once at the center of economic life, has become a place deliberately outside of it, a retreat, a refueling station to which the family members return periodically for spiritual, physical, and psychological sustenance. Such sustenance depends to a large extent on the services of the housewife-mother. These are the services which are "labors of love" and intangible of definition and which supposedly are their own reward. As was discussed earlier (The Lady and the Mill Girl) this 20th-century definition of the home and the homemaker originated in industrializing pre-Civil War America. It was then that the sharper class divisions made possible by industrialization turned middle-class women into "ladies," a status formerly only achieved by the upper classes. Ladies were women who did not work for pay and who could turn all or part of their housework over to other women. At the very time when economic changes had made the contrast between men's work for wages and women's labor for "love" more apparent, middle-class American women were persuaded to upgrade their work by allowing experts to define their tasks and by thinking of themselves as "homemakers" and managers rather than as drudges doing household "chores." Catharine Beecher and her younger sister Harriet were the first to set themselves up as experts and to teach young women "scientific management" of the home.[2] Ministers, newspaper editors, doctors—later psychiatrists and psychologists—would elaborate this "cult of homemaking" into a potent ideology. Scientific nutrition and hygiene, modern methods of child-rearing, home decoration and entertaining according to the "lady-like" standards were now considered essential skills of the homemaker. In the later half of the 19th century, high schools and colleges offered "scientific" training, even degrees in home economics. Housewives who accepted the guidance of the experts were encouraged to feel pride in their achievements through the achievements of their husbands and children. Those who did not or could not were blamed for most of the ills of society and for the failures of the younger generation.

In 1899, the economist Thorstein Veblen brilliantly characterized a lady as one whose function it was to display her husband's wealth by spending. The leisured lady herself had become a status symbol, said Veblen, "a means of conspicuously unproductive expenditure."[3] Veblen, though highly perceptive about the way in which the lady herself was transformed into a species of commodity, was unsympathetic to the ambiguity of her position. For the lady's freedom to engage in community and voluntary activities, to take up recreation or self-improvement, depended on the availability of another woman to do her housework. A woman might be exempt from doing housework herself, as long as she could be replaced by another woman. All over the world upper- and middle-class women had enjoyed the privileges of their class and gained relative freedom by the exploited labor of lower-class women. In America this "solution" was difficult from the beginning and involved not only class but racial tensions. It would, in the 20th century, prove to be no solution at all, so middle-class women would have to look for other means of their own emancipation.

What made the problem of managing servants particularly vexing in America was the absence of a servant class. In Europe there had long existed a servant class derived from feudalism, which had its own tradition, status hierarchy, and professional pride. The relationship of mistress to servant was clear cut and well defined. There was no such servant class in America. The rich had for two centuries tried to meet this problem by the employment of slaves and indentured servants, but the dislike of white workers for servant positions had been a problem to their employers even in colonial times. The South could, for a century, postpone facing the problem because of the prolongation of slavery and the depressed economic conditions of Blacks for the five decades after the end of slavery.

Southern domestic servants were Blacks, so the relationship of employer and employee remained, well into the 20th century, heavily tinged with the heritage of slavery. In the pre-Civil War North, domestic servants were sometimes Blacks, but mostly Irish immigrants. Both groups were victims of economic discrimination and thus particularly vulnerable to exploitation. Native-born American women shunned domestic service, leaving the field to recent immigrants. By the turn of the century, urbanized Blacks moved into competition with immigrant women for domestic employment, changing the job definition from sleep-in service to day work. Regardless of this structural change, domestic service remained, nationwide, one of the most exploited occupations, with substandard wages and working conditions. In the 20th century the tendency of women to avoid domestic service when they had any other choices spread to black women. Whenever industrial employment opportunities were available to them, black women, too, preferred factory work. As a result there has been a constant shrinking of the domestic service work force since World War I.[4]

This fact has placed distinct limits on the class privileges of American women. The unavailability of steady sleep-in help, the irregular availability of day workers and their tendency to work sporadically and part-time, have made it necessary for all women, regardless of their wealth, to do some of their own housework. This has spurred the development and use of electrical gadgets and labor-saving machinery in the home, but has not, on the whole, led to the development of alternative homemaking and cleaning services.[5] Whatever time was gained for the modern housewife by the use of labor-saving machinery and by the employment of domestic workers was reclaimed at once by the increasing pressures of 20th-century consumerism. Today, the homemaker has become the shopper, the decorator, the entertainer, the specialist in gourmet cooking and/or child development.

Being a housewife has different meanings for women of different classes. In the homes of working-class women, the factory workers, the immigrants in the sweated industries, the black women supporting their families as domestics, there was no "scientific homemaking." The wives of workingmen perform quite a different function—their work was and is essential to family survival and to the maintenance of a decent standard of living. Unless the wife provides the free services she does, including comparison bargain-shopping, running to hospital clinics and agencies, making and repairing clothes, the worker's family would quickly sink into poverty. The unpaid services of the blue-collar-worker's wife are in effect what enables him and his family to survive inflation, occasional unemployment, or setbacks due to sickness.[6] In that respect, the lower-class housewife is more closely akin to the farm wife or the frontier housewife of the 19th century than she is to the upper-class homemaker of her own time. Both, however, continue to provide unpaid services for the benefit of others. Another thing they have in common is that each is only one man's heartbeat away from insecurity, even poverty. Occupation housewife, whether on the level of being a homemaker and manager or on the level of being a do-it-yourself housewife, fixes the woman into dependency on a male breadwinner. As tens of thousands of women have found out in the event of divorce or widowhood after decades of dedicated family service, being a housewife is no preparation for self-support in the marketplace. The housewife in modern society represents an economic anachronism. The gap between the efficiency of mechanized mass production and the relative inefficiency of the housewife has widened, resulting in loss of status for her. Regardless of compensatory terminology, her own self-esteem has diminished with her loss of status. This is symbolized by the self-effacing and factually erroneous answer to the question, "Do you work?" given by countless modern women: "No, I'm just a housewife."

The housewife does indeed work. In 1966, economists in a Chase Manhattan Bank study computed the average American housewife's work-week at 99.6 hours. Women employed outside the home worked an additional 34 hours per week doing housework.[7] Ann Oakley in her pioneering sociological study of British housewives finds the full-time housewife working 105 hours per week. The British woman employed full time outside the home works an additional 48 hours per week at domestic chores. On the average, housework requires 77 hours a week, Oakley finds.[8]

This estimate is quite in keeping with worldwide patterns. UNESCO Time Budget Series studies of 12 countries (representing different types of economic organization) show a remarkable consistency in the way men and women distribute their daily activities. Everywhere more employed women than men do housework and child care:

> In no country do employed men spend more than half an hour a
> day on housework, and employed women less than an hour and
> a half, even though women's working hours outside the home
> are sometimes longer than men's.

Elise Boulding, summarizing the findings, concludes that everywhere "women's time is far more constrained than men's."[9] The double (and triple) burden of the working woman-housewife-childbearer is a quantifiable reality. It deprives her of her leisure time, saps her energy during her hours on a paid job, and affects every aspect of her life.

What is the value of her work in economic terms? Economists of the Chase Manhattan Bank of New York have recently calculated that the thirty million American women who do not work outside the home and who list their occupations as "housewives" are each doing unpaid work worth $257.53 a week on the current labor market.[10] The work they do includes twelve different skill categories. Each of the services the housewife performs becomes a legitimate paid occupation when performed by men in the marketplace, from cooking and sewing to window-washing and floor-cleaning. Computing the average housewife's work in terms of hourly wages needed to replace her, the Chase Manhattan economists calculate that each housewife performs a job worth $13,391 a year. Another study computes the aggregate value of earnings forgone by housewives due to their unpaid domestic labor as $105 billion a year. This would be a sizable portion of the Gross National Product, if it were included in it.[11]

Who pays the housewife's support? Who benefits from her unpaid labor?

At first glance it seems obvious that the husband or the male family head (in the case of an unmarried woman) pays for the housewife's support in exchange for her services. Apologists for the institution have explained that this represents an even exchange of bartered services for upkeep, but the figures just cited tend to disprove this argument. Charlotte Perkins Gilman, an important feminist theoretician writing at the turn of the century, pointed out that, were there any rational relationship between the labor performed by the housewife and the amount of financial support she receives, the housewife in the low-income family, who works the hardest, would be the most amply rewarded, and the richest housewife the least.[12] Since the exact opposite is the case, this argument can be disregarded.

Another explanation offered focuses on the "homemaking" aspects of the housewife's work. The rise of modern consumerism has spread to the lower classes the use of the home as a place to display the status of the breadwinner. The ability to acquire and show off the material goods deemed indispensable for respectability is one of the required skills of the housewife. The respect accruing to her from this, as well as from the achievements of her children, is her alleged intangible reward. Such an interpretation sees the housewife as essentially unemployed, a volunteer working for "love" and for the respect gained through the achievements of family members.

Since all occupations also offer intangible rewards in addition to cash payments, such an explanation sidesteps rational economic analysis. It does not highlight the benefits to the husband and the members of the family derived from the housewife's work and thus calls attention to the peculiar way in which the occupation seems to be institutionalized within the family. Some of the major theoretical discussions of the subject by modern feminists have focused on this view. By simplifying the economic relationship of husband and wife, this interpretation makes it appear that the husband is the sole beneficiary of the housewife's unpaid labor. He exploits her and has a vested interest in maintaining her in this occupation.[13] Thus the question "Who does the dishes?" becomes not only an emotionally charged but a politically dynamic issue.

While there is some merit to this approach, it essentially over-simplifies and disregards the way in which family function and structure differ in different classes of society. It makes it appear that the oppression of the housewife and her economic exploitation are primarily located in the family and does not sufficiently recognize the way in which the family is enmeshed in other social institutions.

It is partially true that the male family head benefits from the housewife's work. So do the children, the husband's employer, and the major economic institutions of the society. Husband and children are the immediate beneficiaries of the housewife's labor. They enjoy something she does *not* enjoy—personal services in everyday life. But the housewife's work also provides a hidden benefit to the husband's *employer*. If the husband is in the middle or upper class, the wife's work improves his status and business standing. Her work frequently helps to advance his career and in some cases, such as that of executives' wives, provides tangible services, which would otherwise have to be paid for, such as the entertainment of clients and customers. In the case of workingmen, wives, as we have seen, help to prop up the husband's low income by their unpaid services. If women, as a group, did not provide such services, workers would have to be paid higher wages or companies would have to provide cheap restaurant meals and laundry facilities for their workers. If the work of housewives were to be treated as other work is, in terms of Social Security benefits, pensions, vacations, and health insurance, every institution in the economy would be affected. Alternately, if every man, woman and child were to take care of the equivalent of his/her own personal service, untold hours would have to be deducted from production and recreational pursuits.

Yet, is there not merit in the frequently heard argument that the housewife is simply doing her share of the family's work in exchange for which she is given support by her husband? Strictly speaking on the basis of economics, one can argue that support for services rendered went out as a form of payment with slavery—in modern society cash is the payment for services rendered. No one would argue that the money she gets for her own support is adequate pay for the work done by the housewife.

But economic considerations do not do justice nor do they encompass the work of the housewife. Most women, whether they are full-time housewives by choice or for lack of other choices, do in effect provide a home out of love for their families. They perform innumerable kindnesses and tasks for which they do not expect a monetary reward. Seen in a broader perspective, they make human life caring and warm in a society which is mostly motivated by self-interest and competition. As farm communities have given way to city and suburban living, the housewife's creation of a substitute for community in the privacy of each small home becomes a way of hiding the absence of community in the larger society. The housewife's unpaid labor of love and nurture goes far toward mediating and hiding some of the more glaring contradictions and tensions in society. While this may have the immediate effect of making life more pleasant and more bearable, it also postpones needed reforms and avoids the search for communal solutions to communal problems.

The problem of the 20-century "instituion of the housewife" goes much deeper than who does the dishes. Even the demand of "wages for housework" only touches the surface.[14] The problem is that the human aspect of life—nurtrance, caring for the helpless, the young, the old, and the creation of a livable enviroment—is relegated to women, while other work is given to men. As long as unpaid housework is by definition woman's major work, all the work of women will be downgraded.

Various myths surrounding women workers have traditionally been used to keep their wages low and to keep them from advancing in skills and status. While few today would assert that "women work for pin money," the myth that men are the main breadwinners persists, despite the fact that half the married women in this country are in the work force, the vast majority of them full-time workers. 47 per cent of the work force are women, but the median income of full-time female workers was only 57 per cent of that of full-time male workers in 1974. The myth that women are not steady workers, that they will quit their jobs in order to get married or have babies, has perpetuated the low status of traditional "women's occupations." Most women workers are locked into low-paid, low-status jobs as domestic workers, waitresses, clerical and health service personnel, and office workers. Training for more advanced skills is frequently withheld from women on the assumption that they will be temporary workers, whose major concerns are domestic cares. The absence of adequate child-care facilities, at any price, makes of such predictions self-fulfilling prophecies. Yet the facts are that nearly three-quarters of the women who work for pay are supporting themselves or their families on less than $10,000 a year. Thus the low status of the housewife reinforces the low status of the woman worker and of the woman professional and excuses any discrimination against her in the job market by the assumption that her primary work is as a housewife. The existence of "occupation housewife" as the major female occupation assures the subordinate status of women not just in the family but in every institution in society.

The gender-linking of service functions and child-rearing is at the root of woman's problem in society. The fact that every woman is a housewife, and that every housewife is a woman, structures inequality between the sexes into every institution of society. Anthropological and historical evidence shows that this societal arrangement is not universal.[15] In many societies various arrangements exist for the division of labor, for child care, and for the assignment of domestic chores. It is the development of agricultural settlements and plow agriculture which first institutionalizes the division of labor by sex, in which men enjoy greater mobility than women. The confinement of women to the home and its environments throughout the centuries of pre-industrial agriculture, while reinforcing the gender-linkage of her feeder-breeder role, did not mean her exclusion from public life and aspects of public power. The farm home was the center of production for men and women; the division of labor was *complementary* and frequently permitted women considerable opportunity for the accumulation of property and for the exercise of a great variety of work skills. In certain West African societies, for example, women in their market trader roles still wield considerable control over resources, intertribal networks, and family property.

The separation of public work sphere from private-domestic space is characteristic of industrial capitalism. The transfer of production outside the home and the creation of a cash economy create a new definition of work. Work is what is done for the market in exchange for money payment; it creates goods to bought and sold. All other work, especially the work done for daily maintenance and the reproduction of the species—child-rearing—is no longer defined as work. It is the development of industrial capitalism which fixes the gender-based division of labor which predominates in our society.

Any program for altering the status of women must depend, to a large extent, on the analysis made regarding the housewife. A number of theoretical approaches are worth considering: [16]

Classical Marxism, especially in the works of Engels, Bebel, and Lenin, offers one such theory, which has been very influential as the basis of political programs.[17] According to this analysis the domestic work of women is an archaic remnant of feudal economic relations under the conditions of advanced capitalism, and Socialists advocate its replacement by socialized domestic-work support services. The experience of 20th-century socialism has shown that institutionalized child care, mass feeding, and establishing commercial laundering have not abolished the position of the housewife. In the absence of changes in the basic family structure, it has remained an occupation curiously resistant to change and social engineering.

In societies where collective living and housing conditions were institutionalized, such as in Israel or Communist China, the jobs formerly done by individual housewives for individual families are still being carried out by women, but now for the benefit of larger numbers of people. These approaches on a smaller scale were earlier tried on American soil. In the 19th century some of the most forward-looking social reformers and feminists formed utopian communities, usually after periods of active political struggle which led to frustrating results. One of the characteristics of these utopian communities was that most of them did not accept the patriarchal family model and tried to substitute for it a more democratic model, or at least one in which women had more varied economic and social choices than those prevailing in the general society. Some of the religious and socialist communities went to great lengths to change sexual and child-rearing arrangements. Children were often reared communally in arrangements similar to those now used in Israeli kibbutzim.

Interestingly, the groups which made the most radical sexual reforms, such as the Oneida colony and the Mormon society, were the longest-lasting. All of the others failed within two or three decades. And in even the boldest experiments, whether religiously or Socialist-inspired, women were still in charge of child-rearing and housekeeping.

A different approach toward modernizing and socializing housework was proposed by Charlotte Perkins Gilman in 1898.[18] In her *Women and Economics* she presented the first major feminist analysis of the role of the housewife. Women's oppression was largely due to the institution of housework as woman's major occupation, Gilman asserted, and boldly proposed to abolish the occupation all together. She called for better town and community planning, for kitchenless apartments in apartment houses with restaurant and laundry facilities, for cleaning services by teams of professional workers, and for less emphasis on display and conspicuous consumption.

In the recent past, due largely to the impact of the feminist movement, efforts to upgrade the position of women within the family have led to work-sharing and redefinition of gender-roles in work assignments. Experiments with changing household composition, the upgrading of domestic work-support services, changes in the law, so as to provide housewives with better Social Security and pension benefits, and the recognition of the needs of displaced homemakers, are all reform measures which can and will provide improvements in the status of housewives. But it is doubtful that such relatively minor changes can permanently alter "occupation housewife" and with it the status of women in society. The problems of the housewife, for so long considered insignificant and subject to personal and familial solutions, are actually major social and political problems, which demand large-scale societal solutions.

One country which has gone far toward tackling these problems is Sweden. There, after decades of legal and educational equality for women, they remained economically disadvantaged and the majority of the married women continued in the housewife's role. In an effort to alter traditional attitudes, large-scale experiments in redefining family roles and in attacking sex-role indoctrination of children are now under way in Sweden, including parental leaves for fathers, the recognition of the position of "house-husband" (a man staying at home to do the family's housework). It is too early to judge the success of such measures in a capitalist welfare state or those radical measures enacted in Socialist Cuba designed to upgrade the status of women and change the traditional *machismo* attitudes of Cuban men by requiring them to share household duties with their wives as a political responsibility. It is obvious from historical experience that legal and educational equality for women will not automatically lead to attitudinal changes essential for altering the role of the housewife.

The confinement of women to the sex-linked housewife-breeder-feeder role has been the key element in her subordination in all her other societal roles. The position of women in society can be ameliorated, but it cannot be decisively altered until "occupation housewife" has ceased to be gender-defined and has become supported or supplanted by other arrangements for the raising of children and the nurturance of people. To accomplish this will demand the transforming and restructuring of all institutions of society and the creation of new forms of community.

10

Placing Women in History: Definitions and Challenges

In the brief span of five years in which American historians have begun to develop women's history as an independent field, they have sought to find a conceptual framework and a methodology appropriate to the task.

The first level at which historians, trained in traditional history, approach women's history is by writing the history of "women worthies" or "compensatory history."[1] Who are the women missing from history? Who are the women of achievement and what did they achieve? The resulting history of "notable women" does not tell us much about those activities in which most women engaged, nor does it tell us about the significance of women's activities to society as a whole. The history of notable women is the

This essay, in an earlier version, was presented at the panel, "Effects of Women's History Upon Traditional Concepts of Historiography" at the Second Berkshire Conference on the History of Women, Cambridge, Mass., October 25–27, 1974. It was, in revised form, presented as a paper at the Sarah Lawrence College Workshop-Symposium, March 15, 1975. I have greatly benefitted from discussion with my co-panelists Renate Bridenthal and Joan Kelly-Gadol, and from the comments and critique of audience participants at both conferences. It was revised and published in *Feminist Studies*, Vol. III, Nos. 1–2 (Fall 1975), 5–14.

history of exceptional, even deviant women, and does not describe the experience and history of the mass of women. This insight is a refinement of an awareness of class differences in history: Women of different classes have different historical experiences. To comprehend the full complexity of society at a given stage of its development, it is essential to take account of such differences.

Women also have a different experience with respect to consciousness, depending on whether their work, their expression, their activity is male-defined or woman-oriented. Women, like men, are indoctrinated in a male-defined value system and conduct their lives accordingly. Thus, colonial and early 19th-century female reformers directed their activities into channels which were merely an extension of their domestic concerns and traditional roles. They taught school, cared for the poor, the sick, the aged. As their consciousness developed, they turned their attention toward the needs of women. Becoming woman-oriented, they began to "uplift" prostitutes, organize women for abolition or temperance, and sought to upgrade female education, but only in order to equip women better for their traditional roles. Only at a later stage, growing out of the recognition of the separate interests of women as a group, and of their subordinate place in society, did their consciousness become woman-defined. Feminist thought starts at this level and encompasses the active assertion of the rights and grievances of women. These various stages of female consciousness need to be considered in historical analysis.

The next level of conceptualizing women's history has been "contribution history": describing women's contribution to, their status in, and their oppression by male-defined society. Under this category we find a variety of questions being asked: What have women contributed to abolition, to reform, to the Progressive movement, to the labor movement, to the New Deal? The movement in question stands in the foreground of inquiry; women made a "contribution" to it; the contribution is judged first of all with respect to its effect on that movement and secondly by standards appropriate to men.

The ways in which women were aided and affected by the work of these "great women," the ways in which they themselves grew into feminist awareness, are ignored. Jane Addams' enormous contribution in creating a female support network and new structures for living are subordinated to her role as a Progressive, or to an interpretation which regards her as merely representative of a group of frustrated college-trained women with no place to go. In other words, a deviant from male-defined norms. Margaret Sanger is seen merely as the founder of the birth-control movement, not as a woman raising a revolutionary challenge to the centuries-old practice by which the bodies and lives of women are dominated and ruled by man-made laws. In the labor movement, women are described as "also there" or as problems. Their essential role on behalf of themselves and of other women is seldom considered a central theme in writing their history. Women are the outgroup, Simone de Beauvoir's "Other."

Another set of questions concerns oppression and its opposite, the struggle for woman's rights. Who oppressed women and how were they oppressed? How did they respond to such oppression?

Such questions have yielded detailed and very valuable accounts of economic or social oppression, and of the various organizational, political ways in which women as a group have fought such oppression. Judging from the results, it is clear that to ask the question—why and how were women victimized—has its usefulness. We learn what society or individuals or classes of people have done to women, and we learn how women themselves have reacted to conditions imposed upon them. While inferior status and oppressive restraints were no doubt aspects of women's historical experience, and should be so recorded, the limitation of this approach is that it makes it appear either that women were largely passive or that, at the most, they reacted to male pressures or to the restraints of patriarchal society. Such inquiry fails to elicit the positive and essential way in which women have functioned in history. Mary Beard was the first to point out that the ongoing and continuing contribution of women to the development of human culture cannot be found by treating them only as victims of oppression.[2] It is far more useful to deal with this question as one aspect of women's history, but never to regard it as the *central* aspect of women's history. Essentially, treating women as victims of oppression once again places them in a male-defined conceptual framework: oppressed, victimized by standards and values established by men. The true history of women is the history of their ongoing functioning in that male-defined world *on their own terms*. The question of oppression does not elicit that story, and is therefore a tool of limited usefulness to the historian.

A major focus of women's history has been on women's-rights struggles, especially the winning of suffrage, on organizational and institutional history of the women's movements, and on its leaders. This, again, is an important aspect of women's history, but it cannot and should not be its central concern.

Some recent literature has dealt with marriage and divorce, with educational opportunities, and with the economic struggles of working women. Much of recent work has been concerned with the image of women and "women's sphere," with the educational ideals of society, the values to which women are indoctrinated, and with gender role acculturation as seen in historical perspective. A separate field of study has examined the ideals, values, and prescriptions concerning sexuality, especially female sexuality. Ron Walters and Ben Barker-Benfield have tended to confirm traditional stereotypes concerning Victorian sexuality, the double standard, and the subordinate position of women. Much of this material is based on the study of such readily available sources as sermons, educational tracts, women's magazines, and medical textbooks. The pitfall in such interpretation, as Carl Degler has pointed out is the tendency to confuse prescriptive literature with actual behavior. In fact, what we are learning from most of these monographs is not what women did, felt, or experienced, but what men in the past thought women should do. Charles Rosenberg, Carroll Smith-Rosenberg, and Carl Degler have shown how to approach the same material and interpret it from the new perspective of women's history.[3] They have sharply distinguished between prescription and behavior, between myth and reality.

Other attempts to deduce women's status from popular literature and ideology demonstrate similar difficulties. Barbara Welter, in an early and highly influential article, found the emergence of "the cult of true womanhood" in sermons and periodicals of the Jacksonian era. Many historians, feminists among them, have deduced from this that Victorian ideals of woman's place pervaded the society and were representative of its realities. More detailed analysis reveals that this mass-media concern with woman's domesticity was, in fact, a response to the opposite trend in society.[4] Lower-class women were entering the factories, middle-class women were discontented with their accustomed roles, and the family, as an institution, was experiencing turmoil and crisis. Idealization is very frequently a defensive ideology and an expression of tension within society. To use ideology as a measure of the shifting status of women, it must be set against a careful analysis of social structure, economic conditions, institutional changes, and popular values. With this caution society's attitudes toward women and toward gender-role indoctrination can be usefully analyzed as manifestations of a shifting value system and of tensions within patriarchal society.

"Contribution" history is an important stage in the creation of a true history of women. The monographic work which such inquiries produce is essential to the development of more complex and sophisticated questions, but it is well to keep the limitations of such inquiry in mind. When all is said and done, what we have mostly done in writing contribution history is to describe what men in the past told women to do and what men in the past thought women should be. This is just another way of saying that historians of women's history have so far used a traditional conceptual framework. Essentially, they have applied questions from traditional history to women, and tried to fit women's past into the empty spaces of historical scholarship. The limitation of such work is that it deals with women in male-defined society and tries to fit them into the categories and value systems which consider *man* the measure of significance. Perhaps it would be useful to refer to this level of work as "transitional women's history," seeing it as an inevitable step in the development of new criteria and concepts.

Another methodological question which arises frequently concerns the connection between women's history and other recently emerging fields. Why is women's history not simply an aspect of "good" social history? Are women not part of the anonymous in history? Are they not oppressed in the same way as racial or class or ethnic groups have been oppressed? Are they not marginal and akin in most respects to minorities? The answers to these questions are not simple. It is obvious that there has already been rich cross-fertilization between the new social history and women's history, but it has not been nor should it be a case of subsuming women's history under the larger and already respectable field of social history.

Yes, women are part of the anonymous in history, but, unlike them, they are also and always have been part of the ruling elite. They are oppressed, but not quite like either racial or ethnic groups, though some of them are. They are subordinate and exploited, but not quite like lower classes, though some of them are. We have not yet really solved the problems of definition, but it can be suggested that the key to understanding women's history is in accepting—painful though that may be—that it is the history of the *majority* of humankind.† Women are essentially different from all the above categories, because they are the majority now and always have been at least half of humankind, and because their subjection to patriarchal institutions antedates all other oppression and has outlasted all economic and social changes in recorded history.

†I was quite unaware, in 1974–75, at the time of writing and at the first publication of this article that I used the word "mankind," subsuming women under the term "man." A student brought this to my attention, and I have ever since used the term "humankind." The shift in consciousness this semantic shift caused is astonishing.

Social history methodology is very useful for women's history, but it must be placed within a different conceptual framework. Historians working in family history ask a great many questions pertaining to women, but family history is not in itself women's history. It is no longer sufficient to view women mainly as members of families. Family history has neglected by and large to deal with unmarried and widowed women. In its applications to specific monographic studies, such as the work of Philip Greven, family history has been used to describe the relationships of fathers and sons and the property arrangements between them.[5] The relationships of fathers to daughters and mothers to their children have been ignored. The complex family-support patterns, for example, whereby the work and wages of daughters are used to support the education of brothers and to maintain aged parents, while that of sons is not so used, have been ignored.

Another way in which family history has been interpreted within the context of patriarchal assumptions is by using a vaguely defined "domestic power" of women, power within the family, as a measure of the societal status of women. In a methodologically highly sophisticated article, Daniel Scott Smith discovered in the 19th century the rise of something called "domestic feminism," expressed in a lowered birth rate from which he deduced an increasing control of women over their reproductive lives.[6] One might, from similar figures, as easily deduce a desire on the part of men to curb their offspring due to the demands of a developing industrial system for a more highly educated labor force, hence for fewer children per family. Demographic data can indeed tell us something about female as well as male status in society, but only in the context of an economic and sociological analysis. Further, the status of women within the family is something quite different and distinct from their status in the society in general.

In studying the history of black women and the black family one can see that relatively high status for women within the family does not signify "matriarchy" or "power for women," since black women are not only members of families, but persons functioning in a larger society. The status of persons is determined not in one area of their functioning, such as within the family, but in several. The decisive historical fact about women is that the *areas* of their functioning, not only their status *within* those areas, have been determined by men. The effect on the consciousness of women has been pervasive. It is one of the decisive aspects of their history, and any analysis which does not take this complexity into consideration must be inadequate.

Then there is the impact of demographic techniques, the study of large aggregates of anonymous people by computer technology based on census data, public documents, property records. Demographic techniques have led to insights which are very useful for women's history. They have yielded revealing data on fertility fluctuations, on changes in illegitimacy patterns and sex ratios, and aggregate studies of life cycles. The latter work has been done very successfully by Joseph Kett, Robert Wells, Peter Laslett, and Kenneth Keniston.[7] The field has in the United States been largely dominated by male historians, mostly through self-imposed sex-role stereotyping by women historians who have shared a prejudice against the computer and statistics. However, a group of younger scholars, trained in demographic techniques, has begun to research and publish material concerning working-class women. Alice Harris, Virginia McLaughlin, Judith and Daniel Walkowitz, Susan Kleinberg, and Tamara Hareven are among those who have elicited woman-oriented interpretations from aggregate data.[8] They have demonstrated that social history can be enriched by combining cliometrics with sophisticated humanistic and feminist interpretations. They have added "gender" as a factor for analysis to such familiar concepts as class, race, and ethnicity.

The compensatory questions raised by women's history specialists are proving interesting and valuable in a variety of fields. It is perfectly understandable that, after centuries of neglect of the role of women in history, compensatory questions and those concerning woman's contribution will and must be asked. In the process of answering such questions it is important to keep in mind the inevitable limitation of the answers they yield. Not the least of these limitations is that this approach tends to separate the work and activities of women from those of men, even where they were essentially connected. As yet, synthesis is lacking. For example, the rich history of the abolition movement has been told as though women played a marginal, auxiliary, and at times mainly disruptive role in it. Yet female antislavery societies outnumbered male societies; women abolitionists largely financed the movement with their fund-raising activities, did much of the work of propaganda-writing in and distribution of newspapers and magazines. The enormous political significance of women-organized petition campaigns remains unrecorded. Most importantly, no historical work has as yet taken the organizational work of female abolitionists seriously as an integral part of the antislavery movement.

Slowly, as the field has matured, historians of women's history have become dissatisfied with old questions and old methods, and have come up with new ways of approaching historical material. They have, for example, begun to ask about the actual *experience* of women in the past. This is obviously different from a description of the condition of women written from the perspective of male sources, and leads one to the use of women's letters, diaries, autobiographies, and oral history sources. This shift from male-oriented to female-oriented consciousness is most important and leads to challenging new interpretations. Historians of women's history have studied female sexuality and its regulation from the female point of view, making imaginative use of such sources as medical textbooks, diaries, and case histories of hospital patients. Questions concerning women's experience have led to studies of birth control, as it affects women and as an issue expressing cultural and symbolic values; of the physical conditions to which women are prone, such as menarche and pregnancy and women's ailments; of customs, attitudes, and fashions affecting women's health and women's life experience. Historians are now exploring the impact of female bonding, of female friendship and homosexual relations, and the experience of women in groups, such as women in utopian communities, in women's clubs and settlement houses. There has been an interest in the possibility that women's century-long preoccupation with birth and with the care of the sick and dying have led to some specific female rituals.[9]

Women's history has already presented a challenge to some basic assumptions historians make. While most historians are aware of the fact that their findings are not value-free and are trained to check their biases by a variety of methods, they are as yet quite unaware of their own sexist bias and, more importantly, of the sexist bias which pervades the value system, the culture, and the very language within which they work.

Women's history presents a challenge to the periodization of traditional history. The periods in which basic changes occur in society and which historians have commonly regarded as turning points for all historical development, are not necessarily the same for men as for women. This is not surprising when we consider that the traditional time frame in history has been derived from political history. Women have been the one group in history longest excluded from political power and they have, by and large, been excluded from military decision-making. Thus the irrelevance of periodization based on military and political developments to their historical experience should have been predictable.

Renate Bridenthal's and Joan Kelly-Gadol's work confirms that the history of women demands different periodization than does political history. Neither the Renaissance, it appears, nor the period during which women's suffrage was won, were periods in which women experienced an advance in their status. Recent work of American historians, such as Linda Kerber's and Joan Hoff Wilson's work on the American Revolution and my own work, confirms this conclusion. For example, neither during nor after the American Revolution nor in the age of Jackson did women share the historical experience of men. On the contrary, they experienced in both periods a loss of status, a restriction of options as to occupations and role choices, and certainly in Jacksonian America, there were restrictions imposed upon their sexuality, at least in prescriptive behavior. If one applies to both of these cases the kind of sophisticated and detailed analysis Kelly-Gadol attempts—that is, differentiations between women of different classes and comparisons between the status of men of a given class and women of that class—one finds the picture further complicated. Status loss in one area—social production—may be offset by status gain in another—access to education.[10.]

What kind of periodization might be substituted for the periodization of traditional history in order for it to be applicable to women? The answer depends largely on the conceptual framework in which the historian works. Many historians of women's history, in their search for a unifying framework, have tended to use the Marxist or neo-Marxist model supplied by Juliet Mitchell and recently elaborated by Sheila Rowbotham.[11] The important fact, says Mitchell, which distinguished the past of women from that of men is precisely that until very recently sexuality and reproduction were inevitably linked for women, while they were not so linked for men. Similarly, child-bearing and child-rearing were inevitably linked for women and still are so linked. Women's freedom depends on breaking those links. Using Mitchell's categories we can and should ask of each historical period: What happened to the link between sexuality and reproduction? What happened to the link between child-bearing and child-rearing? Important changes in the status of women occur when it becomes possible through the availability of birth-control information and technology to sever sexuality from inevitable motherhood. It may be the case, however, that it is not the availability and distribution of birth control information and technology so much as the level of medical and health care which is the determinant of change. That is, when infant mortality decreases, so that raising every child to adulthood becomes the normal expectation of parents, family size declines.

The above case illustrates the difficulty that has vexed historians of women's history in trying to locate a periodization more appropriate to women. Working in different fields and specialities, many historians have observed that the transition from agricultural to industrializing society and then again the transition to fully developed industrial society entails important changes affecting women and the family. Changes in relations of production affect women's status as family members and as workers. Later, shifts in the mode of production affect the kinds of occupations women can enter and their status within them. Major shifts in health care and technological development, related to industrialization, also affect the lives of women. It is not too difficult to discern such patterns and to conclude that there must be a causal relationship between changes in the mode of production and the status of women. Here, the Marxist model seems to offer an immediately satisfying solution, especially if, following Mitchell, "sexuality" as a factor is added to such factors as class. But in the case of women, just as in the case of racial castes, ideology and prescription internalized by both women and men seem to be as much a causative factor as are material changes in production relations. Does the entry of lower-class women into industrial production really bring them closer to "liberation"? In the absence of institutional changes such as the right to abortion and safe contraception, altered child-rearing arrangements, and varied options for sexual expression, changes in economic relations may become oppressive. Unless such changes are accompanied by changes in consciousness, which in turn result in institutional changes, they do not favorably affect the lives of women.

Is smaller family size the result of "domestic freedom" of choice exercised by women, the freedom of choice exercised by men, the ideologically buttressed coercion of institutions in the service of an economic class? Is it liberating for women, for men, or for corporations? This raises another difficult question: What about the relationship of upper-class to lower-class women? To what extent is the relative advance in the status of upper-class women predicated on the status loss of lower-class women? Examples of this are: the liberation of the middle-class American housewife in the mid-19th century through the availability of cheap black or immigrant domestic workers: the liberation of the 20th-century housewife from incessant drudgery in the home through agricultural stoop labor and the food-processing industry, both employing low-paid female workers.

Is periodization then dependent as much on class as on gender? This question is just one of several which challenge the universalist assumptions of all previous historical categories. There is no ready answer, but I think the questions themselves point us in the right direction.

All conceptual models of history hitherto developed have only limited usefulness for women's history, since all are based on the assumptions of a patriarchal ordering of values. The structural-functionalist framework leaves out class and sex factors, the traditional Marxist framework leaves out sex and race factors as *essentials,* admitting them only as marginal factors. Mitchell's neo-Marxist model includes these but slights ideas, values, and psychological factors. Still, her four-structures model and the refinements of it proposed by Bridenthal are an excellent addition to the conceptual working tools of the historian of women's history. They should be tried out, discussed, refined. But they are not, in my opinion, the whole answer.

Kelly-Gadol offers the useful suggestion that attitudes toward sexuality should be studied in each historical period. She considers the constraints upon women's sexuality imposed by society a useful measure of women's true status. This approach would necessitate comparisons between prescribed behavior for women and men as well as indications of their actual sexual behavior at any given time. This challenging method can be used with great effectiveness for certain periods of history and especially for upper- and middle-class women. It is doubtful whether it can be usefully employed as a general criterion, because of the difficulty of finding substantiating evidence, especially as it pertains to lower classes.

I raised the question of a conceptual framework for dealing with women's history in 1969,[12] reasoning from the assumption that women were a subgroup in history. Neither caste, class, nor race quite fits the model for describing us. I have now come to the conclusion that the idea that women are some kind of a subgroup or particular is wrong. It will not do—there are just too many of us. No single framework, no single factor, four-factor or eight-factor explanation can serve to contain all that the history of women is. Picture, if you can, an attempt to organize the history of men by using four factors. It will not work; neither will it work for women.

Women are and always have been at least half of humankind, and most of the time have been the majority. Their culturally determined and psychologically internalized marginality seems to be what makes their historical experience essentially different from that of men. But men have defined their experience as history and have left women out. At this time, as during earlier periods of feminist activity, women are urged to fit into the empty spaces, assuming their traditional marginal, "subgroup" status. But the truth is that history, as written and perceived up to now, is the history of a minority, who may well turn out to be the "subgroup." In order to write a new history worthy of the name, we will have to recognize that no single methodology and conceptual framework can fit the complexities of the historical experience of all women.

The first stage of "transitional history" may be to add some new categories to the general categories by which historians organize their material: Sexuality, reproduction, the link between childbearing and child-rearing; role indoctrination; sexual values and myths: female consciousness. Further, all of these need to be analyzed, taking factors of race, class, ethnicity, and, possibly, religion into consideration. What we have here is not a single framework for dealing with women in history, but new questions to all of history.

The next stage may be to explore the possibility that what we call women's history may actually be the study of a separate women's culture. Such a culture would include not only the separate occupations, status, experiences, and rituals of women but also their consciousness, which internalizes partiarchal assumptions. In some cases, it would include the tensions created in the culture between the prescribed patriarchal assumptions and women's efforts to attain autonomy and emancipation.

The questions asked about the past of women may demand interdisciplinary approaches. They also may demand broadly conceived group research projects that end up giving functional answers; answers that deal not with slices of a given time or society or period, but which instead deal with a functioning organism, a functioning whole, the society in which both men and women live.

A following stage may develop a synthesis: a history of the dialectic, the tensions between the two cultures, male and female. Such a synthesis could be based on close comparative study of given periods in which the historical experience of men is compared with that of women, their tensions and interactions being as much the subject of study as their differences. Only after a series of such detailed studies can we hope to find the parameters by which to define the new universal history. My guess is that no one conceptual framework will fit so complex a subject.

Methods are tools for analysis—some of us will stick with one tool, some of us will reach for different tools as we need them. For women, the problem really is that we must acquire not only the confidence needed for using tools, but for making new ones to fit our needs. We should do so relying on our learned skills and our rational skepticism of handed-down doctrine. The recognition that we had been denied our history came to many of us as a staggering flash of insight, which altered our consciousness irretrievably. We have come a long way since then. The next step is to face, once and for all and with all its complex consequences, that women are the majority of humankind and have been essential to the making of history. Thus, all history as we now know it, is, for women, merely prehistory.

11

The Majority Finds Its Past

Women's experience encompasses all that is human; they share— and always have shared—the world equally with men. Equally in the sense that half, at least, of all the world's experience has been theirs, half of the world's work and many of its products. In one sense, then, to write the history of women means documenting all of history: women have always been making history, living it and shaping it. But the history of women has a special character, a built-in distortion: it comes to us refracted through the lens of men's observations; refracted again through values which consider man the measure. What we know of the past experience of women has been transmitted to us largely through the reflections of men: how we see and interpret what we know about women has been shaped for us through a value system defined by men. And so, to construct a new history that will with true equality reflect the dual nature of humankind—its male and female aspect—we must first pause to reconstruct the missing half—the female experience: women's history.

Women's history must contain not only the activities and events

This essay first appeared in *Current History*, Vol. 70, No. 416 (May 1976), 193–96, 231.

in which women participated, but the record of changes and shifts in their perception of themselves and their roles. Historically, women began their public activities by extending their concerns from home and family to the larger community. With this broadening of female concerns came the questioning of tradition, often followed by tentative steps in new directions: Anne Hutchinson holding weekly meetings for men and women in which she, not the male clergy, commented on the Bible; Frances Wright daring to assert women's freedom of sexual choice; Margaret Sanger discovering in one moment of insight and empathy that societally enforced motherhood was a wrong no longer to be tolerated.

Then came the reaching out toward other women: sewing circles and female clubs; women workers organizing themselves; women's rights conventions; the building of mass movements of women. By such steps women became "woman-oriented." Out of such activities grew a new self-consciousness, based on the recognition of the separate interests of women as a group. Out of communality and collectivity emerged feminist consciousness—a system of ideas that not only challenged patriarchal values and assumptions, but attempted to substitute for them a feminist system of values and ideas.

The most advanced conceptual level by which women's history can now be defined must include an account of the female experience as it changes over time and should include the development of feminist consciousness as an essential aspect of women's historical past. This past includes the quest for rights, equality, and justice which can be subsumed under "women's rights," i.e., the civil rights of women. But the quest for female emancipation from patriarchally determined subordination encompasses more than the striving for equality and rights. It can be defined best as the quest for autonomy. Autonomy means women defining themselves and the values by which they will live, and beginning to think of institutional arrangements that will order their environment in line with their needs. It means to some the evolution of practical programs, to others the reforming of existing social arrangements, to still others the building of new institutions. Autonomy for women means moving out from a world in which one is born to marginality, bound to a past without meaning, and prepared for a future detemined by others. It means moving into a world in which one acts and chooses, aware of a meaningful past and free to shape one's future.

The central question raised by women's history is: what would history be like if it were seen through the eyes of women and ordered by values they define?

Is one justified in speaking of a female historical experience different from that of men?[1] To find an answer to this basic question, it is useful to examine the life cycles and the turning points in individual lives of men and women of the past. Are there significant differences in childhood, education, maturity? Are social expectations different for boys and girls? Taking full cognizance of the wide range of variations, are there any universals by which we can define the female past? Material for answering such questions as far as they pertain to women can be found in many primary sources, some virtually untapped, other familiar. Autobiographical letters and diaries, even those frequently used, yield new information if approached with these questions and rearranged from the female point of view.[2]

There are basic differences in the way boys and girls now and in the past experienced the world and, more important, the social roles they were trained to fulfill. From childhood on, the talents and drives of girls were channeled into different directions from those of boys. For boys, the family was the place from which one sprang and to which one returned for comfort and support, but the field of action was the larger world of wilderness, adventure, industry, labor, and politics. For girls, the family was to be the world, their field of action was the domestic circle. He was to express himself in his work, and through it and social action help to transform his environment; her individual growth and choices were restricted to lead her to express herself through love, wifehood, and motherhood—through the support and nurturance of others who would act for her. The ways in which these gender-differentiated patterns would find expression would change in the course of historical development; the differences in the function assigned to the sexes might widen or narrow, but the fact of different sex role indoctrination remained.

Throughout most of America's past, life was experienced at a different rhythm by men and women. For a boy, education was directed toward a vocational or professional goal, his life ideally moved upward and outward in a straight line until it reached a plateau of fulfillment; the girl's education was sporadic and often interrupted: it did not lead to the fulfillment of her life role, but rather competed with it. Her development was dependent on her relationship to others and was often determined by them; it moved in wavelike, circuitous motion. In the boy's case, life crises were connected to vocational goals: separation from the family for purposes of greater educational opportunity; success or failures in achievement and career; economic decisions or setbacks. For the girl, such crises were more closely connected to stages in her biological life: the transition from childhood to adolescence, and then to marriage, which usually meant, in the past, greater restraint rather than the broadening out which it meant for the boy. Love and marriage for her implied a shifting of domesticity from one household to another, and the onset of her serious responsibilities: childbirth, child-rearing, and the nurture of the family. Finally came the crisis of widowhood and bereavement which could, depending on her economic circumstances, mean increasing freedom and autonomy or a difficult struggle for economic survival.

All people, in every society, are assigned specific roles and indoctrinated to perform to the expectations and values of that society. But for women this has always meant social indoctrination to a value system that imposed upon them greater restrictions of the range of choices than those of men. During much of the historic past, some of these restrictions were based on women's function as childbearers and the necessity of their bearing many children in order to guarantee the survival of some. With a declining infant mortality rate and advances in medical knowledge that made widely accessible birth-control methods possible, the gender-based role indoctrination of women was no longer functional but anachronistic. Women's indoctrination to motherhood as their primary and life-long function became oppressive, a patriarchal cultural myth. Additionally, even after educational restrictions were removed, women have been trained to fit into institutions shaped, determined, and ruled by men. As a result, their definitions of selfhood and self-fulfillment have remained subordinated to those of others.

American women have always shared in the economic life of the nation: in agriculture as equal partners performing separate, but essential work; in industry usually as low-paid unskilled workers; and in the professions overcoming barriers formed by educational discrimination and traditional male dominance. Although the majority of women have always worked for the same reasons as men— self-support and the support of dependents—their work has been characterized by marginality, temporariness, and low status. Typically, they have moved into the male-defined work world as outsiders, often treated as intruders. Thus, after each of the major wars in which the nation engaged, women who during wartime did all essential work and services, were at war's end shunted back to their traditional jobs. As workers, women have been handicapped by direct discrimination in hiring, training, and advancement, and, more profoundly, by their sex-role indoctrination that made them consider any work they did as subsidiary to their main job: wife and motherhood.

Thus, women often participated in their own subordination by internalizing the ideology and values that oppressed them and by passing these on to their children. Yet they were not *passive* victims; they always involved themselves actively in the world in their own way. Starting on a stage defined by their life cycle, they often rebelled against and defined societal indocrination, developed their own definitions of community, and built their own female culture.

In addition to their participation in the economic life of society, women have shaped history through community-building and participation in politics. American women built community life as members of families, as carriers of cultural and religious values, as founders and supporters of organizations and institutions.[3] So far, historians have taken notice mostly of the first of these functions and of the organizational work of women only insofar as they "contributed" to social reforms. Women's political work has been recognized only as it pertains to women's rights and woman suffrage.

Historical interpretation of the community-building work of women is urgently needed. The voluminous national and local records that document the network of community institutions founded and maintained by women are available. They should be studied against the traditional record of institution-building, which focuses on the activities of men. The research and the monographic work that form the essential groundwork for such interpretations have yet to be done.

The history of women's struggles for the ballot has received a good deal of attention by historians, but this narrow focus has led to the impression that the main political activity in which women engaged in the past was working for woman suffrage.[4] While the importance of that issue is undeniable, it is impossible to understand the involvement of American women in every aspect of the nation's life, if their political activity is so narrowly defined. Women were involved in most of the political struggles of the 19th century, but the form of their participation and their activities were different from those of men. It is one of the urgent and as yet unfulfilled tasks of women's history to study the ways in which women influenced and participated in political events, directly or through the mass organizations they built.

The involvement of American women in the important events of American history—the political and electoral crises, the wars, expansion, diplomacy—is overshadowed by the fact of the exclusion of women from political power throughout 300 years of the nation's life. Thus women, half of the nation, are cast in the marginal role of a powerless minority—acted upon, but not acting.

That this impression of the female past is a distortion is by now obvious. It is premature to attempt a critical evaluation or synthesis of the role women played in the building of American society. It is not premature to suggest that the fact of the exclusion of women from all those institutions that make essential decisions for the nation is itself an important aspect of the nation's past. In short, what needs to be explained is not why women were so little evident in American history as currently recorded, but why and how patriarchal values affected that history.

The steps by which women moved toward self-respect, self-definition, a recognition of their true position and from there toward a sense of sisterhood are tentative and varied and have occurred throughout our history. Exceptional women often defied traditional roles, at times explicitly, at other times simply by expressing their individuality to its fullest. The creation of new role models for women included the development of the professional woman, the political leader, the executive, as well as the anonymous working woman, the club woman, the trade unionist.[5] These types were created in the process of changing social activities, but they also were the elements that helped to create a new feminist consciousness. The emergence of feminist consciousness as a historical phenomenon is an essential part of the history of women.

The process of creating a theory of female emancipation is still under way. The challenges of modern American women are grounded in past experience, in the buried and neglected female past. Women have always made history as much as men have, not "contributed" to it, only they did not know what they had made and had no tools to interpret their own experience. What is new at this time, is that women are fully claiming their past and shaping the tools by means of which they can interpret it.

Women are not a marginal "minority," and women's history is not a collection of "missing facts and views" to be incorporated into traditional categories. Women are at least half and often a majority of all Americans and are distributed through all classes and categories of American society. Their history inevitably reflects variations in economic class, race, religion, and ethnicity. But the overriding fact is that women's history is the history of the *majority* of humankind.

12

The Challenge of Women's History

There is an ironic significance in the fact that the very term used to describe the new field Women's History is a misnomer. The unavailability of proper terminology is of itself a mark of the difficulties we have in conceptualizing the novel and somewhat daring enterprise in which we are engaged. There are women in history, and there are men in history, and one would hope that no historical account of a given period could be written that would not deal with the actions and ideas of both men and women. Were this the case, there would indeed be no need for Women's History.

But history as traditionally recorded and interpreted by historians has been, in fact, the history of the activities of men ordered by male values—one might properly call it "Men's History." Women have barely figured in it; the few who were noticed at all were members of families or relatives of important men and, very occasionally and exceptionally, women who performed roles generally reserved for men. In the face of such monumental neglect, the effort to reconstruct a female past has been called "Women's History." The term must be understood not as being descriptive of a

This essay is based on a lecture delivered at the Aspen Institute for Humanistic Studies, Paepcke Auditorium, August 25, 1977.

past reality but as both a conceptual model and a strategy by which to focus on and isolate that which traditional history has obscured.

I. The first challenge of Women's History to traditional history, then, is the assertion that women *have* a history, and that this history has been obscured and misunderstood because of the patriarchal values that pervade our culture and our ideas. These values are, of course, shared to such an extent by most men and women in our culture as to remain unconscious.

What are patriarchal values? Simply, the assumption that the fact of biological sex differences implies a God-given or at least a "natural" separation of human activities by sex, and the further assumption that this leads to a "natural" dominance of male over female. But women are half, and sometimes more than half, of humankind. Common-sense observation and reasoning tell us that half of the world's work, half of the world's experience, has been theirs. And yet in recorded history, as defined by historians, women appear only as marginal "contributors" to human development. This is so because patriarchal values dominate and order the writing of history. It is assumed that "man is the measure of significance," so that the activities of men are seen as being inherently more significant than the activities of women—i.e. war and politics are seen as more significant to the history of humankind than child-rearing—thus it is not surprising to find that history yields little information about the past of women.

The first step toward finding the history of women, then, is to become aware of these patriarchal assumptions and go beyond them. Once we move away from the assumption that women can be subsumed under the category "man," we begin to think of women as a separate, different, but equally significant segment of humanity, which must have had a history, as men did. How can we find that history? What questions must we ask of the past?

What did the past mean to men? What did it mean to women? How did their experience of particular events—such as wars, revolutions, depressions—differ? Or did it differ at all? What were significant periods of change for men? For women? These are some of the questions that will elicit information about women and their past.

II. Anyone attempting to find the answers to such questions is at once confronted by the challenging question, how to think about women in history. How are they to be conceptualized, since they are obviously not visible among those making decisions in areas traditionally considered decisive for the course of civilization?

Somehow women do not quite fit into any of the categories appropriate to minorities of one sort or another. Although historians of women's history have by no means reached a consensus on the subject, let me state my conclusion. Women are not a minority in any sense. Women are a sex. They have experienced educational, legal, and economic discrimination, as have members of minority groups, but they, unlike truly marginal groups, are distributed through every group and class in society. The mistress of the plantation and her female slave, the mill-owner's wife and the mill girl, are all part of women's history. Women are more closely allied to men of their own group than they are to women of other classes and races. Finally, women have always indoctrinated their children of both sexes in the very values by which they themselves have been indoctrinated to subordination. There is no question that women represent a special problem for the historian.[1] There is no question that they must be treated as full-fledged partners in the making of history.

Because of their numbers and their dispersement throughout society and because of their close and essential ties to men, the subordination of women to men could continue for as long as it did only with the assent and collaboration of women. It must therefore be essentially different in nature from other forms of human subordination. How can it be described and understood?

It may be useful to reflect on the fact that throughout history *men and women* have struggled to emancipate themselves from biological necessity—that is to free themselves from hunger, cold, competition for scarce resources—and to amass enough surplus to survive as a group. For most of historical time, most men and women lived in a state of oppression. Rights and personal liberties had to evolve slowly, first as concepts and possibilities, then as values instituted as law. For the majority of human beings such rights have had to be won through social struggle of the subordinate group, piecemeal and over resistance. It is only a few centuries since the possibilities for widespread economic comfort exist, upon which the demand of individual liberty and self-fulfillment as a human right can be raised. Thus, throughout the millennia of preindustrial society, whatever subordination women experienced must be described and analyzed within the context of the oppression of the males of their group.

Yet woman's position, whether as a member of the oppressed lower classes or as a member of the ruling elite, was always different in essentials from that of the male of her group. To understand precisely and to interpret with sophistication the shifts and changes in this relation of the sexes at different periods is one of the major tasks of women's history.

For most of historical time, woman is oppressed not through her reproductive sexuality—that is, through the need of society to assign most of a woman's adult lifespan to tasks of child-bearing and child-rearing—but through the *de-valuing* of such activities by men as they institute organized society. Women are oppressed also through sexual exploitation, as manifested in the rape of women of the conquered group by the victors, the rape of women of subordinate classes by the masters, in the millennia of organized prostitution, and in the constant pressure on single women to make marriage and family service their main career. Women as a group are oppressed through the denial to them of access to educational opportunities on an equality with men and, finally, through the denial to them—for longer than to any other group—of political representation and power in government.

III. The third challenge of Women's History is the need to add new questions to those asked by traditional history in order to elicit information about women.

Gender must be added as an analytical category to history.[2] When gender is considered with race, class, ethnicity, and religious affiliation in analyzing any given period or event, an entirely new dimension is added to social history. How were women affected by changes in family life, employment opportunities, education, law, and institutional structures? How did their changing status affect social values? These and similar questions yield much information about women and throw a new light on traditional interpretations.

IV. The fourth challenge of Women's History is a challenge to traditional sources.

The excuse of traditional historians for their neglect of women in history—that this reflected nothing more than a dearth of sources—has long since become untenable. It is true that, because of the special nature of their subordination, most women have remained among the anonymous in history. The usual sources for demographic history—census figures, parish and birth records, property and tax records, wills—have yielded important information about the life cycles, birth rates, marriage behavior patterns, and economic activities of anonymous men and women in the past. Other useful sources for finding women and their activities are the records of churches and educational institutions, minutes of organizations, police and criminal records, hospital and medical records, and the like. The increased interest in diaries, family letters, autobiographical and local history sources has invigorated historical scholarship. There is no shortage of material pertaining to the past of women.

Yet historians concerned with uncovering this past have faced tangible and concrete difficulties in regard to sources. One of these is that most historical sources were written by and collected by men. Libraries and archives organized their materials within the traditional categories of male-oriented history. There were few entries under "women," and women were generally subsumed under the "male" category. Thus, the activities of trade-union women would have to be laboriously reconstructed by reading through volumes of organizational minutes. Women's work was not usually separately categorized. Women's auxiliaries of whatever "male" organizations (often made up of men *and* women) did not usually keep records. As in the case of the female antislavery societies, the organizational work of women was seldom worthy of attention, except when it created tensions within the "main" organization.[3] In this way, women would surface as marginals or disrupters.

Since married women carry their husbands' names, they tend to disappear in family correspondences, which are organized by the names of male family members. Finders' guides, bibliographical tools, and major aids to historical research such as the "Union List of Manuscripts" reflect and reinforce the tendency to assign women to invisibility. The cataloguing and indexing of manuscripts have great impact on defining themes and sources of importance in historical scholarship. The major papers of historical figures, which have been preserved, catalogued, and indexed and thus made available to scholars usually through long-range projects financed by public grants, are skewed by patriarchal bias and consign women to the limbo of historical nonexistence.[4] This attitude is slowly yielding under the impact of the new scholarship, and some remedial efforts are now under way. But it will take decades before the foundations upon which historical scholarship is built can be cleared of their unacknowledged bias against women.

One of the most important remedial efforts is the Women's History Sources Survey, a National Endowment for the Humanities-funded project now near completion—in its first stage—at the University of Minnesota. The survey seeks to identify and compile a guide to primary sources for the study of the history of women in America. The guide will describe sources in 3500 repositories, with emphasis on the less well-known and less-used collections.

The research necessary for its compilation has led to a massive team effort of historians and archivists and has caused a number of archives to recatalogue their own holdings so as to make their women's history sources more visible. More than any previous effort, this research project has proven the existence of rich, hitherto untapped sources, which will ultimately benefit historical scholarship in general.

As we have noted earlier, women's history is more than finding data about women and fitting it into the empty spaces within patriarchal history. Women's History is a new vantage point, a stance, a way of looking at traditional material with new questions. Androcentric bias pervades not only the interpreters but also the sources. Much of what traditional sources tell us about women has come to us refracted through the lens of men's observation. The historian of women must question her sources for androcentric bias and must seek to counteract such bias by seeking primary sources which provide women's points of view.

It is, of course, not always possible to find such sources. Historians, eager to avoid such limitations, have welcomed the use of quantitative data, which are not only authoritative but seemingly value free. Yet even statistics can be interpreted within the confines of a male-centered value system, as this example will indicate. Recently, male demographic historians have interpreted falling birth rates in Europe during the 18th century and in the United States during the 19th century as indicating an increased "domestic power of women," since they supposedly influenced their husbands to curb sexual intercourse, as a means of birth control.[5] Women-oriented historians have questioned this approach and pointed out that nothing in the statistical data tells us how these bedroom decisions were made. It is just possible that men, active in industrializing society and seeing at first hand how important education of their male offspring is for upward mobility, would conclude that to limit the number of children in order to offer them better education was in their own interest.[6] We really do not know how women felt and thought about this, nor are we entitled to conclude that these figures indicate their wielding greater power within the home.

V. Women's history challenges the traditional periodization of history.

Traditional history is periodized according to wars, conquests, revolutions, and/or vast cultural and religious shifts. All of these categories are appropriate to the major activities of men, especially political men. What historians of women's history have learned is that such periodization distorts our understanding of the history of women.

Events that advance the position of men in society, adding to their economic opportunities, their liberties and their social standing, frequently have the *opposite* effect on women. Thus, recent studies of the Renaissance have shown that this period, in which men have experienced an unfolding of opportunity and knowledge, was one in which women were subject to greater restraints and restrictions than they had experienced during earlier centuries. The fact that a few upper-class women occupied positions usually reserved for men in no way contradicts these findings. In the United States, the American Revolution and the political and economic changes of the age of Jackson affected American women in a similar way.[7] Opportunities for education and upward mobility for men coincided with the exclusion of women from such advances. Professionalization of medicine and law had the effect on women of excluding them for almost a century from professional life. The political rights gained by large groups of white men, hitherto excluded from voting and representation by property restrictions, resulted only in widening the gap between the opportunities afforded men and those afforded women in society. Women were now excluded by law, not only as formerly by custom, from voting and representation. This fact was clearly perceived by middle-class women and was one of the prime motivating forces of the woman's rights movement.

Similarly: early capitalism, in Europe in the 15th and 16th centuries, in the United States during the late 18th century, freed masses of men from economic deprivation and from the struggle for mere survival, enabling them to consider liberty, opportunity, and upward mobility as something belonging to them by right. For women, this development could not take place until they could be freed from the biological necessity of producing as many children as they were capable of producing in order to guarantee that some would survive. The preconditions for this decisive development were improved medical knowledge and distribution of services, such as improved sanitation, which would lower infant morality and lower the risk of death in childbirth. Modernization helped to create these *pre-conditions* for woman's emancipation, but they benefitted women of different classes at different times: European middle-class women in the 18th century, American white middle-class women in the 19th century, and lower-class and black women in the 20th. This variation of the pre-conditions for woman's emancipation explains, in part, why lowered infant mortality rates and lowered fertility rates do not proceed in parallel curves. In America, fertility rates declined throughout the 19th century, for white women from 7.04 in 1800 to 5.42 in 1850 to 3.56 in 1900. The fertility of black women declined more sharply, but *later*, beginning only in 1880.[8] Infant mortality declined less dramatically and later for both white and black women. Since national birth statistics are not available for the 19th century, these figures have to be estimated roughly. According to authoritative estimates, about 78 per cent of white infants around 1800 survived from birth to about 2½ years; 84 per cent survived in 1901; and 97 per cent in 1950.[9]

This shows that the most dramatic reduction in infant mortality for whites occurred in the 20th century, while the birth rate fell most dramatically in the first half of the 19th century. The major reduction in infant mortality for Blacks occurred much later, between 1940 and 1970.

The "demographic transition," the period when lower mortality rates make family-planning decisions independent of necessity, does not necessarily lead to a drop in fertility rates, although it did so in the United States. The causes for the falling birth rate are complex, and historians do not agree in their explanations. There is also controversy over the role of women in the making of family-planning decisions.[10] The point here is not to offer a simple causal explanation but to show that the very potential for making decisions depends, for women, on lowering infant mortality and on having access to education. Only after these conditions prevail, can women aspire to self-fulfillment and upward mobility apart from their reproductive function. Historian Linda Gordon has shown persuasively that the technical means of fertility control were available to women throughout historical time, although such means were often brutal and dangerous (i.e. infanticide and self-induced abortions). Gordon suggests that the "desire for and the problems in securing abortion and contraception made up a shared female experience. . . . the desire was so passionate that women would take severe risks to win a little space and control in their lives."[11] Yet on the mass level, women's ability to have impact on fertility rates depended on changing societal attitudes and needs. The periods when these changes occur mark the "Renaissance" for women and they occur at different periods than did the "Renaissance" of men. It is worth noting in passing that only after this period does woman's indoctrination to motherhood as a lifelong and primary function become oppressive, a patriarchal cultural myth.

VI. A redefinition of categories and values is necessary.

It should be obvious by now that the effort to conceptualize women's history as a collection of "missing facts and views" to be incorporated into the empty spaces of traditional history is too limited, even fallacious. To anyone seriously concerned with the implication of research done in the past eight years, it is clear that we

need a redefinition of historical categories and historical significance. This is the sixth and most basic challenge of women's history.

Women have been left out of history not because of the evil
conspiracies of men in general or male historians in particular, but
because we have considered history only in male-centered terms.
We have missed women and their activities, because we have asked
questions of history which are inappropriate to women. To rectify
this and to light up areas of historical darkness we must, for a
time, focus on a *woman-centered* inquiry, considering the possibility
of the existence of a female culture *within* the general culture
shared by men and women. History must include an account of the
female experience over time and should include the development of
feminist consciousness as an essential aspect of women's past. This
is the primary task of women's history. The central question it
raises is: What would history be like if it were seen through the
eyes of women and ordered by values they define?

When the historian adopts such a stance, even as a temporary
strategy, the darkness of history lifts and the historical experience
of women becomes visible, different from that of men and yet in-
tegrally a part of it. Different life cycles, different turning points,
different expectations, different opportunities, even different consciousness of self and others. In their work, too, women have experienced history differently than did men. Women have always done
and still do two kinds of work—work for pay and unpaid service.
In the marketplace women's work has been characterized by
marginality, temporariness, and low status. This has resulted in
their predominance in low-paying job categories, being last hired,
first fired, and in the persistence of wage and salary differentials
which disadvantage working women. The other work of women,
that which society defined as their "main" work—housework and
child-rearing—has remained financially unrewarded and historically invisible.

But child-rearing is an essential economic and social function
without which no society could exist. The multitude of economic

and social services performed by the housewife are indispensable to the ability of men to perform wage labor. In a male-centered value system we only call work that which is performed for wages, thereby obliterating from consideration and view the work performed by most women. Why has there never been a history of housework? Why have we only in the past two years had work done on the history of child-rearing? A woman-centered approach would deal with such questions and would, for example, insist that any history written about the Civil War or World War II must include an account of the work of women at the front or on the home front.

Women also have shaped history through community-building. While men conquered territory and built institutions which managed and distributed power, women transmitted culture to the young and built the social network and infra-structures that provide continuity in the community.

A typical pattern would be that women perceived a social or community need, began to meet it in practical, unstructured ways, then continued to expand their efforts into building a small institution, often financed by funds they raised through voluntary activities. Thus, women built orphanages, homes for wayward children, old-age homes, kindergartens, libraries in community after community. Usually, when the institution had existed long enough and established itself, it became incorporated, registered, licensed, possibly taken over as a community institution. At that point it would usually be taken over by a male board of directors. It would also—incidentally—enter history, its official status making of its records historical sources. The women who had done the work, if they appeared in the record at all, would be visible only as a ladies' auxiliary group or as unpaid, unrecognized volunteers. A woman-centered inquiry can elicit this hidden story in community after community, and lead us to a new and different understanding of the history of our society. Voluminous records are available in every locality, but the essential research and monographic work have yet to be done.

It should be obvious by now that Women's History is not an "exotic specialty," a temporary, politically inspired "fad." It will not be sidetracked; it will not go away. Women's History is a strategy necessary to enable us to see around the cultural blinders which have distorted our vision of the past to the extent of obliterating from view the past of half of humankind.

For these reasons, women's history poses a final, most serious challenge to scholarship and societal values.

VII. Women's history asks for a paradigm shift.

It demands a fundamental re-evaluation of the assumptions and methodology of traditional history and traditional thought. It challenges the traditional assumption that man is the measure of all that is significant, and that the activities pursued by men are by definition significant, while those pursued by women are subordinate in importance. It challenges the notion that civilization is that which men have created, defended, and advanced while women had babies and serviced families and to which they, occasionally and in a marginal way, "contributed."

Civilization consists of the integrated activities of men and women, based on a gender-based division of labor. Changes in the division of labor and in the relation of the sexes are in themselves historical phenomena and must be treated as such.

What is needed is a new universal history, a holistic history which will be a synthesis of traditional history and women's history. It will be based on close comparative study of given periods in which the historical experiences of men are compared with those of women, their interactions being as much the subject of study as their differences and tensions. Only after a series of such detailed studies has been done and their concepts have entered into the general culture can we hope to find the parameters by which to define the new universal history. But this much can be said already: Only a history based on the recognition that women have always been essential to the making of history and that *men and women* are the measure of significance, will be truly a universal history.

Notes

Introduction

1. Gerda Lerner, *The Grimké Sisters from South Carolina: Rebels against Slavery* (Boston, 1967); published as a paperback with new subtitle: *Pioneers for Woman's Rights and Abolition* (New York, 1971).
2. Mary R. Beard, *Woman as Force in History* (New York, 1946; reprint 1962).
3. Ann Lane (ed.), *Mary Ritter Beard: A Sourcebook* (New York, 1977), p. 204.
4. *Ibid.*, p. 207.
5. Mary R. Beard, *A Short History of the American Labor Movement* (New York, 1930; reprint, Westport, Conn., 1971); *On Understanding Women,* (New York, 1931); *Laughing Their Way: Women's Humor in America* (New York, 1934); *America Through Women's Eyes* (New York, 1933); *The Force of Women in Japanese History* (Washington, D.C., 1953). See also: *Women's Work in Municipalities* (New York, 1915).
6. Eleanor Flexner, *Century of Struggle: The Woman's Rights Movement in the United States* (Cambridge, Mass., 1959).
7. Betty Friedan, *The Feminine Mystique* (New York, 1963); cf: *No More Fun and Games: A Journal of Female Liberation,* 371 Somerville Avenue, Somerville, Mass. 02143; "Notes From the First Year," *Journal of New York Radical Women* (June 1968).
8. Gerda Lerner, *The Woman in American History* (Reading, Mass., 1971).
9. Juliet Mitchell, *Women: The Longest Revolution* (Boston, 1966; reprint from *New Left Review,* Vol. 40, Nov.–Dec. 1966).
10. Gerda Lerner (ed.), *Black Women in White America: A Documentary History* (New York, 1972).
11. Gerda Lerner, *The Female Experience: An American Documentary* (New York and Indianapolis, 1977).

Chapter 1. New Approaches to the Study of Woman in American History

1. Cf. Arthur Schlesinger, Sr., *New Viewpoints in American History* (New York, 1922), chap. 6. For a contemporary historian's viewpoint, see David M. Potter, "American Women and the American Character," in *American History and Social Sciences,* ed. Edward N. Saveth (New York, 1964), pp. 427–28.

2. The most important feminist tracts before the launching of the woman's rights movement are: Charles Brockden Brown, *Alcuin: A Dialogue* (Boston, 1798); Sarah M. Grimké, *Letters on the Equality of the Sexes and the Condition of Woman* (Boston, 1838); and Margaret Fuller, *Woman in the Nineteenth Century* (Boston, 1844). The publications of the feminist movement are too numerous to list here; a representative collection is incorporated in Elizabeth C. Stanton, Susan B. Anthony, and Matilda J. Gage, *History of Woman Suffrage* (6 vols.; New York, 1881–1922); hereafter referred to as *HWS.*

3. Typical of the "compilers" are: Lydia M. Child, *History of the Condition of Women* (2 vols.; New York, 1835); Sarah J. Hale, *Woman's Record.* . . . . (New York, 1853); Phebe A. Hanaford, *Daughters of America, or Women of the Century* (Augusta, Me., n.d.); and Frances E. Willard and Mary A. Livermore, *American Women* (New York, 1897).

4. Cf. Eleanor Flexner, *Century of Struggle: The Woman's Rights Movement in the United States* (Cambridge, Mass., 1959); Aileen S. Kraditor, *The Ideas of the Woman Suffrage Movement* (New York, 1965).

5. Mary R. Beard, *Woman as Force in History* (New York, 1946).

6. Mary R. Beard, *America Through Women's Eyes* (New York, 1933), *On Understanding Women* (New York, 1931), and *Women's Work in Municipalities* (New York, 1915); Charles R. and Mary R. Beard, *The Rise of American Civilization* (New York, 1927). For a recent interpretation of Mary Beard's work see Ann Lane (ed.), *Mary Ritter Beard: A Sourcebook* (New York, 1977).

7. For the economic life of colonial women see: Elisabeth A. Dexter, *Colonial Women of Affairs: Women in Business and Professions in America before 1776* (Boston, 1931), and *Career Women of America: 1776–1840* (Francestown, N.H., 1950); Richard B. Morris, *Government and Labor in Early America* (New York, 1946); and Julia C. Spruill, *Women's Life and Work in the Southern Colonies* (Chapel Hill, 1938). For women's economic role in 19th- and 20th-century America, see: Edith Abbott, *Women in Industry* (New York, 1918); J. B. Andrews and W. D. P. Bliss, *Report on Condition of Woman and Child Wage-Earners in the United States* (19 vols.; Doc. No. 645, 61st Congress, 2nd Session; Washington, D.C., 1910); and Elizabeth Baker, *Technology and Women's Work* (New York, 1964).

8. For women in reform movements, see: Robert Bremmer, *American Philanthropy* (Chicago, 1960); Clarke E. Chambers, *Seedtime of Reform: American*

Social Service and Social Action, 1918–1933 (Ann Arbor, 1963); Christopher Lasch, The New Radicalism in America: 1889–1963 (New York, 1965); and Daniel Levine, Varieties of Reform Thought (Madison, Wis., 1964).

9. For a history of the family, see Arthur W. Calhoun, A Social History of the American Family (3 vols.; Cleveland, 1918); Sidney Ditzion, Marriage, Morals, and Sex in America (New York, 1953); Paul H. Jacobson, American Marriage and Divorce (New York, 1959); and William O'Neill, Divorce in the Progressive Era (New Haven, 1967).

It is worth noting how small the historiography on the American family was in 1969. The growth of the field of family history and the explosion of scholarly interest in the subject occurred after this essay was written.

10. Harriet Martineau, Society in America (New York, 1837), I, 158.

11. Helen Hacker, "Women as a Minority Group," Social Forces, XXX (1951–52), 60–69.

12. See Kraditor, Ideas and Lasch, New Radicalism.

13. A full bibliography of colonial women is to be found in Eugenie A. Leonard, Sophie H. Drinker, and Miriam Y. Holden, The American Woman in Colonial and Revolutionary Times: 1565–1800 (Philadelphia, 1962).

Chapter 2. The Lady and the Mill Girl

1. Keith E. Melder, "The Beginnings of the Women's Rights Movement in the United States: 1800–1840" (Dissertation, Yale, 1963, and published under the title Beginnings of Sisterhood: The American Woman's Rights Movement (New York, 1977); Elisabeth A. Dexter, Colonial Women of Affairs: Women in Business and Professions in America before 1776 (Boston, 1931) and Career Women of America: 1776–1840 (Francestown, N.H., 1950)

2. Herbert Moller, "Sex Composition and Corresponding Culture Patterns of Colonial America," William and Mary Quarterly, Ser. 3, II (April 1945), 113–53.

3. The summary of the status of colonial women is based on the following sources: Mary Benson, Women in 18th Century America: A Study of Opinion and Social Usage (New York, 1935); Arthur Calhoun, A Social History of the American Family (3 vols.; Cleveland, 1918); Dexter, Colonial Women; Dexter, Career Women; Edmund S. Morgan, Virginians at Home: Family Life in the 18th Century (Williamsburg, 1952); Julia C. Spruill, Women's Life and Work in the Southern Colonies (Chapel Hill, 1938).

4. E. M. Boatwright, "The Political and Legal Status of Women in Georgia: 1783–1860," Georgia Historical Quarterly, XXV (April 1941); Richard B. Morris, Studies in the History of American Law (New York, 1930), chap. 3. A summary of travelers' comments on American woman may be found in: Jane

Mesick, *The English Traveler in America: 1785–1835* (New York, 1922), pp. 83–99.

5. For facts on colonial medicine the following sources were consulted: Wyndham B. Blanton, *Medicine in Virginia* (3 vols.; Richmond, 1930); N. S. Davis, M.D., *History of Medical Education and Institutions in the United States* . . . (Chicago, 1851); Dexter, *Career Women;* K. C. Hurd-Mead, M.D., *A History of Women in Medicine: from the Earliest Times to the Beginning of the 19th Century* (Haddam, Conn., 1938); Geo. W. Norris, *The Early History of Medicine in Philadelphia* (Philadelphia, 1886); Joseph M. Toner, *Contributions to the Annals of Medical Progress in the United States before and during the War of Independence* (Washington, D.C., 1874). The citation regarding Mrs. Allyn is from Hurd-Mead, *Women in Medicine,* p. 487.

6. Fielding H. Garrison, M.D., *An Introduction to the History of Medicine* (Philadelphia, 1929). For licensing legislation: Davis, *History,* pp. 88–103; see also: Martin Kaufman, "American Medical Diploma Mills," *The Bulletin of the Tulane University Medical Faculty,* Vol. 26, No. 1 (Feb. 1967), 53–57.

7. Among the alternate institutions founded are: New England Female Medical College (1848); Female (later Women's) Medical College of Philadelphia (1850); Women's Medical College and New York Infirmary for Women (1865); Woman's Hospital of Philadelphia (1861); New England Hospital for Women and Children (1862).

   For information on the training of pioneer women physicians see: James R. Chadwick, M.D., *The Study and Practice of Medicine by Women* (New York, 1879).

   For intances of discrimination see: Harriot K. Hunt, M.D., *Glances and Glimpses or Fifty Years Social including Twenty Years Professional Life* (Boston, 1856); Elizabeth Blackwell, *Pioneer Work in Opening the Medical Profession to Women* (New York, 1865); "Preamble and Resolution of the Philadelphia County Medical Society Upon the Status of Women Physicians with *A Reply by a Woman*" (Philadelphia, 1867), pamphlet;

   See also biographies of women physicians in Edward and Janet James (eds.), *Notable American Women, 1607–1950: A Biographical Dictionary* (3 vols.; Cambridge, Mass., 1972).

   For a recent work offering a somewhat different interpretation see Mary Roth Walsh, *Doctors Wanted: No Women Need Apply: Sexual Barriers in the Medical Profession, 1835–1975* (New Haven, 1977).

8. George Daniels, "The Professionalization of American Science: The Emergent Period, 1820–1860," paper delivered at the joint session of the History of Science Society and the Society of the History of Technology, San Francisco, December 28, 1965.

9. Hurd-Mead, *Women in Medicine,* p. 391.

10. *Ibid.,* p. 486.

11. Betsy E. Corner, *William Shippen Jr.: Pioneer in American Medical Education* (Philadelphia, 1951), p. 103.

12. *Ibid.*

13. Benjamin Lee Gordon, *Medieval and Renaissance Medicine* (New York, 1959), pp. 689–91. Blanton, *Medicine*, II, 23–24; Hurd-Mead, *Women in Medicine*, pp. 487–88; Annie Nathan Meyer, *Woman's Work in America* (New York, 1891); Harriot K. Hunt, M.D., *Glances* . . . pp. 127–40; Eleanor Flexner, *Century of Struggle: The Woman's Rights Movement in the United States* (Cambridge, Mass., 1959), pp. 115–19.

14. Sophie H. Drinker, "Women Attorneys of Colonial Times," *Maryland Historical Society Bulletin*, vol. LVI, No. 4 (Dec. 1961).

15. Dexter, *Colonial Women*, pp. 34–35, 162–65.

16. Harriet W. Marr, *The Old New England Academies* (New York, 1959), chap. 8; Thomas Woody, *A History of Women's Education in the United States* (2 vols.; New York, 1929), pp. 100–109, 458–60, 492–93.

17. Matthew Carey, *Essays on Political Economy* . . . (Philadelphia, 1822), p. 459.

18. The statements on women industrial workers are based on the following sources: Edith Abbott, *Women in Industry* (New York, 1910), pp. 66–80, and "Harriet Martineau and the Employment of Women in 1836," *Journal of Political Economy*, XIV (Dec. 1906), 614–26; Matthew Carey, *Miscellaneous Essays* (Philadelphia, 1830), pp. 153–203; Helen L. Sumner, *History of Women in Industry in the United States*, in *Report on Condition of Woman and Child Wage-Earners in the United States* (19 vols., Washington, D.C., 1910), IX; also: Elizabeth F. Baker, *Technology and Woman's Work* (New York, 1964), chaps. 1–5.

19. Emily Putnam, *The Lady: Studies of Certain Significant Phases of Her History* (New York, 1910), pp. 319–20; Barbara Welter, "The Cult of True Womanhood: 1820–1860," *American Quarterly*, Vol. XVIII, No. 2, Part I (Summer 1966), 151–74.

20. Veblen generalized from his observations of the society of the Gilded Age and fell into the usual error of simply ignoring the lower-class women, whom he dismissed as "drudges . . . fairly content with their lot," but his analysis of women's role in "conspicuous consumption" and of the function of women's fashions is unsurpassed. For references see: Thorstein Veblen, *The Theory of the Leisure Class* (New York, 1962, first printing, 1899), pp. 70–71, 231–32, and "The Economic Theory of Woman's Dress," *Essays in Our Changing Order* (New York, 1934), pp. 65–77.

21. Like most groups fighting status oppression women formulated a compensatory ideology of female superiority. Norton Mezvinsky has postulated that this was clearly expressed only in 1874; in fact this formulation appeared in the earliest speeches of Elizabeth Cady Stanton and in the speeches and reso-

lutions of the Seneca Falls conventions and other pre-Civil War woman's rights conventions. Rather than a main motivating force, the idea was a tactical formulation, designed to take advantage of the popularly held male belief in woman's "moral" superiority and to convince reformers that they needed the votes of women. Those middle-class feminists who believed in woman's "moral" superiority exploited the concept in order to win their major goal—female equality. For references see: Norton Mezvinsky, "An Idea of Female Superiority," *Midcontinent American Studies Journal*, Vol. II, No. 1 (Spring 1961), 17–26; Stanton *et al.*, *HWS*, I, 72, 479, 522, 529, and *passim;* Alan P. Grimes, *The Puritan Ethic and Woman Suffrage* (New York, 1967), chaps. 2 and 3.

22. Stanton *et al.*, *HWS*, I, 70.
23. Betty Friedan, *The Feminine Mystique* (New York, 1963).

Chapter 3. The Feminists: A Second Look

1. William O'Neill, *The Woman Movement: Feminism in the United States and England* (New York, 1969); see also O'Neill's *Everyone Was Brave* (Chicago, 1969).
2. Aileen Kraditor, *The Ideas of the Women's Suffrage Movement: 1890–1920* (New York, 1965); Anne F. and Andrew M. Scott, *One Half the People: The Fight for Woman's Suffrage* (Philadelphia, 1975).
3. For a summary of women's status and roles in the 20th century, see William H. Chafe, *The American Woman: Her Changing Social, Economic, and Political Roles, 1920–1970* (New York, 1972).
4. For a more recent analysis of modern feminism see Gayle Yates, *What Women Want: The Ideas of the Movement* (Cambridge, Mass., 1975).
5. "Redstockings Manifesto," in *Notes from the Second Year: Radical Feminism* (New York, NOTES, PO Box AA, Old Chelsea Station, N.Y. 10911, May 1970).
6. "I Am Furious Female," Radical Education Project (Detroit, n.d.).
7. Helen Hacker "Women as a Minority Group," *Social Forces*, XXX (1951–52), 60–69.
8. Matina Horner, "Woman's Will To Fail," *Psychology Today* (Nov. 1969), 36–41.
9. Judy Bernstein, "Sisters, Brothers, Lovers . . . Listen" (New England Free Press).
10. "The Myth of the Vaginal Orgasm," in *Notes from the Second Year*. . . .

Chapter 4. Women's Rights and American Feminism

1. Aileen S. Kraditor, *Ideas of the Women Suffrage Movement* (New York, 1965); William O'Neill, *Everyone Was Brave* (Chicago, 1969).

2. For biographical information on all the women mentioned in this section, consult *Notable American Women, 1607–1950*. See also: A. Perkins and T. Wolfson, *Frances Wright: Free Enquirer* (New York, 1939).

3. Stanton *et al., HWS*.

4. John Humphrey Noyes, *History of American Socialisms* (Philadelphia, 1970 reprint).

5. Emanie Sachs, *The Terrible Siren* (New York, 1928); Johanna Johnston, *Mrs. Satan: The Incredible Saga of Victoria C. Woodhull* (New York, 1967); Madeleine B. Stern, *We, the Women: Career Firsts of the Nineteenth Century* (New York, 1963).

6. Charlotte Perkins Gilman, *Women and Economics* (Boston, 1898; reprint New York, 1966), *The Home; Its Work and Influence* (New York, 1903; reprint Urbana, Ill., 1972), and *The Living of Charlotte Perkins Gilman; An Autobiography* (New York, 1935).

7. Margaret Sanger, *Margaret Sanger: An Autobiography* (New York, 1938) and *My Fight for Birth Control* (New York, 1931); David M. Kennedy, *Birth Control in America: The Career of Margaret Sanger* (New Haven, 1970).

8. Richard Drinnon, *Rebel in Paradise: A Biography of Emma Goldman* (Chicago, 1961); Emma Goldman, *Living My Life* (2 vols.; New York, 1931); Alix K. Shulman, *Red Emma Speaks: Selected Writing and Speeches* (New York, 1972).

   For a recent and revisionist interpretation of Goldman's role in the birth control movement see Linda Gordon, *Woman's Body, Woman's Right: A Social History of Birth Control in America* (New York, 1976), pp. 212–30, and esp. fn. 87.

9. Mirra Komarovsky, *Blue Collar Marriage* (New York, 1964); Lee Rainwater, Richard P. Coleman, and Gerald Handel, *Workingman's Wife* (New York, 1962); Nancy Seifer, *Nobody Speaks for Me! Selfportraits of American Working Class Women* (New York, 1976).

10. Betty Friedan, *The Feminine Mystique* (New York, 1963).

11. "Working Women and the War: Four Narratives," *Radical America*, IX (1975), 133–62; Paddy Quick, "Rosie the Riveter: Myths and Realities," *ibid.*, 115–32. William H. Chafe, *The American Woman* (New York, 1972), Part Two.

Chapter 5. Black Women in the United States

1. For a list of biographies and autobiographies of, and articles on black women see Gerda Lerner, *Bibliography in the History of American Women* (Bronxville, N.Y., 1978), pp. 59–65.

   Primary sources on black women are made available in B. J. Lowenberg and R. Bogin (eds.), *Black Women in Nineteenth-Century American Life: Their Words, Their Thoughts, Their Feelings* (University Park, Pa., 1976) and in

Gerda Lerner, *Black Women in White America: A Documentary History* (New York, 1972), a collection of primary sources.

2. Two of the earliest anthologies are L. C. Scruggs, M.D., *Women of Distinction* (Raleigh, N.C., 1893) and N. F. Mossell, *The Work of the Afro-American Woman* (Philadelphia, 1908). Sadie Iola Daniel, *Women Builders* (Washington, D.C., 1931), consists of brief biographical sketches of outstanding black women. Hallie Quinn Brown, *Homespun Heroines and Other Women of Distinction* (Xenia, Ohio, 1926), although uncritical, contains a wealth of information about community, religious, and educational leaders. Among the more recent compilations the most comprehensive and useful are: Sylvia G. L. Dannett, *Profiles of Negro Womanhood: Vol. I, 1619–1900* (Chicago, 1964) and Wilhelmina S. Robinson, *Historical Negro Biographies: International Library of Negro Life and History* (New York, 1967). There are brief biographical sketches of important black women in Marcus H. Boulware, *The Oratory of Negro Leaders: 1900–1968* (Westport, Conn., 1969) and in Roy L. Hill, *Rhetoric of Racial Revolt* (Denver, 1964).

3. John W. Blassingame, *The Slave Community: Plantation Life in the Ante-Bellum South* (New York, 1972); Angela Davis, "Reflections on the Black Woman's Role in the Community of Slaves," reprinted from *Black Scholar*, Vol. 3, No. 4 (Dec. 1971); Dorothy Porter, "The Organized Educational Activities of Negro Literary Societies, 1828–1846," *Journal of Negro Education,* V (Oct. 1936), 556–66.

4. See the recently completed dissertation by Tullia Hamilton, "The National Association of Colored Women's Clubs" (dissertation, Emory University, 1978). Other dissertations now under way reflect an increasing recognition of the role of black women as builders of community and institutions. These include: Linda Perkins, "A Biography of Fanny Jackson Coppin" (Univ. of Illinois, Urbana), and Elaine Smith, "Mary McLeod Bethune" (Howard University).

5. The generalizations in this paper are based on my study of primary sources in preparation for my book, *Black Women.* These are listed therein in more detail in "Notes on Sources." Among them are: Charles S. Johnson and W. E. B. Du Bois papers at Fisk University; Carter G. Woodson papers at the Library of Congress; Monroe Work Papers at Tuskegee Institute; manuscript and printed sources at the Schomburg Collection, New York Public Library, and at Howard University.

All the major antislavery collections were studied including: Theodore Dwight Weld Papers at William L. Clements Library, University of Michigan, and the papers of the American Missionary Association at the Amistad Research Center, Dillard University.

Major sources read on women's history include those at the Schlesinger

Library, Radcliffe College; Sophia Smith Collection, Smith College; Blackwell Family Papers; Elizabeth Cady Stanton Papers, Library of Congress; Lucy Chase Manuscript, American Antiquarian Society. The organizational records of the major black women's organizations were studied and those of some interracial organizations, including the YWCA papers, Smith College; NAACP papers, Library of Congress; Committee on Interracial Cooperation and the Neighborhood Union Papers at Atlanta University. A thorough reading of the major black newspapers, magazines, and publications of the past, as well as of abolitionist and women's rights newspapers yielded much valuable information.

6. Lerner, *Black Women,* pp. 27–29, 30–33.

7. Primary sources on these institution builders can be found in Lerner, *Black Women,* pp. 85–92, 118–46. For background information on these institutions see: Carter G. Woodson, *The Education of the Negro Prior to 1861* (New York, 1915) and Henry A. Bullock, *A History of Negro Education in the South, from 1619 to the Present* (Cambridge, Mass., 1967). My generalizations are based on extensive reading in the papers of Mary McLeod Bethune, Amistad Research Center, Dillard University, and Rosenwald Fund Papers, Fisk University; the Margaret Murray Washington Papers, which are found in the Booker T. Washington Papers, Library of Congress; the Charlotte Hawkins Brown Papers at the Schlesinger Library, Radcliffe College. Much information can be found in the publications of the Tuskegee Institute, Alabama, Departments of Records and Research, Nos. 1–10 (Tuskegee, 1949–61) and in the publication of the Hampton Institute, *The Southern Workman* (1872–1939).

Note the absence of any historical biographies on these women. There are three popular biographies of Mary McLeod Bethune. Rackham Holt, *Mary McLeod Bethune* (New York, 1964); C. O. Peare, *Mary McLeod Bethune* (New York, 1951); Emma Gelders Sterne, *Mary McLeod Bethune* (New York, 1959).

A useful bibliography of secondary sources on Mary McLeod Bethune can be found in Dolores Leffall and Janet Sims, "Mary McLeod Bethune—the Educator; also including an annotated bibliography," *Journal of Negro Education* 45 (Summer 1976), 342–59.

A major archival and research project is now under way, sponsored by the National Council of Negro Women, to establish a Mary McLeod Bethune Archives and to collect her scattered papers and those of other black women leaders.

8. First citation: Frances E. W. Harper, letters, March 29, 1870, and March 1871, as cited in William Still, *The Underground Railroad* (Philadelphia, 1872), pp. 776–78. The second citation is from Stanton *et al., HWS,* II,

391, and refers to the 1869 meeting of the Equal Rights Association.

9. Elsie Johnson Douglas, "The Double Task: The Struggle of Negro Women for Sex and Race Emancipation," *Survey Graphic,* Vol. 6, No. 6 (March 1925), 691.

10. On the institution-building of black women see: Elizabeth L. Davis, *Lifting as They Climb: The National Association of Colored Women* (n.p., 1933) and *The Story of the Illinois Federation of Colored Women's Clubs: 1900–1922* (n.p.: n.d. [1922]), an uncritical and disorganized assemblage of records and documents pertaining to the NACW and one of its subsidiaries; Emma Field, "The Women's Club Movement in the United States: 1877–1900," M.A. Thesis in History, Howard University, 1948. See also: *National Cyclopedia of the Colored Race,* ed. Clement Richardson (Montgomery, Ala., 1919); N. F. Mossell, *The Work of the Afro-American Woman* (Philadelphia, 1908).

11. On Ida B. Wells see: Alfreda M. Duster (ed.), *Crusade for Justice: The Autobiography of Ida B. Wells* (Chicago, 1970). For Ida B. Wells's view on rape and lynchings, see: Ida B. Wells, *A Red Record* (Chicago, 1895). This and the views of other women's club leaders on lynching are cited in Lerner, *Black Women,* pp. 193–215.

12. For expressions of these ideas by contemporary black women see: Josephine Carson, *Silent Voices: The Southern Negro Woman Today* (New York, 1969); Tony Cade (ed.), *The Black Woman: An Anthology* (New York, 1970); Inez Smith Reid, *Together Black Women* (New York, 1972); Joyce Ladner, *Tomorrow's Tomorrow: The Black Woman* (New York, 1971).

13. I have here omitted from consideration the complex personal relationships between black women and black men, because of the scanty historical evidence available to me.

14. Anne Firor Scott, *The Southern Lady: From Plantation to Politics* (Chicago, 1970). The direct quote is from Mary Boykin Chesnut, *A Diary from Dixie,* ed. Ben Ames Williams (Boston, 1949), pp. 21–22.

15. Generalizations about the condition of slave women are based on extensive reading of slave narratives, travelers' accounts, and oral history sources. For a detailed summary of these, see Lerner, *Black Women,* pp. 618–21, and chap. 1 for documents pertaining to slave women. See also Willie Lee Rose, *A Documentary History of Slavery in North America* (New York, 1976), pp. 324–27, 417–49.

References to frequent childbirths by slave women occur in: Frances Ann Kemble, *Journal of a Residence on a Georgian Plantation in 1838–1839,* ed. John A. Scott (New York, 1961), pp. 224–41; Charles Ball, *Slavery in the United States: A Narrative of the Life and Adventures of Charles Ball, a Black Man* (Lewistown, Pa., 1836), pp. 150–51; George P. Rawick, *The American Slave: A Composite Autobiography* (Westport, Conn., 1972), p. 88; and Norman R. Yetman, *Life Under the Peculiar Institution: Selections from the Slave Narrative Collection* (New York, 1970), pp. 228, 262. Both Rawick and Yetman are based on oral testimony of ex-slaves in the Federal Writers Project *Slave Narratives.*

On miscegenation, see Rawick, p. 88; Yetman, pp. 13, 37, 75, 127, 232, 307–8, 317, 325, 327. See also Charles H. Nichols, *Many Thousand Gone: The Ex-Slaves' Account of Their Bondage and Freedom* (Bloomington, Ind., 1963), pp. 36, 39–40, 49, 54, 68, 79; Blassingame, *The Slave Community*, pp. 83–84. For more recent interpretations see Robert W. Fogel and Stanley L. Engerman, *Time on the Cross: The Economics of American Negro Slavery* (2 vols., Boston, 1974), I, pp. 78–86; Eugene Genovese, *Roll, Jordan, Roll: The World the Slaves Made* (New York, 1974), pp. 413–31 and Herbert Gutman, *The Black Family in Slavery and Freedom, 1750–1925* (New York, 1976), pp. 392–402.

The following slave narratives offer insights into the condition of slave women: L. M. Child (ed.), Harriet Brent Jacobs, *Incidents in the Life of a Slave Girl, Written by Herself* (Boston, 1861); Sarah Bradford, *Harriet Tubman: The Moses of Her People* (New York, 1961; reprinted from 1886 ed.); William Craft, "Running a Thousand Miles for Freedom, or The Escape of William and Ellen Craft from Slavery," reprinted from the 1860 edition in Arna Bontemps (ed.), *Great Slave Narratives* (Boston, 1969); *A Narrative of the Life of Frederick Douglass, An American Slave, Written by Himself* (New York, 1845); *An Autobiography of the Reverend Josiah Henson* (Reading, Mass., 1969, reprinted from 1881 ed.): *Narrative of the Life of Moses Grandy* (Boston, 1844); *Narrative of Solomon Northup, Twelve Years a Slave . . .* (Auburn, N.Y., 1853).

16. There are many examples of forcible rape of black women during race riots. See "Memphis Riot and Massacre," U.S. Document 1274, 39th Congress, 1st Session, 1865–66. House Reports, Vol. 3, No. 101. KKK Hearings, Vol. 5, "Report of the Joint Select Committee to Inquire into the Condition of Affairs in the Late Insurrectionary States," 42 Congress, 2nd Session, 1871.

17. Blassingame, *The Slave Community*, p. 88; H. Jacobs, *Incidents . . .* , p. 49.

18. W. J. Cash, *The Mind of the South* (New York, 1941); Lillian Smith, *Killers of the Dream* (New York, 1949; revised 1962); Eldridge Cleaver, *Soul on Ice* (New York, 1968); Richard Wright, *Black Boy* (New York, 1937); Winthrop Jordan, *White Over Black: American Attitudes Toward the Negro, 1550–1812* (Chapel Hill, 1968), explores the early history of racism, including a full discussion of its sexual aspects; Gunnar Myrdal, *An American Dilemma: The Negro Problem and Modern Democracy* (New York, 1944), chaps. 3, 5, 24, 26, 27. Calvin C. Hernton, *Sex and Racism in America* (New York,

1965), approaches the subject from the black point of view. Albert Memmi, *Dominated Man* (New York, 1968), discusses sex-caste oppression and compares it to race-caste oppression. Robert Staples, "The Myth of the Impotent Black Male," in *Black Scholar,* Vol. II, No. 10 (June 1971), 2–8, is particularly interesting and insightful.

19. On Ida B. Wells, see note 11, above.

20. For the traditional interpretation of the black family see: Jessie Bernard, *Marriage and Family Among Negroes* (Englewood Cliffs, N.J., 1966); Andrew Billingsley, *Black Families in White America* (Englewood Cliffs, N.J., 1968); Kenneth Clark, *Dark Ghetto* (New York, 1965); and Franklin Frazier, *The Negro Family in the United States* (Chicago, 1939).

For a revisionist position which challenges the Frazier thesis see Gutman, *Black Family,* chap. 1 and Afterword; Joe R. Feagin, "The Kinship Ties of Negro Urbanites," and David A. Shulz, "Variations in the Father Role in Complete Families of the Negro Lower Class," both in Norval D. Glenn and Charles M. Bonjean (eds.), *Blacks in the United States* (San Francisco, 1969); Nancy L. Gonzales, "Toward a Definition of Matrifocality," and Carol B. Stack, "The Kindred of Viola Jackson: Residence and Family Organization of an Urban Black American Family," both in Norman Whitter, Jr., and John F. Szwed (eds.), *Afro-American Anthropology: Contemporary Perspectives* (New York, 1970). See also: Carole B. Stack, "Black Kindreds: Parenthood and Personal Kindreds Among Blacks Supported by Welfare," *Journals of Comparative Family Studies,* Vol. III, No. 2 (Summer 1972), 194–206; Charles Valentine, *Culture and Poverty* (Chicago, 1968); Frank F. Furstenberg, Jr., Theodore Hershberg, and John Modell, "The Origins of the Female-Headed Black Family: The Impact of the Urban Experience," *Journal of Interdisciplinary History,* Vol. VI, No. 2 (Aug. 1975), 211–33; Justin Labinjoh, "The Sexual Life of the Oppressed: An Examination of the Family Life of Ante-Bellum Slaves," *Phylon,* XXXV (Dec. 1974), 375–97.

21. Claudia Goldin, "Female Labor Force Participation: The Origin of Black and White Differences, 1870 and 1880," *Journal of Economic History,* XXXVII (March 1977). Goldin shows that in a study of seven Southern cities in 1870 and 1880, "black women participated in the labor force on the average of three times more than did white women, and married black women averaged almost six times the rate of married white females."

22. Jeanne L. Noble, *The Negro Woman's College Education* (New York, 1956); Marion V. Cuthbert, *Education and Marginality: A Study of the Negro Woman College Graduate* (New York, 1942); and E. Wilbur Bock, "Farmer's Daughter Effect: The Case of the Negro Female Professionals," *Phylon,* XXX (Spring 1969), 17–26.

23. W. Bock (*ibid.*) first observed this phenomenon and coined the phrase. See

also: Jessie Bernard, "The Impact of Sexism and Racism on Employment Status and Earnings," Warner Module #25 (New York, MSS Modular Publication, 1973). Bernard concluded a thorough analysis of census data pertaining to race and sex in employment with the following observations: 1) Racism is more serious for black men than for black women; 2) Sexism is a more serious handicap for white women than for black women; 3) While both racism and sexism handicap black women, sexism is more serious than racism; 4) Among educated black women there is evidence of "reverse racism"— black women earn more than white women in the same employment categories.

A somewhat different conclusion is reached by Albert W. Niemi in "Sexist Earnings Differences: The Cost of Female Sexuality," *American Journal of Economics and Sociology*, 36 (Jan. 1977), 38. "Sexist earning differentials are very costly for females . . . Black families appear to encounter a much lower degree of sexist discrimination but this largely reflects racial discrimination against Black males. When earnings of Black females are compared to the standard for White males, they too appear to face a high sexist differential."

24. There is one exception, that of educational attainment. A comparison of the college graduates by race and sex, show that in the past black families tended to favor their daughters educationally compared with white families. In 1960 8.3% of white females and 15.8% of white males finished four or more years of college, while the figures for Blacks were 4% females, 4.1% males. In other words, a black male had about an equal chance for a college education with a black female, while a white male was twice as likely to complete college than was a white female.

By 1974, as a result of civil rights movement gains, black males had advanced into educational opportunity at a faster rate than black females. 17.2% of white females and 24.9% of white males would complete college as compared to 7.6% black females and 8.5% black males. Statistics from U.S. Dept. of Commerce/Bureau of the Census, *The Social and Economic Status of the Black Population in the United States 1974* (Washington, D.C., 1975), Tables 67 and 68.

25. *Ibid.*, Table 49.

26. Figures for 1965: U.S. Department of Labor, Wage and Labor Standards Administration, and Women's Bureau, *Negro Women . . . in the Population and in the Labor Force* (Washington, D.C., 1967).

Figures for 1970: *Bureau of the Census Income in 1970 of Families and Persons in the United States*, Series P-60, #80 (Oct. 3, 1971), Table 52.

27. U.S. Census, *Black Population in the U.S.*, 1974, Table 39.

28. *Ibid.*, Tables 80 and 84.

29. The myth of black matriarchy was elevated to the level of governmental pol-

icy following the publication of Daniel Patrick Moynihan, *The Negro Family: The Case for National Action* (Washington, D.C., 1967). The theory and its critics are fairly represented in Lee Rainwater and William L. Yancey, *The Moynihan Report and the Politics of Controversy . . . Including the Full Text of "The Negro Family: The Case for National Action" by Daniel Patrick Moynihan* (Cambridge, Mass., 1967).

Among more recent critics are: Angela Davis, "Reflections . . . ,"; Robert Staples, "The Myth of the Black Matriarchy," *Black Scholar*, Vol. 1, Nos. 3–4 (Jan.–Feb. 1970), 9–16; Herbert, Gutman, "Persistant Myths about the American Negro Family," *Journal of Interdisciplinary History*, VI (Autumn 1975), 181–210; and Joyce Ladner, *Tomorrow's Tomorrow*. The last, a sociological study, is unique in treating the subject from the point of view of the black woman.

Chapter 6. Community Work of Black Club Women

1. Fannie Barrier Williams, "Club Movement Among Negro Women," in J. W. Gibson and W. H. Crogman (eds.), *Progress of a Race* (Atlanta, 1903); Mary Church Terrell, "The History of the Club Movement," *The Afro-American Women's Journal*, 1940. Typescript copy in Mary Church Terrell Papers, Library of Congress.

2. L. C. Scruggs, M. D., *Women of Distinction* (Raleigh, N.C., 1893); N. F. Mossell, *The Work of the Afro-American Woman* (Philadelphia, 1908); *National Encylopedia of the Colored Race*, ed. Clement Richardson (Montgomery, Ala. 1919); and Hallie Quinn Brown, *Homespun Heroines and Other Women of Distinction* (Xenia, Ohio, 1926), are among the earlier books listing outstanding black women.

3. Elizabeth L. Davis, *Lifting as They Climb: The National Association of Colored Women* (n.p., 1933); Elizabeth Lindsay Davis, *The Story of the Illinois Federation of Colored Women's Clubs: 1900–1922* (n.p.: n.d. [1922]), an uncritical and disorganized assemblage of records and documents pertaining to the NACW and one of its subsidiaries; Emma Field, "The Women's Club Movement in the United States: 1877–1900." M.A. Thesis in History, Howard University, 1948. A recently completed unpublished dissertation by Tullia Hamilton, "The National Association of Colored Women's Clubs," provides the first coherent scholarly account.

4. For background information on these institutions see: Carter G. Woodson, *The Education of the Negro Prior to 1861*, (New York, 1915) and Henry A. Bullock, *A History of Negro Education in the South, from 1619 to the Present*, (Cambridge, Mass., 1967). See also notes 6 and 7, chapter 5 above.

5. Report of the Tuskegee Women's Club; 1904–1905 (n.p., 1906), pamphlet.

6. On Ida B. Wells see Alfreda M. Duster. *Ida B. Wells* (Chicago, 1970). For Ida B. Wells's view on rape and lynchings, see note 11, chapter 5 above.

7. Duster, *Ida B. Wells,* pp. 78–81.

8. Davis, *Illinois Federation* . . . , pp. 95–96, 99–101. See also Alan H. Spear, *Black Chicago: The Making of a Negro Ghetto: 1890–1920* (Chicago, 1967), pp. 101–2.

9. On Victoria Earle Matthews see: J. E. Bruce, "Noted Race Women I Have Known and Me," J. E. Bruce Manuscript, Schomburg Collection, New York Public Library, and *Woman's Era,* Vol. II, No. 5 (Aug. 1895) and Vol. III, No. 5 (Jan. 1897). On Colored Woman's League of Washington D.C., see: Andrew F. Hilyer (ed.), *The 20th Century Union League Directory: A Historical, Biographical and Statistical Study of Colored Washington* (Washington, D.C., 1901), pp. 155–56.

10. All information about the Atlanta Neighborhood Union is based on study of the Neighborhood Union Papers, Trevor Arnett Library, Atlanta University. Also on a typescript in these papers, "Survey of the Work of the Neighborhood Union" by W. Walter Chivers (undated). Excerpts from the Neighborhood Union Papers are reprinted in Gerda Lerner, *Black Women in White America* (New York, 1972), pp. 500–509.

11. "Plan of Work: Atlanta Colored Women's War Council," Neighborhood Union Papers, in *ibid.,* pp. 498–500.

12. The summary of the work in the YWCA is based on a study of the YWCA Papers, Smith College and of the YWCA Manuscript in the Neighborhood Union Papers. Some of these items are reprinted in *ibid.,* pp. 477–89.

13. Quote, undated manuscript [probably 1921], YWCA Manuscript, Box 5, Neighborhood Union Papers.

14. This summary is based on a study of the papers of the Commission on Interracial Cooperation, Atlanta, University of Atlanta. See also reprints from these papers in Lerner, *Black Women,* pp. 461–67.

Chapter 7. Black and White Women in Interaction and Confrontation

1. William Chafe, *Women and Equality: Changing Patterns in American Culture* (New York, 1977), discusses this aspect of the comparison in detail.

2. M. Chesnut, *A Diary from Dixie* (Boston, 1949), pp. 21–22.

3. For a fuller discussion of this theme see Lillian Smith, *Killers of the Dream* (New York, 1949; revised 1962), I, 1, 2; II, 1–4; III, 1–4; W. J. Cash, *Mind of the South* (New York, 1941), pp. 87–89; Winthrop Jordan, *White Over Black* (Chapel Hall, 1968), chap. 4.

4. F. A. Kemble, *Journal* . . . (New York, 1961), pp. 224–41.

5. For childhood and youth of the Grimké sisters, see Gerda Lerner, *The Grimké*

Sisters from South Carolina: Rebels Against Slavery (Boston, 1967), chaps. 1–5; citation from Angelina E. Grimké, *An Appeal to the Women of the Nominally Free States* (New York, 1837), p. 161.

6. The first public lecture tour of record was undertaken by Salome Lincoln, a Massachusetts-born textile worker who, after leading a successful strike of female workers, left the mill in 1829. She became an itinerant preacher and in 1830 held twelve public prayer meetings in Boston. The next American-born woman to speak in public was a Black, Maria Stewart, who gave four lectures. Both women and the Scottish-born Frances Wright, who lectured during the same years, 1829–32, were subject to severe censure and attacks. For more information on Salome Lincoln, see Gerda Lerner, *Female Experience: An American Documentary* (New York and Indianapolis, 1977), pp. 162–70, 275–77. For information on Maria Stewart, see Gerda Lerner, *Black Women in White America* (New York, 1972), pp. 526–30.

7. Lerner, *Grimké Sisters: Rebels,* p. 162.

8. Proceedings, Anti-Slavery Convention of American Women . . . 1837 (New York, 1837).

9. *Narrative of Sojourner Truth* (Battle Creek, 1884), p. 135.

10. Sarah and Angelina Grimké to Sarah Douglass (undated), Mss, Weld-Grimké Papers, Wm. L. Clements Library, University of Michigan.

11. *Provincial Freeman,* vol. I, No. 39, (Dec. 16, 1854).

12. *Ibid.*

13. *Ibid.*

14. Frederick Douglass, speech before Equal Rights Association, New York City, May 1869, as cited in *The Revolution,* May 20, 1869.

15. *Woman's Journal,* Sept. 27, 1890.

16. A. Kraditor, *Ideas* . . . (New York, 1965), chap. 7.

17. Letters by Daisy Lampkin to Heywood Broun (Aug. 28, 1924) and to Walter White (Aug. 18, 1924) describe several incidents of discrimination in the years 1913–24. NAACP Mss., Library of Congress.

18. The generalizations concerning the teachers of the freedmen are based on the study of manuscript sources, particularly those of the American Missionary Association; Amistad Research Center, Dillard University; Freedmen's Aid Commission, Papers, Cornell University; and the *Freedmen's Record.* Also, diaries and letters of Charlotte Forten, Lucy Chase, Susie King Taylor, Frances E. W. Harper, Virginia Randolph, Laura Mobley, and others.

19. Undated letter fragment, Charlotte Hawkins Brown Mss., Schlesinger Library, Radcliffe College. Also letters by Mary McLeod Bethune in the Rosenwald Fund Papers, Fisk University.

20. Margaret M. Washington to Edna D. Cheney, Nov. 23, 1896, Cheney Papers, Boston Public Library.

21. Information on Negro women's clubs comes from a study of the organizational records of the National Association of Colored Women, the Atlanta Neighborhood Union, the Tuskegee Woman's Club, the Boston New Era Club, and others.

22. Mrs. Booker T. Washington, "Club Movement among Negro Women," in J. L. Nichols and W. H. Crogman (eds.), *Progress of the Race* (Naperville, Ga., 1929), pp. 220–26.

23. The Willard incident is described in several issues of the *Woman's Era* (Feb.– July 1895).

24. The foregoing is based on manuscript materials, chiefly: YWCA organizational files, Sophia Smith Collection, Smith College; Neighborhood Union papers, Commission on Interracial Cooperation papers and the files of the Association of Southern Women for the Prevention of Lynching, all at Atlanta University. See also: Henry E. Barber, "The Association of Southern Women for the Prevention of Lynching," *Phylon,* Vol. XXXIV, No. 4 (Winter 1973), 378–89.

Chapter 8. The Political Activities of Antislavery Women

1. Dwight L. Dumond, *Antislavery: The Crusade for Freedom in America* (Ann Arbor, 1961), chap. 33.

   For more studies of political antislavery see: Frederick J. Blue, *The Free Soilers: Third Party Politics, 1848–54* (Urbana, 1973); Eric Foner, *Free Soil, Free Labor, Free Men: The Ideology of the Republican Party before the Civil War* (New York 1970); Richard Sewell, *John P. Hale and the Politics of Abolition* (Cambridge, Mass., 1965); Theodore Smith, *The Liberty and the Free Soil Parties in the Northwest* (Cambridge, Mass., 1897); James B. Stewart, *Holy Warriors: The Abolitionist and American Slavery* (New York, 1976), and *Joshua Giddings and the Tactics of Radical Politics, 1795–1864* (Cleveland, 1969); Bertram Wyatt-Brown, *Lewis Tappan and the Evangelical War Against Slavery* (New York, 1969).

   For emphasis on the impact of ideological and organizational division in the antislavery movement see: Gilbert H. Barnes, *The Anti-Slavery Impulse: 1830–1844* (New York, 1939), chaps. 15, 16; Aileen Kraditor, *Means and Ends in American Abolitionism: Garrison and His Critics on Strategy and Tactics, 1824–1850* (New York, 1967).

   For a critical interpretation of abolitionists as anti-institutional see: Stanley Elkins, *Slavery: A Problem in American Intellectual and Institutional Life* (Chicago, 1959); Willie Lee Rose, *Rehearsal for Reconstruction: The Port Royal Experiment* (New York, 1964).

2. Figures based on Annual Reports of the American Anti-Slavery Society

198 NOTES

1834–39, as cited in Louis Filler, *The Crusade Against Slavery: 1830–1860* (New York, 1960), p. 67.

3. Dumond, *Antislavery,* chaps. 33, 34 and Barnes, *Anti-Slavery Impulse,* chaps. 15, 16.

For a factual description of the schisms see: Filler, *Crusade Against Slavery,* chap. 6.

For a view minimizing the impact of the split of 1840 see: Gerda Lerner, *The Grimké Sisters from South Carolina: Rebels Against Slavery* (Boston, 1967); and Ronald Walters, *The Antislavery Appeal: American Abolitionism after 1830* (Baltimore; 1976).

4. See, for example, Eleanor Flexner, *Century of Struggle: Woman's Rights Movement in the United States* (Cambridge, Mass., 1959), and Keith Melder, *The Beginning of Sisterhood: The American Women's Rights Movement, 1800–1850* (New York, 1977).

5. David Donald, "Toward a Reconsideration of Abolitionists, in *Lincoln Reconsidered* (New York, 1956), pp. 28–36; Alice Hatcher Henderson, *The History of the New York State Anti-Slavery Society,* unpublished Dissertation (University Microfilms, Ann Arbor, Michigan, 1963); Gerald Sorin, *The New York Abolitionists: A Case Study of Political Radicalism* (Westport, Conn. 1971).

6. The literature focusing on women in the antislavery movement is sparse. Except for a few biographies of female abolitionists, the subject is treated as a minor aspect of the general antislavery movement in separate chapters of the monographs cited in note 3 above. See also: Alma Lutz, *Crusade for Freedom: Women in the Antislavery Movement* (Boston, 1968); Jane H. and Wm. H. Pease, *Bound with Them in Chains: A Biographical History of the Antislavery Movement* (Westport, Conn., 1972), chap. 3 "The Boston Bluestocking: Maria Weston Chapman"; William Loren Katz, "The Black/White Fight Against Slavery and for Women's Rights in America," *Freedomways,* Vol. XVI, No. 4 (1976), 230–36; Carol Thompson, "Women and the Anti-Slavery Movement," *Current History,* LXX (May 1976), 198–201. A recent book focusing on women abolitionists is: Blanche Glassman Hersh, *"The Slavery of Sex": Feminist Abolitionists in America* (Chicago, 1978).

7. Dumond, *Antislavery,* chap. 33; Barnes, *Antislavery Impulse,* chaps. 15, 16.

8. Judith Wellman, "To the Father and the Rulers of Our Country, Abolitionist Petitions and Female Abolitionists in Paris, New York, 1835–45," Unpublished Paper, Berkshire Conference on Women's History, Bryn Mawr College, June 1976.

9. Angelina Emily Grimké, *Appeal to the Christian Women* (New York, 1836).

10. Dates based on the Annual report of the Board of Managers of the Massachusetts Anti-Slavery Society (Boston, Mass., 1838) and the Proceedings of the Anti-Slavery Convention of American Women, held in New York City, May 9–12, 1837 (New York, 1837).

11. Proceedings, p. 8.

12. *Ibid.*, pp. 11–12.

13. *Ibid.*

14. *Congressional Globe*, 24th Congress, VIII, p. 337.

15. Barnes, *Antislavery Impulse*, p. 266, fn. 34 and 39.

16. Petitions to the 25th Congress, 1–3 Sessions, House Records HR-25 A and Senate Records 25-H-H1, National Archives. Petitions to Congress 1821–38 were examined and scanned, but are not included in the count.

17. For a discussion of these petitions see Dumond, *Antislavery*, pp. 245–48. Dumond discusses 1496 petitions, but these are often duplicates as to the signatures, since he lists the totals for petitions on various antislavery topics. Thus, his figures and mine differ.

    I chose to concentrate on the petitions opposing the annexation of Texas, considering this the most political issue of the time and the kind women would least likely be concerned with. I reason that whatever the number of women concerned with this issue, *more* women could be found signing petitions on other issues.

    The 402 petitions I examined represent a random sampling of the larger total discussed by Dumond. I believe the sample is large enough to permit the making of generalizaitons as to patterns, but it would be desirable to do a more thorough study comprising all the petitions for a selected year.

18. A scan of the petitions revealed the pattern of origin and of male-female participation. The signature count on the outside of the petition was not always accurate; the errors were in omitting female names. Several petitions which listed "male" on the outside actually contained female names, probably an effort on the part of the petition gatherer to maximize the political pressure on his Congressman by making it appear that all signers were voters. This convinced me that if I accepted the outside notation and gender count, I would be erring on the conservative side, with respect to female participation.

    Petitions are designated "male" or "female" depending on the notation on the outside or the count inside. If persons of both sexes sign a petition it is here designated as "mixed."

19. For a detailed account of Ohio abolitionism see: Douglas A. Gamble, "Garrisonian Abolitionists in the West: Some Suggestions for Study," *Civil War History*, Vol. XXII, No. 1 (March 1977), 52–68; James Brewer Stewart, "Peaceful Hopes and Violent Experience: The Evolution of Reforming and Radical Abolitionism, 1831–1837," *ibid.*, Vol. XVII, No. 4 (Dec. 1971), 293–309.

20. Patricia Heard, "One Blood All Nations' Antislavery Petitions in Sandwich": *Fifty-ninth Annual Excursion of the Sandwich Historical Society*, Sunday, Aug. 27, 1978 (n.p., n.d.), 26–31; and Ellen Langenheim Henle, "Forget Not the Matron: Sandwich Women and Antislavery in the Antebellum Years,"

ibid., 32–38. I am indebted to Dr. Ellen Henle for bringing this item to my attention.

21. Judith Wellman, "Are We Aliens Because We Are Women: Female Abolitionists and Abolitionist Petitions in Upstate New York," Paper presented to the National Archives Conference, April 1976. Unpublished.

22. Journal of the United States Senate of America, 1st Session, 25 Congress (Washington, D.C., 1837), p. 63, Oct. 12, 1837.

23. This is a conservative figure. There were five county petitions, which likely included some of the towns the sisters visited, but did not so designate.

24. For a more detailed account, see Lerner, *The Grimké Sisters: Rebels,* chaps. 12–14.

25. Juliana A. Tappan to Anne Weston, July 21, 1837, Weston Papers, Boston Public Library.

26. Hanna H. Smith to Abby Kelley, July 25, 1839, Abby Kelley Foster Papers, American Antiquarian Society, Worcester, Mass.

27. M. E. Robbins to Abby Kelley, Jan. 21, 1839, *ibid.* The writer was the corresponding secretary to the Lynn Female Antislavery Society.

28. Antoinette Brown, Oct. 1852, Blackwell Family Papers, Box 54, Library of Congress.

29. Amy Swerdlow, "Abolition's Conservative Sisters: The Ladies' New York City Anti-Slavery Societies, 1834–1840." Paper presented at the Third Berkshire Conference on the History of Women, Bryn Mawr College, June 9–11, 1976. Unpublished.

30. Wellman, "Are We Aliens . . . ," 7,11.

31. Wellman, "Fathers and Rulers. . . ."

32. Minutes of the Ashtabula County Female Anti-Slavery Society, Manuscript, Western Reserve Historical Society, Cleveland, Ohio.

Chapter 9. *Just a Housewife*

1. Robert V. Wells, "Demographic Changes and the Life Cycles of American Families," *Journal of Interdisciplinary History,* Vol. II, No. 2 (Autumn 1971), 282–92.

2. Catharine Beecher and Harriet Beecher Stowe, *The American Woman's Home, or Principles of Domestic Science* (New York, 1869). See also Catharine Beecher, *Letters to Persons Who Are Engaged in Domestic Service* (New York, 1842).

3. Thorstein Veblen, *The Theory of the Leisure Class* (New York, 1962; reprint of 1899 ed.), pp. 70–71.

4. For a full discussion of the problems and the history of domestic service see David M. Katzman, *Seven Days a Week: Women and Domestic Service in Industrializing America* (New York, 1978). "A Note on Sources" offers a valuable bibliography.

The main historical source is Lucy M. Salmon, *Domestic Service* (New York, 1897). A new analytical model for the discussion of women and work can be found in Patricia Branca, "A New Perspective on Women's Work: A Comparative Typology," *Journal of Social History,* IX (Winter 1975), 129–53. See also, Lerner, *Black Women in White America* (New York, 1972), "Doing Domestic Work," pp. 227–39.

For a comparison with changes in the status of housewives in Europe see: Joan W. Scott and Louise Tilly, "Women's Work and the Family in 19th Century Europe," *Comparative Studies in Society and History,* XVII (1975), 36–64.

5. The impact of technological changes on housework is discussed in Ruth Schwartz Cowan, "A Case Study of Technological and Social Change: The Washing Machine and the Working Wife," in Mary S. Hartman and Lois Banner (eds.), *Clio's Consciousness Raised: New Perspectives on the History of Women* (New York, 1974), pp. 245–53; Wm. D. and D. C. Andrews, "Technology and the Housewife in 19th Century America," *Women's Studies,* Vol. II, No. 3 (1974), 309–28.

6. For detailed accounts of the work and the economic contributions of working-class housewives see Lee Rainwater, Richard P. Coleman, and Gerald Handel, *Workingman's Wife* (New York, 1962), and Mirra Komarovsky, *Blue Collar Marriage* (New York, 1964).

7. Sylvia Porter, "What's a Wife Worth?" *New York Post Magazine,* July 13, 1966, p. 2. Also, updated figures in Ann Crittenden Scott, "The Value of Housework—For Love or Money," *Ms.,* Vol. I, No. 1 (July 1972), 56–59.

8. Ann Oakley, *Woman's Work: The Housewife, Past and Present* (New York, 1974), p. 6. An earlier sociological study is Helena Z. Lopata, *Occupation Housewife* (New York, 1971).

9. Alexander Szalai, *The Use of Time* (The Hague, 1972), as cited in Elise Boulding, "Familiar Constraints on Women's Work Roles," *Signs: Journal of Women in Culture and Society,* Vol. I, No. 3, Pt. 2, 112–13.

10. Porter, "What's a Wife Worth?"

11. Estimates of the value of housework vary greatly, depending on the basis on which the salaries are computed. These range from unskilled wages to calculations which consider the work of the housewife and child-rearer as equivalent to the professional and semi-professional services of nursery school teachers, child psychologists, chauffeur, chef, waitress, etc. See: Wm. D. and D. C. Andrews, "Technology and the Housewife in 19th Century America"; Juanita Kreps, *Sex in the Marketplace: American Women at Work* (Baltimore, 1971); C. S. Pyun, "The Monetary Value of a Housewife," *American Journal of Economics and Sociology,* Vol. 28, No. 3 (1969), 271–84; Harvey S. Rosen, "The Monetary Value of a Housewife: A Replacement Cost Approach," *American Journal of Economics and Sociology,* Vol. 33, No. 1 (1974),

65–73; Kathryn E. Walker and William H. Gauger, *The Dollar Value of Household Work,* Cornell University Information Bulletin No. 60 (Ithaca, 1973); Jo Ann Vanek, "Time Spent in Housework," *Scientific American,* Vol. 231, No. 5 (Nov. 1974), 116–20.

12. Charlotte Perkins Gilman, *Women and Economics* (New York, 1966; reprint of 1898 ed.).

13. Pat Mainardi, "The Politics of Housework," in *Sisterhood Is Powerful,* ed. Robin Morgan (New York, 1970); and Meredith Tax, "Woman and Her Mind: The Story of Daily Life," in Roberta Salper (ed.), *Female Liberation, History and Current Politics* (New York, 1972).

For more recent Marxist interpretations along similar lines, see Jean Gardiner, "Women's Domestic Labor," *New Left Review,* No. 89 (Jan.–Feb. 1975), 47–58 and bibliography.

14. On wages for housework see "Recognition of the Economic Contribution of the Homemaker," Clearinghouse on Women's Issues, 1346 Conn. Ave. N.W., No. 924, Washington, D.C. 20036. Also see Carol Lopate, "Pay for Housework?" in David Mermilstein (ed.), *Economics: Mainstream Readings and Radical Critiques,* 3rd ed. (New York, 1976), pp. 479–86.

15. Esther Boserup, *Women's Role in Economic Development* (London, 1970); Judith K. Brown, "A Note on the Division of Labor by Sex," *American Anthropologist,* Vol. 72, No. 5 (Oct. 1970), 1073–78; Ernestine Friedl, *Women and Men: An Anthropologist's View* (New York, 1975); M. K. Martin and B. Voorhis, *Female of the Species* (New York, 1975); and Peggy R. Sanday, "Female Status in the Public Domain," in M. Z. Rosaldo and L. Lamphere, *Woman, Culture and Society* (Stanford, 1974), pp. 189–206.

16. See Nona Glazer-Malbin, "Housework," *Signs,* Vol. I, No. 4 (Summer 1976), 905–22, for an excellent review of the literature on the subject in the different disciplines.

17. The theoretical analyses of the topic "Housework" deserve a separate article and cannot be adequately dealt with here. Marxist analysis, which has been very influential on this topic, falls into two categories: classical and feminist-revisionist.

For the classical Marxist theory see: Frederick Engels, *The Origin of the Family, Private Property and the State* (New York, 1942; reprint of 1884 ed.); August Bebel, *Women Under Socialism* (New York, 1971; reprint of 1904 ed.); V. I. Lenin, *Women and Society* (New York, 1938).

For feminist-revisionist Marxist theory see: Margaret Benston, "Political Economy of Women's Liberation," *Monthly Review,* Vol. XXI, No. 4 (Sept. 1969); Mariarosa Dalla Costa, *The Power of Women and the Subversion of the Community* (Bristol, Eng., 1973); Barbara Ehrenreich and Deirdre English, "Manufacture of Housework," *Socialist Revolution* XXVI (1975); Jean Gar-

diner, "Women's Domestic Labor"; Ira Gerstein, "Domestic Work and Capitalism," *Radical America,* Vol. 7, Nos. 4-5 (July–Oct. 1973), 101–28; Wally
Secombe, "The Housewife and Her Labour under Capitalism," *New Left
Review,* No. 83 (Jan.–Feb. 1974), 3–24; Eli Zaretsky, "Capitalism, the Family, and Personal Life," *Socialist Revolution,* Vol. 3, Nos. 1–2 (Jan.–April
1973), 69–125, and *idem.,* Vol. 3, No. 3 (May–June 1973), 19–70.

18. C. P. Gilman, *Women and Economics,* and *The Home: Its Work and Influence*
(New York, 1903).

Chapter 10. Placing Women in History

1. For the term "women worthies," I am indebted to Natalie Zemon Davis,
Stanford University. For the terms "compensatory history" and "contribution
history" I am indebted to Mari Jo Buhle, Ann G. Gordon, and Nancy
Schrom, "Women in American Society: An Historical Contribution," *Radical
America,* Vol. 5, No. 4 (July–Aug. 1971), 3–66.

2. Mary R. Beard, *Woman as Force* (New York, 1946). See also a further discussion of this question in Chapter 1 of this book.

3. Ronald G. Walters (ed.), *Primers for Prudery* (Englewood Cliffs, N.J., 1974);
Ben Barker-Benfield, "The Spermatic Economy: A Nineteenth Century View
of Sexuality," *Feminist Studies,* Vol. 1, No. 1 (1972), 45–74; Carl Degler,
"What Ought To Be and What Was: Women's Sexuality in the Nineteenth
Century," *American Historical Review,* Vol. 79, No. 5 (Dec. 1974), 1467–90.
For a different approach see also: Carroll Smith-Rosenberg and Charles Ro-
senberg, "The Female Animal: Medical and Biological Views of Women in
Nineteenth Century America," *Journal of American History,* Vol. 60, No. 2
(Sept. 1973), 332–56; Carroll Smith-Rosenberg, "The Hysterical Woman:
Some Reflections on Sex Roles and Role Conflict in 19th Century America,"
Social Research, Vol. 39, No. 4 (Dec. 1972), 652–78; Charles Rosenberg,
"Sexuality, Class and Role," *American Quarterly,* Vol. 25, No. 2 (May 1973),
131–53.

4. Barbara Welter, "Cult of True Womanhood," *American Quarterly,* Vol. 18
(Summer 1966), 151–74.

5. Philip J. Greven, Jr., *Four Generations: Population, Land and Family in Colonial Andover, Massachusetts* (Ithaca, 1970). For a good sampling of recent
work in family history, see Michael Gordon (ed.), *The American Family in
Social-Historical Perspective* (New York, 1973).

6. Daniel Scott Smith, "Family Limitation, Sexual Control and Domestic
Feminism in Victorian America," *Feminist Studies,* Vol. 1, Nos. 3/4 (Winter–
Spring 1973), 40–57.

By somewhat similar reasoning Edward Shorter has defined "women's liberation" as "Disregarding outside controls upon personal freedom of action and sexuality for the sake of individual self-fulfillment." He argues that attitudinal changes of this sort were induced in lower-class women by their involvement in the market economy and that these in turn led to higher legitimate and illegitimate fertility in late 18th-century Europe. He explains the drop in fertility rates in the 19th century by the diffusion of birth control knowledge from middle-class women to lower-class women. What is important here is his argument that women were responsible for and in control of decisions relating to their fertility and that their liberation meant, in fact, sexual liberation. See Edward Shorter, "Female Emancipation, Birth Control, and Fertility in European History," *American Historical Review*, LXVIII (1973), 605–40.

For a feminist critique of his reasoning and his evidence see Louise Tilly, Joan Scott, and Miriam Cohen, "Women's Work and Fertility Patterns," *Journal of Interdisciplinary History*, VI (Winter 1976), 447–76.

7. See *Journal of Interdisciplinary History*, Vol. II, No. 2 (Autumn 1971), for articles by Joseph Kett, Robert Wells, Peter Laslett, and Kenneth Keniston.

8. Virginia Yans McLaughlin, "Patterns of Work and Family Organization: Buffalo's Italians," *ibid.*, pp. 219–314. Tamara Hareven, "The History of the Family as an Interdisciplinary Field," *ibid.*, pp. 399–414; Susan Kleinberg, "Women's Work: The Lives of Working Class Women in Pittsburgh, 1870–1900" (unpublished paper); Alice Kessler-Harris, "Stratifying by Sex: Notes on the History of Working Women" in Richard Edwards *et al.* (eds.), *Labor Market Segmentation* (New York, 1975). A shorter version of this is in B. Carroll, *Liberating Women's History* (Urbana, 1976); and, Alice Kessler-Harris, "Where Are the Organized Women Workers?", *Feminist Studies* (Fall 1975), 92–110.

9. Linda Gordon, *Woman's Body, Woman's Right: A Social History of Birth Control in America* (New York, 1976); James C. Mohr, *Abortion in America: The Origins and Evolution of National Policy* (New York, 1978); Carroll Smith-Rosenberg, "The Hysterical Woman . . ." pp. 652–78; Ann Douglas Wood, "The Fashionable Diseases: Women's Complaints and Their Treatment in 19th Century America," *Journal of Interdisciplinary History*, IV (Summer 1973), 25–52.

For a discussion of female bonding see: Carroll Smith-Rosenberg, "The Female World of Love and Ritual: Relations Between Women in Nineteenth Century America," *Signs*, Vol. I, No. 1 (Fall 1975), 1–30.

10. See papers by Marilyn Arthur, Renate Bridenthal, Gerda Lerner, Joan Kelly-Gadol in *Conceptual Framework in Women's History* (Bronxville, N.Y., 1976); Joan Kelly-Gadol, "Did Women Have a Renaissance?," in Renate Bridenthal and Claudia Koonz, *Becoming Visible: Women in European History* (Boston, 1977), pp. 137–64; Joan Kelly-Gadol, "The Social Relation of the Sexes:

Methodological Implications of Women's History," *Signs,* Vol. I, No. 4 (Summer 1976), 809–24; Linda K. Kerber, "Daughters of Columbia: Educating Women for the Republic," in *The Hofstadter Aegis: A Memorial* (New York, 1974); and Joan Hoff Wilson, "The Illusion of Change: Women and the American Revolution," in Alfred F. Young (ed.), *The American Revolution: Explorations in the History of American Radicalism* (De Kalb, Ill., 1976).

11. Juliet Mitchell, *Woman's Estate* (New York, 1972), Sheila Rowbotham, *Woman's Consciousness, Man's World* (Baltimore, 1973); S. Rowbotham, *Women, Resistance and Revolution* (New York, 1972).

12. Gerda Lerner, Chapter 1 of this book.

Chapter 11. *The Majority Finds Its Past*

1. See Carroll Smith-Rosenberg, "The New Woman and the New History," *Feminist Studies,* Vol. III, No. 1/2 (Fall 1975), 185–98, for a methodological discussion.

   For historical work which has accepted the concept of a female culture or highlighted aspects of it, see Nancy Cott, "Young Women in the Second Great Awakening in New England," *Feminist Studies,* Vol. III, No. 1/2 (Fall 1975), 15–29; C. Smith-Rosenberg, "Beauty, the Beast and the Militant Woman," *American Quarterly,* Vol. 23, No. 3 (Oct. 1971), 562–84; C. Smith-Rosenberg, "Female World . . . ," *Signs* (Fall 1975; Anne Firor Scott, *The Southern Lady: From Pedestal to Politics, 1830–1930* (Chicago, 1970); Kathryn Kish Sklar, *Catharine Beecher: A Study in American Domesticity* (New Haven, 1973); Barbara Welter, "Feminization of American Religion: 1800–1860," in William O'Neill (ed.), *Problems and Issues in American Social History* (Minneapolis, 1974); Ann Douglas Wood, "The Scribbling Women and Fanny Fern: Why Women Wrote," *American Quarterly,* Vol. 23, No. 3 (Oct. 1971), 3–24.

2. G. Lerner, *Female Experience: An American Documentary* (New York and Indianapolis, 1977), Part I.

3. The first historian to call attention to this aspect of Women's History was Mary Beard. Her *Woman's Work in Municipalities* (New York, 1915; reprint 1972) merely indicates the availability of sources without organizing or interpreting them. This weakness is shared by other early collections of women's club activities, such as Jane Cunningham Croly, *The History of the Women's Club Movement in America* (New York, 1898); Elizabeth Lindsay Davis, *Lifting as They Climb* (n.p., 1933); Maud Nathan, *The Story of an Epoch-Making Movement* (New York, 1926).

   Also see: Clarke A. Chambers, *A Seedtime of Reform* (Ann Arbor, 1967), chaps. 2, 5, 6; Jill Conway, "Women Reformers and American Culture,

1870–1930," *Journal of Social History*, Vol. V, No. 2 (Winter 1971–72), 164–77; Richard Jensen, "Family, Career and Reform: Women Leaders of the Progressive Era," in Michael Gordon (ed.), *The American Family in Social-Historical Perspective* (New York, 1973); Keith Melder, "Ladies Bountiful: Organized Women's Benevolence in Early 19th Century America," *New York History* (*July* 1967), 231–54; Gerda Lerner, *Black Women in White America* (New York, 1972), chap. 8; Frances Willard, *Glimpses of Fifty Years* (Chicago, 1899); Mildred White Wells, *Unity in Diversity: The History of the General Federation of Women's Clubs* (*Washington, D.C.*, 1953).

An indication of the range of available untapped sources on the community and institution-building work of women can be gleaned from perusing the biographies in James (eds.), *Notable American Women* (Cambridge, Mass., 1972) of women listed under one or all of the following headings: "Kindergartners," "Religious Founders and Leaders," "School Founders and Administrators," "Social and Civic Reformers," "Temperance Advocates," "Welfare Work Leaders," "Women's Club Leaders."

4. For monographs on woman suffrage see: Carrie Chapman Catt and Nattie R. Schuler, *Women Suffrage and Politics* (New York, 1926); William Chafe, *Women and Equality* (New York, 1977); Alan P. Grimes, *The Puritan Ethic and Woman Suffrage* (New York, 1967); Ida Husted Harper, *Story of the National Amendment for Woman Suffrage* (New York, 1919); Mrs. Inez Haynes Irwin, *The Story of the Woman's Party* (New York, 1921), and *Up Hill with Banners Flying* (Penobscot, Me., 1964); Aileen S. Kraditor, *Ideas . . .* (New York, 1965); David Morgan, *Suffragists and Democrats in America* (East Lansing, 1972); Anne F. Scott and Andrew Scott, *One Half the People: The Fight for Woman's Suffrage* (Philadelphia, 1975); Doris Stevens, *Jailed for Freedom* (New York, 1920; reprint, 1976).

For a broader-based treatment of the subject see: Barbara Berg, *The Remembered Gate: Origins of American Feminism: The Woman and the City, 1800–1860* (New York, 1978); Ellen Dubois, *Feminism and Suffrage: The Emergence of an Independent Women's Movement in America, 1848–1869* (Ithaca, 1978); Eleanor Flexner, *Century of Struggle* (Cambridge, Mass., 1959); Keith Melder, *Beginnings of Sisterhood* (New York, 1977); William O'Neill, *Everyone Was Brave* (Chicago, 1969); Ross Evans Paulson, *Woman's Suffrage and Prohibition* (Glenview, Ill., 1973).

5. Lerner, *Female Experience*, Part III.

Chapter 12. *The Challenge of Women's History*

1. For a full discussion of these issues, see Chapters 1 and 4 of this book. Other historians who have attempted definitions of women as a category have expe-

rienced similar perplexities. See the essays by Juliet Mitchell, Hilda Smith, and Sheila Johansson in Berenice Carroll, *Liberating Women's History: Theoretical and Critical Essays,* (Urbana, Ill., 1976), pp. 369–427. Also; Chafe, *Women and Equality* (New York, 1977), chap. 1 and 3, and Carl Degler, "Is There a History of Women?", An Inaugural Lecture delivered before the University of Oxford in March 14, 1974 (Oxford, 1975).

2. The definition of "relation of the sexes" as an essential category to be added to historical analysis was first succinctly stated by Joan Kelly-Gadol in "The Social Relation of the Sexes: Methodological Implications of Women's History," *Signs,* Vol. I, No. 4, (Summer 1976), 809–24.

3. See Chapter 8 of this book.

4. They share this invisibility with racial and ethnic minorities and with lower-class groups, but with the *differences* earlier noted. See: Jesse Lemisch, "The Papers of Great White Men" and "The Papers of a Few Great Black Men and a Few Great White Women," *The Maryland Historian,* Vol. VI, No. 1 (Spring 1975), 43–50, 60–66.

5. Articles by Shorter ("Female Emancipation . . .") and D. S. Smith ("Family Limitation . . ."), see note 6, Chapter 10, this book.

6. Tilly, Scott, Cohen, "Women's Work . . . ," see note 6, Chapter 10, this book.

7. See Chapter 2 of this book.

8. Ansley J. Coale and Melvin Zelnik, "New Estimates of Fertility and Population in the United States" (Princeton, 1963), Table 2, p. 36, quoted in Daniel Scott Smith, "Family Limitation . . .", 44.

9. Wilson H. Grabill, Clyde V. Kiser, and Pascal K. Whelpton, "Demographic Trends, Marriage, Birth and Death," in Michael Gordon (ed.), *The American Family in Social-Historical Perspective* (New York, 1973), p. 383.

   See also: Stanley L. Engerman, "Black Fertility and Family Structure in the United States, 1880–1940," *Journal of Family History,* Vol. II, No. 2 (Summer 1977), 117–38.

10. See notes 5 and 6 above.

11. Linda Gordon, *Woman's Body* . . . (New York, 1976), p. 70.

Index

National Conference of Colored Women, 87

National Congress of Neighborhood Women, 59n

National Federation of Afro-American Women, 87

National Organization of Women (NOW), 32

Neighborhood Union, Atlanta, Ga., 88-92

New England Federation of Women's Clubs, 108

New Era Club, 87, 108

Noyes, John Humphrey, 53, 55

Nurses, 23

Oakley, Ann, 136

Oneida community, 55, 143

O'Neill, William, 33, 52

Oppression of women, 36-42, 81, 111
black, 58, 63, 66, 68, 69, 81, 111

Organizations of women, 32, 33, 161
antislavery societies, 115-116, 118, 120, 123-127
black, 58, 68-69, 73, 83-93
working women, 52-53, 59-60

"Other," xxxi, 147

Overpopulation, 61

Owen, Robert Dale, 53, 55

Palmer, Alice Freeman, 106

Palmer Memorial Institute, 67, 106

Patriarchal values, 169, 177

Paul, Alice, xxiv

Phillips, Wendell, 124n

Phillis Wheatley Association, 87

Phillis Wheatley Club, 86

Porter, Dorothy, 65

Preston, Dr. Ann, 20

Preston, William C., 117

Primitive societies, sexual division of labor, 50, 141

Progressive period, 60, 86

Property rights of women, 17, 28, 49

Psychology:
Freudian, 5, 9n, 29, 35, 40
of women, 8-9

Puritans, 16

Quakers, 51, 99

Race discrimination, 74-76
in antislavery movement, 101-103
in education in South, 105-106
petitions against, in antislavery movement, 124
sex loophole in, 75-77, 193n
of white women, 95
in woman's rights movement, 34, 106-107
and woman's suffrage, 104-105
in women's organizations, 108, 109

Race riots, 109

Rape, double standard for blacks and whites, 72-73, 109

Renaissance, 154, 175

Roles, male and female, see Men; Women

Rose, Ernestine, 4, 53, 55

Rosenberg, Charles, 148

Rowbotham, Juliet, 155

Ruffin, Josephine St. Pierre, 86, 87, 108

Sanger, Margaret, xxiv, 53, 147, 161
birth control campaign, 55-56

Schlesinger, Elizabeth, xxiv

Seneca Falls Convention (1848), 27, 30, 33, 98, 126

Servants, domestic, 133-135, 156

Sexism, 40-42, 193n
restrictions imposed by sex, 49
in roles of men and women, 40, 42, 44, 46

Sexual exploitation:
of black women, 69-73, 85-86, 95-97, 101-103
of lower-class women, 71-72

Sexual morality:
of black women, 57, 108, 109
and woman suffrage, 52
and women's emancipation, 53-55
working-class standards, 57

Sexuality:
and feminism, 36, 37, 44-47
of women, 45, 155
in women's history, 148, 155-157

Shadd, Mary Ann, 101-103